BLOOMINGDALE'S ILLUSTRATED 1886 CATALOG

BLOOMINGDALE'S ILLUSTRATED 1886 CATALOG

Fashions, Dry Goods and Housewares

by

BLOOMINGDALE BROTHERS

New Introduction by Nancy Villa Bryk

Published in association with
Henry Ford Museum & Greenfield Village, Dearborn, Michigan
by Dover Publications, Inc., New York

HENRY
FORD
MUSEUM
&
GREENFIELD
VILLAGE

Copyright © 1988 by Dover Publications, Inc.

Published in Canada by General Publishing Company, Ltd., 30 Lesmill Road, Don Mills, Toronto, Ontario.

Published in the United Kingdom by Constable and Company, Ltd.

This Dover edition, first published in 1988 in association with Henry Ford Museum & Greenfield Village, Dearborn, Michigan, is a slightly abridged republication of the Spring and Summer 1886 catalog published by Bloomingdale Brothers, New York. Pages 3–6, 111–112 and 163–164 were missing from the copy of the catalog used for reproduction. The remaining pages have been renumbered consecutively and the Index and Index to Advertisers have been changed to reflect the new page numbers. A new Introduction has been written specially for this edition.

Manufactured in the United States of America
Dover Publications, Inc., 31 East 2nd Street, Mineola, N.Y. 11501

Library of Congress Cataloging-in-Publication Data

Bloomingdale's illustrated 1886 catalog : fashions, dry goods, and housewares / by Bloomingdale Brothers.
      p.   cm.
  Includes index.
  ISBN 0-486-25780-0 (pbk.)
    1. Manufactures—Catalogs 2. Bloomingdale's (Firm)—Catalogs.
3. Clothing and dress—Catalogs. 4. House furnishings—Catalogs.
I. Bloomingdale's (Firm)
TS199.B53   1988   88-16217
380.1'45'0294—dc19   CIP

INTRODUCTION

Today, "Bloomie's" is equated with "chic." The affluent, with charge cards ready for action, flock to Bloomingdale's on New York's Upper East Side. However, Bloomingdale's Department Store was not always patronized by the fashionable. From its founding in the late nineteenth century until just after the Second World War, Bloomingdale's was known for catering to the working class by selling rather ordinary items of good quality at low prices. This reprinted "price list," from Henry Ford Museum's trade literature collections, is really a mail-order catalog. It documents the firm's conventional stock preferred by housewives of modest means and conservative taste.

Lyman and Joseph Bloomingdale founded their store in 1872 at 938 Third Avenue near 57th Street, far from New York City's main shopping district near Union Square (14th Street). They soon outgrew the store they called "The Great East Side Bazaar" (which had a hoopskirt attached to the flagpole) and moved in 1877, then again in 1880 to a five-story rented building on Third Avenue and 56th Street. The firm occupied this building when this catalog was issued.

The catalog shows the variety of goods the store could offer at this larger facility. Forty-five departments are represented here, primarily dry goods, clothing, and sundries. However, Bloomingdale's also sold items such as furniture which are not depicted here. Larger items may not have been sold by mail by this company because of difficulty with or cost in shipping them. The U.S. Mail Service would only deliver packages under four pounds, so private express companies were employed to deliver larger goods (see the advertisement on page 158).

The firm soon outgrew even this five-floor building at Third Avenue and 56th Street. Tired of renting inadequate facilities, Lyman and Joseph had a building constructed to their specifications a few blocks away, at the corner of Third Avenue and 59th Street. The new building was under construction when this catalog was printed,

and the Bloomingdale Brothers proudly featured it on the cover of this price list. They moved to their new location in late 1886, and this building, with additions, still serves as the firm's flagship store.

Other merchants thought the Bloomingdale Brothers were foolish for remaining so far from the shopping district, but the Bloomingdales were confident that a rapidly expanding city and transit system would mitigate this distance factor. The key was to make the store a destination for shoppers. They aggressively advertised their commitment to quality goods at low prices, and the business thrived. Clients were largely blue-collar families who found bargains at Bloomingdale's.

The new store was spacious enough to accommodate everything from pianos to a book department. The large windows at street level were attractively arranged to lure the pedestrian inside. The store advertised heavily and held large promotions. Lyman grabbed publicity by installing "sky carriages" (elevators) of glass, mahogany, and plush upholstery, later adding escalators (quite a spectacle at the turn of the century). They used the first neon sign in the city. Despite the gimmicks, the brothers remained committed to offering well-priced goods. Bloomingdale Brothers' formula was a success; the store grossed about $800,000 in 1883, and over $1 million at the end of 1887.

This catalog reveals that the new store included a "country orders department" to expedite mail orders. Department stores like Bloomingdale's and Wanamaker's fought hard for rural customers. They knew that many farmers despised country stores, which often stocked inferior goods at high prices. Bloomingdale's reliable, inexpensive goods offered the rural consumer a viable alternative. The catalog also describes amenities offered to Bloomingdale's out-of-town visitors, including a "luxurious parlor" for those just visiting for the day, and transportation to the ferry or train depot.

Items in this catalog were considered fairly fashionable in their day. While the very stylish probably did not shop at Bloomingdale's, the practical housewife who enjoyed pretty things was delighted with the store's goods. The 1886 ladies' fashions consisted of "suits" of tight-fitting bodice and heavily bustled skirt. Women's undergarments seen here are a wonder—corsets with dozens of bones, bustles, and "dress forms" (essentially falsies). Gentlemen's and children's fashions are extensively illustrated. The household furnishings departments feature heavy portieres to be hung in doorways, mantel lambrequins, white lace curtains, and a host of metal goods rarely seen in catalogs—curtain poles, stair corners and stair buttons, and drapery hooks. Perhaps most intriguing is the Hair Goods Department, which offers women's hair switches, curls, braids, and "back coiffures" (many ventilated for comfort).

What is remarkable about the catalog is the degree to which goods were customized to satisfy the purchaser. The Dressmaking Department asked for careful measurements so their products would fit well. It noted, too, that fabrics and colors could be altered, "with estimates cheerfully furnished on application." Wedding outfits would be selected and sent according to directions of the customer. Those who ordered trims for a dress were told to include a fabric swatch so that a perfect match could be obtained. If a trimmed hat was ordered, the purchaser was to state her complexion so that one that flattered her coloring could be sent. Such heady decisions were often not left to the customer; Bloomingdale's was willing to make the choice for her.

The Bloomingdale's considered so stylish today is the result of a post-Second World War decision to upgrade the store's image and clientele. Higher-ticket items replaced lower-priced stock, the most fashionable goods were sought, and brilliant window artists employed. While Lyman Bloomingdale would have enjoyed the revitalized store's promotion and advertising techniques, he might be surprised that today's Bloomingdale's is practically synonymous with "trendy."

In our age of discount stores and enclosed malls, it is difficult to imagine the wonder engendered by the late nineteenth-century urban department stores. Characterized as "grand palaces," stores like Bloomingdale's were huge, magnificently furnished, and stocked with thousands of items some had never seen before. Young women left home for employment as store clerks. Middle-class matrons spent endless hours shopping, intoxicated by the array of goods offered by these grand emporiums. One immigrant, Mary Antin, described the magic of the department store in her published memoirs. She wrote of her transformation from a foreigner into an American, part of which took place in a "dazzlingly beautiful palace called a 'department store.'" There she and her sister "exchanged our hateful homemade European costumes . . . for real American machine-made garments, and issued forth glorified in each other's eyes."

Nancy Villa Bryk
Curator
Division of Domestic Life
Henry Ford Museum & Greenfield Village

NOTE

The arrival of the department stores' "wish books" or mail-order catalogs was an event in rural communities. Such catalogs were pored over countless times and often lent to friends and neighbors. Because of the hard use they received, few catalogs have survived to the present day. Those that have often feature torn, cut, or missing pages. Such is the case with the copy of the catalog reproduced here. The four pages at the front of the book that contained the illustrations of the suits and hats described on page 3, one page of braids and trims, one page of men's clothing, and two pages of non-Bloomingdale advertising are missing. For the modern reader's convenience, in this edition the pages have been renumbered and the indexes corrected to reflect the new page numbers (and better alphabetical order!).

BLOOMINGDALE'S
ILLUSTRATED
1886
CATALOG

SPRING & SUMMER, 1886

Bloomingdale Brothers'

PRICE LIST.

DEPARTMENTS.

Cloaks and Wraps—
  Ladies' Misses' and
  Children's.
Clocks and Watches.
Clothing—Gentlemen's
  Youths' and Boys'.
Confectionery.
Corsets.
Crockery.
Cutlery.
Dry Goods.
Fans.
Feathers and Flowers.
Fire-arms.
Fringes.
Furnishing Goods—
  Gents' and Boys'.
Gloves.
Hats—Ladies', Gents'
  and Children's
Hair Goods.
House-Furn'g Goods.
Housekeeping Goods.
Hosiery.
Infants' Wear.
Jerseys.

DEPARTMENTS.

Jewelry.
Laces and Lace Goods
Leather Goods.
Millinery.
Notions.
Parasols.
Ribbons.
School Supplies,
Shawls.
Shoes.
Silverware.
Stationery.
Smoking Articles.
Suits—Ladies', Misses'
  and Children's.
Toilet Articles.
Toys.
Umbrellas.
Underwear—Ladies',
  Gents' & Children's.
Upholstery Goods.
White Goods.
Willow Ware.
Walking Sticks.
Zephyr Worsteds and
  Fancy Articles.

WE WILL REMOVE ABOUT AUGUST 15TH TO OUR NEW BUILDING 3RD AVENUE, COR. 59TH STREET.

The Publishers are convinced that the within prices are from 5 to 25 per cent. cheaper than in any other Catalogue, for the reason that the prices given are exactly the same as those charged to persons buying in the store, and that means

The Lowest Prices in the United States.

BLOOMINGDALE BROTHERS

924, 926 AND 928 THIRD AVENUE,
160, 162 AND 164 East, 56th St., NEW YORK.

For Index to Bloomingdale Brothers' Price List refer to pages 145 and 146.

INDEX TO ADVERTISERS.

Do not cut or mutilate this book; by simply referring to the number of the page and article you desire, you will be fully understood.

VERY IMPORTANT.

PLEASE READ CAREFULLY THE FOLLOWING NOTE:

When sending an order, write it upon a separate sheet of paper from the letter, and be as explicit as possible in giving descriptions of style, color, size, price and the exact measurement for ready-made garments, also enclose bill of last purchase if you have it.

Send full name, Post Office, County and State, plainly written.

No goods sent on approval, unless by special arrangement; we guarantee all goods to be as represented.

Bonnets, Hats, Feathers, Flowers and goods cut according to sample, *cannot be exchanged.*

Complete wedding outfits selected, plain or elaborate, according to directions.

Mourning of all descriptions carefully selected, and sent at the shortest notice.

In returning goods bear in mind that *one word* of writing subjects the entire package to full letter postage. Direct to the firm, and place your name after the word *from*, in one corner of the envelope or wrapper.

All goods sent and returned at the expense and risk of the purchaser, as our responsibility ceases after we have delivered the package, plainly and properly addressed, at the New York Post Office or Express Office.

Articles that would be injured by opening or handling in the mail should be sent as registered matter, as the expense is only ten cents for each package.

Ladies are particularly requested to always send samples of goods for which fringe and trimmings, buttons, hose and ribbons are required, as a perfect match can then be given.

When ordering corsets or gloves do not forget to give the size required.

When ordering underwear, give bust measurement.

When ordering a cloak, suit, or wrapper, give measurement, as per directions on page 3. If ordering for a child, state age also.

When ordering a hat state whether the lady has a large or small head. If a trimmed hat, give complexion also.

When ordering collars, give size, if possible. We always send medium where size is not given.

When ordering from samples, return particular sample selected, and state if any goods can be substituted in case the special piece ordered has been sold. Fasten sample to your letter; either pin it on, or, if zephyr, tie it through a hole in the margin.

Remember that our sales are very large; our goods, except on some standard styles, are constantly changing. Often when we lay in a large supply of some special article enough to last, as we suppose, for some time, there is a run made upon it until all is sold, and when gone we may not be able to replace it exactly. In view of this fact, it is well, especially in ordering fringes, laces, ladies' neckties, bows, dress goods, etc., to state whether we will be allowed to substitute something similar in quality, color, or pattern, if the particular article ordered has been sold prior to our receipt of the order.

Send postal note, Post Office or Express money order, draft on New York, or money by registered letter; direct the letter to us plainly, and we will be sure to receive it.

Address,   BLOOMINGDALE BROS ,
Third Ave, and 56th St., New York.

For Index to Bloomingdale Brothers' Price List refer to pages 145 and 146.

REMOVAL.

About August 15th, 1886, we shall remove to our New Building, now in course of erection, at the N. W. Corner of 3d Avenue and 59th Street, which will be, when completed, one of the largest buildings in the world devoted to the exclusive use of one firm. It will cover seven city lots, and there will be seven stories occupied for the manufacture and sale of almost every article that can be used by man, woman or child, for their personal use, or for use in their homes.

Particular attention has been paid to the arrangement of our Country Order Department, which will occupy sufficient space for its systematic management, and for the expeditious handling of the thousands of articles of every conceivable kind which daily pass through it, so that customers may rely upon having their orders filled with the utmost promptness. We trust that should you visit New York, you will not fail to honor our establishment with a call, and we may add that persons who remain for a day only, need not go to a hotel, as we shall have a luxurious parlor where they may rest; cloak rooms where all parcels may be left and checked; a restaurant where light refreshments may be had, and direct transportation for passengers and freight to Ferry or Railroad Depot. As a guarantee of our responsibility and permanency we may mention that the building and the ground on which it stands is our own property, and since the saving in rent thus effected will be over $30,000 per annum, we shall be enabled to do our business at a minimum profit, which in these days of sharp competition, means that our customers will surely receive the benefit of this great reduction in our expenses.

BLOOMINGDALE BROTHERS.

ON THE FRONT COVER WE GIVE AN ILLUSTRATION OF OUR BUILDING NOW IN COURSE OF ERECTION

924 TO 928 THIRD AVE., AND 160 TO 164 EAST 56th St., NEW YORK.

3

Ladies', Misses' and Children's Suit Department.

The most successful branch of our business is our Dressmaking department; a notable feature therein, is that neither pains or expense are spared in securing the services of the most skillful artists, who are able to reproduce the original European designs, and competent to design modes to suit the demands of this fashionable country. No pains are spared in the execution of orders entrusted to us, which are completed in the shortest possible time compatible with good taste and excellence in finish. Through our catalogue we receive hundreds of orders daily and we are proud to say that we have given satisfaction in almost every instance.

In addition. we plainly assert that our moderation in prices is not at all in discordance with what we have just cited, having the best materials and finest wokmanship that capital can secure, and the experience and discrimination of the most perfect management.

Our patrons will please remember that the ordinary measure for costumes, wraps, etc., runs from 32 inch to 40 inch bust measure; larger sizes will cost a proportionate advance.

Directions for Measurement.

In ordering dresses. please give all measurements as illustrated.
Cloaks do not require measurement round waist.

FRONT.

With a tape measure ascertain the following measurements:
1—Around the neck.
1 to 2—Neck to waist.
2 to 2—Size of waist all round.
3 to 4—Across the bust.
3 to 3—Around entire bust and back under the arms.
4 to 5—Inside length of sleeve.
6 to 7—Length of waist under arm.
Side of neck to 8 for length of shoulder.
8 to 9—From shoulder to elbow.
9 to 10—From elbow to wrist, with the arm bent.

BACK.

A to B—Across back from sleeves.
C to D—Length of back from collar to waist.

In addition the above, and in order to avoid mistakes, we require the following measurements, viz:
Measurement around hips taken over the dress.
Length of skirt in front from waist.
" " back " "
' " on side " "

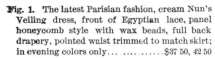

Recolect that as we manufacture all our own garments, we can make up any design in different materials than those described in this catalogue. Estimates cheerfully furnished on application.

DESCRIPTION AND PRICES OF SUITS ILLUSTRATED ON FASHION PLATE..

Fig. 1. The latest Parisian fashion, cream Nun's Veiling dress, front of Egyptian lace, panel honeycomb style with wax beads, full back drapery, pointed waist trimmed to match skirt; in evening colors only... .... $37 50, 42 50

Fig. 2. Embroidered Chambray Dress, skirt trimmed with deep embroidery on bottom and sides, side drapery basque with separate vest and embroidered front........ $10 75, 12 50

Fig. 3. White Lawn Suit, plain skirt with deep embroidery, all-over embroidered back, sash with embroidered ends.............. $9 75, 11 50

Fig. 4. Very Pretty Lawn Suit, skirt 3 rows of embroidered ruffles. baby waist with satin ribbon bows, embroidered yoke and sleeves,
$8 75, 10 25, 12 50

Fig. 5. Very Pretty Lawn Suit, 2 embroidered ruffles on bottom, long overdress trimmed with embroidery, full draped back round basque trimmed with insertion in front.... $11 25, 13 50

Fig. 6. Lawn Suit, trimmed with plaiting, embroidery and tucks, plaited back trimmed with tucks, waist as illustrated.......... $14 25, 16 50

Fig. 7. Elegant Lawn Suit, deep ruffle on bottom, long embroidered over dress in front, all-over embroidered basque with ribbon bow.... $18 50

Fig. 8. Very Pretty Lawn Suit, Peasant skirt. deep flounces of embroidery at bottom, headed by tucks and Hamburg edging; baby waist with embroidered yoke and sleeves........ ... $17 50

Fig. 9. Handsome Lawn Suit, skirt with two rows of knife plaits headed by a band, over dress trimmed with tucks and embroidery; waist with vest insertion and trimmings of embroidery,
$6 25

Fig. 10. Handsome Lawn Suit, skirt consisting of 3 tucked ruffles trimmed with embroidery, full back, waist with tucks and embroidery,
$6 75

Fig. 11. Very Handsome Lawn Suit, front of all over embroidery, back of tucks and Hamburg edging; embroidered waist with inside basque of plain goods, trimmed with satin ribbon bows
....$19 75

Fig. 12. Very Handsome Costume, made of Lawn, Nun's Veiling, Albatross Cloth or Cashmere, elaborately trimmed with lace and satin ribbon; White Lawn, $15 00 and $18 00; Nun's Veiling, Albatross Cloth or Cashmere, in white or evening shades..............$17 50, 20 00, 22 50

Fig. 13. Pretty Style Lawn Suit, skirt and overdress trimmed with tucks, full back, plaited blouse with belt.. ....$5 95

Fig. 14. Lawn Suit, skirt tucked front and side. as illustrated; plaited basque with belt .. $6 25

Fig. 15. Lawn Suit, skirt 4 tucked ruffles edged with embroidery, basque trimmed with embroidery and insertion....................$10 75

Fig. 16. Stylish Lawn Suit, skirt of tucks with two rows of Irish point insertion, deep flounce of embroidery round bottom, short front drapery trimmed with embroidery, back trimmed to correspond, waist of Irish point with plain vest front........................ .... $21 50

Fig. 17. Lawn Suit. skirt trimmed with folds and deep embroidered plaiting; baby waist with embroidered yoke and sleeve $8 75

Fig. 18. Lawn Suit, skirt 3 tucked ruffles, tucked back, basque trimmed with tucks and ruffles of the same material.........................$5 25

SPECIAL.

White Lawn Suit, tucked skirt, basque trimmed with tucks and belt...... ....$3 25

Fig. 19. Handsome Lawn Suit, skirt trimmed with embroidered and plain flounces, pointed waist with separate "Zouave" front, bag sleeves
....$14 00

Fig. 20. Stylish Lawn Suit, skirt with two flounces of embroidery, long front tucked drapery, with deep flounce of embroidery, full draped back, vest trimmed with Hamburg edge and embroidered sleeves...........$12 50

Fig. 21. Elegant Costume of cream lace with colored flowers, plain skirt with overdress artistically draped and trimmed with satin ribbon bows, pointed waist...........$23 50, 27 50

Fig. 22. Stylish Costume of Escurial Lace, skirt 3 deep flounces of short front drapery and long full back drapery looped at side with ribbon bow, pointed waist trimmed with ribbon,
22 75, 24 00
Same, of Oriental or Egyptian Lace,
$17 50 and 21 00

Fig. 23. Very Neat Seaside Costume of cream or white Lawn, with colored embroidery, skirt with tucks and edging on side, long front drapery, trimmed with colored embroidery, waist with bodice and trimmed to correspond, $14 25

Fig. 24. Handsome Lawn Suit, richly trimmed with embroidery. waist with loose front of embroidery and trimmed with satin ribbon,
$12 75

DESCRIPTION OF HATS ILLUSTRATED ON ABOVE FIGURES.

Fig. 19. White Straw Hat, trimmed with Oriental lace and roses.... .. ..$5 50, 6 00

Fig. 20. Straw Hat, faced with velvet, trimmed with ribbon........ ... .$4 75, 5 75

Fig. 21. Oriental Lace Poke, trimmed with ribbon and aigrettes........ ....$5 50 to 8 00

Fig. 22. Flare Hat, mull shirring, ribbon trimming and bird.....................$3 50 to 5 00

Fig. 23. Black Lace Poke, trimmed with ribbon and flowers.... ....$6 00 to 9 00

Fig. 24. Straw flare, lace facing, trimmed with lace and flowers.................$4 75 to 7 00

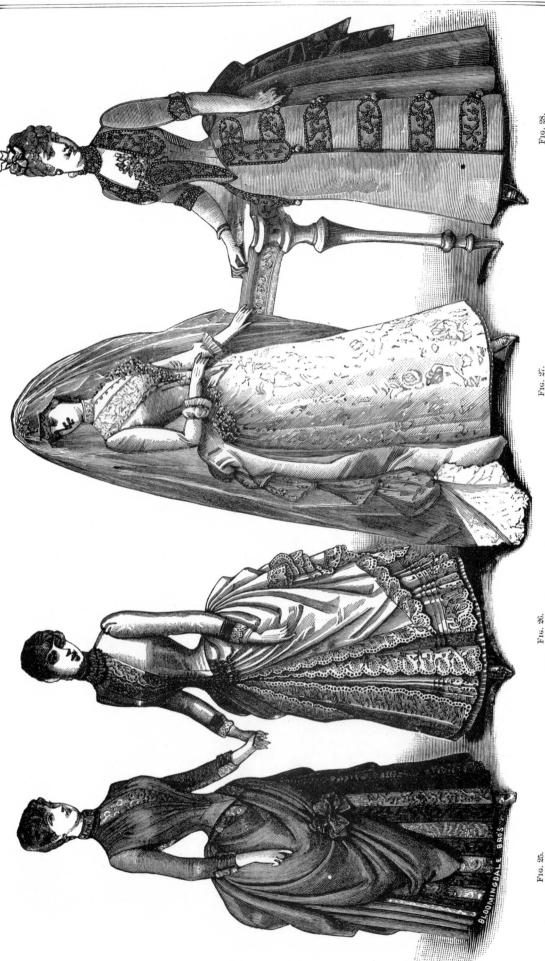

FIG. 25.

No. 1. Elegant Reception Costume, skirt of watered silk; front and back drapery and waist of gros grain silk; waist trimmed to match skirt; black only, ... $35.00, 37.50 and 42.00

No. 2. Same of plain silk, all colors.
. . . . $27.50 and 32.50

FIG. 26.

No. 3. Very Rich Costume of Nun's Veiling, trimmed with Egyptian Lace; skirt with one row knife plaiting round bottom; princess drapery in front and handsomely draped in back, short waist with postillion back, cream and evening shades, ... $18.50, 22.50 and 25.50

No. 4. Same of Cashmere white and evening shades, ... $20.00, 25.00, 27.50

FIG. 27.

No. 5. Elegant Bridal Suit of white brocaded and plain satin; skirt with front of brocade satin; full train of plain puffed in back; pointed waist trimmed with lace and flowers,
. . . . $40.00, 45.00 and 50.00

No. 6. Same in Gros Grain Silk, with lace front . . . . $37.50 and 42.50

No. 7. Same of White Nun's Veiling or Cashmere, ... $22.50 and 25.00

FIG. 28.

No. 8. Elegant Reception Costume of Gros Grain Silk or Satin; skirt with plain front, panel on side trimmed with 6 bands of jet gimp, heavily folded in back and trimmed with satin ribbon bow; waist as illustrated or with high neck; trimmed to match skirt, in black, navy blue, brown and garnet, ... $35.00, 38.50 and 42.50

924 TO 928 THIRD AVE., AND 160 TO 164 EAST 56th St., NEW YORK.

5

Fig. 29.

No. 9. Very pretty Walking Costume, skirt with a row of plaits round bottom, and 3 elegant deep lace flounces with pointed folds between trimmed with satin ribbon bows, plaited back, short waist trimmed with lace and satin ribbon scarf; gros-grain silk or satin with Spanish lace, in black and all the fashionable shades.....$32 50, 37 50 and 42 50

No. 10. Same style of French all wool cashmere, trimmed with Chantilly lace; all colors.....$17 50, 22 50 and 25 00

No. 11. Drarp d'Alsace, all colors, $14 50. 17 50 and 20 00

Fig. 30.

No. 12. Neat Walking Costume; skirt of white flannel with polonaise of contrasting color, trimmed with velvet ribbon bow and buckles; can also be had all one of shade if desired $18 00, 20 50 and 22 75

Fig. 31.

No. 13. Elegant Costume of gros-grain silk; plaited skirt with narrow plaited panel on side, and straps of ribbon extending across, short waist with "Fedora," front and short or long sleeves; can be had in a combination of black and cardinal, or all of one shade. $34 00, 37 50 and 41 00

No. 14. Same style of Crape La Favor, in all the new and fashionable shades, $15 00 and 17 50

No. 15. Of all wool French cashmere, black and colored.........$16 50, 19 00 and 22 50

Fig. 32.

No. 16. Very handsome Combination Suit; made of worsted lace and plain material; skirt of lace with knife plaiting round bottom pointed front and full back drapery, of the plain goods, pointed basque of lace with a plaited yoke insertion of plain material; can be had in blue, brown, black and cream. In cashmere or Nun's veiling, $17 50 and 22 50

Fig. 33.

No. 17. Stylish Silk Suit: skirt with front of brocade goods edged with panel of velvet, paniers in front, full back drapery, long cutaway basque with plaited vest insertion and revers of velvet; all fashionable shades,— $29 50, 32 50 and 35 00

No. 18. Same. of cashmere with brocaded silk, all colors $18 50 and 22 50

BLOOMINGDALE BRO'S

Fig. 34.

No. 10. Very Elegant Suit of Albatross Nun's Veiling or Albatross Cloth, skirt with two deep ruffles of Egyptian or Oriental lace, panier drapery; pointed Basque, trimmed with lace to match skirt, in cream, light blue and pink, $19 75, 22 50 and 26 50

Fig. 35.

No. 20. Latest Style Costume, made of imported French fancy material with silk border, plain skirt with long pointed front drapery, looped at side panel of watered ribbon over a full back drapery; waist with ribbon scarf fastened with a handsome buckle; in white with ribbon of contrasting color,
$24 50, 26 75 and 30 00

No 21. Same, in tan, brown, blue de beige, colors,
$19 75, 22 50 and 25 00

Fig. 36.

No. 22. Very Neat Suit of white material, box plaited skirt, with several rows of colored silk stitching, shawl drapery in front with colored stitching and fringe; artistically draped in black; pointed waist, with plaited scarf stitched to match skirt; Flannel........$24 50 and 27 50

No. 23. Nun's Veiling or Albatross Cloth.........$21 75 and 25 00

Fig. 37.

No. 24. Handsome Suit of French Sateen, skirt knife plaited bottom, overdress artistically draped and scalloped, waist with yoke and shirred in front, satin ribbon belt and bow.....$14 50

Fig. 38.

No. 25. Elegant Costume of Nun's Veiling or Albatross Cloth; skirt of lace flouncing; short waist, satin ribbon belt and bow of contrasting colors; cream and light colors only,
$27 50 and 32 50

Fig. 39.

No. 26. Elaborate Suit of imported fancy goods, front of skirt embroidered, apron front drapery, side puffs and full back drapery, "Zouave" waist with Fedora front; white and high colors only
$8 75, 33 50 and 36 00

BLOOMINGDALE BROS.

FIG. 40.

No. 27. Rich Costume, made of plain and brocade Silk, plaited skirt with side of brocade silk; heavy ribbon sash falling over plaited back ;short waist with brocade silk insertion; edged by velvet revers in all fashionable shades,
..............$31.50, 34.00 and 37.50
No. 28. Same, all wool cashmere or brocaded silk................$17.50 and 22.50

FIG. 41.

No. 29. Elegant suit of plain material, handsomely trimmed with beads; skirt with deep knife plaiting in front and 4 rows of beads on each side; short front drapery and plaited back; waist trimmed to correspond; in silk, with jet beads. all colors,
..............29.50, 32.50, 36.00 and 40.00
No. 30. Same, in Cashmere or Homespun, with rosary beads....$18.75, 21.50 and 24.75

FIG. 42.

No. 31. Elaborate Walking Costume: knife plaited skirt shawl drapery: pointed waist; trimmed with ribbon bows, flannel, white and all the leading shades,
..............$14.50 and 16.75

FIG. 43.

No. 32. Elegant suit of plain and figured French Sateen; skirt with front of figured goods and pointed drapery; back of plain with drapery of figured material; waist trimmed with revers of velvet; all colors
..............$12.75 and 14.50

FIG. 44.

No. 33. Handsome costume of plain and brocade goods, skirt knife plaited round bottom; with front drawn at side and trimmed with ribbon bows; side box plaited, artistic drapery in front and back of brocade goods; waist with bodice and yoke; trimmed with ribbon bows; buttoned in back. The most fashionable suit of the season, plain and brocade silk; all colors,
..............$31.50 and 34.75
No. 34. Same in Worsted goods, with striped or brocade to match .....$18.00, 20.50 and 23.75

BLOOMINGDALE BRO'S

Fig. 45.

No. 35. Stylish Suit of striped and plain material; skirt of fancy stripes, box-plaited round bottom; short front drapery and side puffs; bows extending to bottom; full back drapery; waist trimmed with clasps and revers of striped material; all-wool cashmere and striped velvet goods,
...........$18.50, 20.75 and 23.50

No. 36. Same, striped camel's hair goods,
........................$22.50 and 26.00

Fig. 46.

No. 37. Very elegant Gros Grain. Silk Suit; trimmed with beaded gimp; skirt box-plaited in front; plain side trimmed with gimp; pointed front drapery with silk cord and tassels; puffed back drapery; waist as illustrated; richly trimmed with gimp, black only,
...........$34.50, 37.50 and 41.00

No. 38. Same, all-wool French Cashmere,
...........$22.50. 25.00 and 27.50

Fig. 47.

No. 39. Handsome Combination Suit; skirt of striped goods; long drapery of plain; looped at side with an elegant clasp; back drapery with trimming of striped material; waist with revers of striped goods; postillion back; French all-wool cashmere and fancy striped, all colors,......... $17.50, 22.00 and 25.75

No. 40. English Cashmere and striped goods,...............$18.75 and 16.50

Fig. 48.

No. 41. Very handsome suit of plain material, trimmed with yak-lace; skirt with 3 rows of lace flouncing; short front drapery looped at side with ribbon bows; puffed back drapery; plain jersey waist; camel's hair or homespun,
...........$21.75 and 24.50

No. 42. Same of Cashmere or Nun's Veiling, trimmed with Egyptian or oriental lace,.......$16.50, 18.75 and 20.50

Fig. 49.

No. 43. Broaded Silk Suit, skirt trimmed with deep flounces of lace; overdress of brocaded silk, falling in heavy folds in front and looped at side, with rich beaded ornaments; waist as illustrated, or high neck, velvet vest. In black,
...........$27.50, 32.50 and 35.00

No. 44. Colors.....$32.00, 36.75 and 39.00

924 TO 928 THIRD AVE., AND 160 TO 164 EAST 56th St., NEW YORK.

9

REDMAN & KENNY N.Y.

FIG. 50.

No. 46. Mourning Suit, trimmed with crape skirt with a row of narrow box plaits round bottom, headed by a deep band and 5 tucks above; folded apron drapery trimmed with crape, full draped back, basque coat front with separate waist. In all wool cashmere.
......$16.75, 19.50 and 22.50
No. 47. In English cashmere,
......$12.50 and 15.00
No. 48. In Henrietta cloth.
......$21.75 and 24.50

FIG. 51.

No. 49. Elaborate Walking Costume made of plain goods and velvet, plain skirt with panel of velvet on side trimmed with 7 clasps pleated long front drapery looped at side artistically draped in back; basque can be had scalloped, trimmed with velvet and clasps as illustrated or plain, buttoned in centre. In all wool diagonal or camels hair.
......$22.50, 24.75 and 27.50
No. 50. In all wool French cashmere......$17.25 and 20.00
No. 51. In English cashmere and velveteen..........$14.75 and 18.75

FIG. 52.

No. 52. Mourning Costume of French all wool cashmere and English crape, skirt with entire front of crape, long apron front drapery and full draped back, short basque trimmed with bands of crape........$16.75, 18.50 and 21.75
No. 53. Same, of Henrietta cloth.
......$21.50, 24.00 and 27.50
No. 54. English cashmere.
......$18.50 and 15.75

FIG. 53.

No. 55. Tailor Made Costume, bound with braid, skirt with knife plaits round bottom, plain front with plaited fans on sides, long pointed front and full back draperies round basque with coat collar and tailor finished. Assabet cloth or Tricot.
......$15.50, 17.50 and 22.50
No. 56. Gilbert's flannel homespun or cheviot...$14.50, 16.50 and 18.00

FIG. 54.

No. 57. Mourning Suit, trimmed with yoke of lace, skirt box plaited round bottom, headed by a deep flounce of lace; plaits of cashmere trimmed with lace, long apron drapery in front and full back drapery, plain basque trimmed with lace round bottom. In all wool cashmere....$14.50, 16.75 and 19.50
No. 58. In English cashmere.
......$11.25 and 13.75

FIG. 55.

No. 59. Very stylish Suit of cashmere and brocade silk, plain skirt with panel of brocaded silk on side, draped as illustrated and trimmed with fancy buttons; plain waist with vest of brocade silk. In French all wool cashmere, $14.50, 16.75 and 19.50
No. 70, In English cashmere.
......$14.50 and 16.75

Fig. 56.   **Fig. 57.**

No. 61. Very Neat Suit of plain material, trimmed with ornaments; skirt knife plaited round bottom, front with plaits and large folds between fastened on one side with 4 cord ornaments and trimmed with buttons; short front and full back draperies, pointed basque with 3 ornaments to match skirt, postillion back. All-wool Assabet Cloth or Tricot.....$16 50, 19 75, and 22 50
No. 62, Flannel or Homespun, $13 75 and 16 25
No. 63. Cashmere, $15 00, and 17 50

No. 64. Handsome Suit of plain material, trimmed with braid, front of skirt hangs in narrow pointed folds, plaited panels on both sides trimr.ed with braid full draped back: basque as illustrated. In Assabet, or Tricot....$17 50, 19 75, 22 50
No. 65. Same, in Flannel, all-wool Cashmere or Homespun, $14 50, 16 75

Fig. 58.   **Fig. 59.**

No. 66. Very Handsome Walking Suit of plain goods, trimmed with velvet and wooden beads, front drapery extending to bottom of skirt, panel of velvet edged with wooden beads, with heavy folds on both sides, pointed waist with postillion back, separate zouave cape trimmed with wooden beads; in Tricot or Cloth,
$19 50, 22 50 and 26 00
No. 67. In Flannel or Cashmere, $15 00, 17 50
No. 68. In Serge or English Cashmere.........$12 00, 14 00

No. 69. Stylish Walking Suit, skirt plain front with border on side, plaited back with narrow border; plain waist buttoned diagonally, trimmed with narrow border, in Cheviot or Camel's Hair.. $14 50, 16 75

Fig. 60.   **Fig. 61.**

No. 70. Handsome Suit, plain goods, trimmed with Hercules braid, knife plaiting on bottom of skirt and six rows of wide Hercules braid in front, 2 panels on each side trimmed with Hercules braid, pointed waist buttoned diagonally and trimmed to match skirt; in Tricot or Assabet Cloth,
$17 75, 20 25, 23 00
No. 71. Same, Cashmere, Homespun or Flannel.. $13 75, 16 00
No. 72. Serge or English Cashmere.........$10 75, 12 50

No. 73. Tailor Made Suit, front of skirt consists of a row of narrow folds, plaited side with straps across, trimmed with fancy buttons, full back drapery; pointed waist with coat back; in Tricot or Cloth,
$15 50, 17 75
No. 74. Same, in Cashmere, Flannel or Homespmn,
$12 25, 14 50
No. 75. Same, in English Cashmere or Serge..... $9 50, 11 25

FIG. 62.

No. 76. Very pretty Seersucker Suit, in different colors, fancy stripes; skirt, 2 knife plaitings round bottom apron drapery looped on side with ribbon bows, full back, waist trimmed with lace and vest insertion, ... $4 75 and 6 25

FIG. 63.

No. 77. Handsome Chambray Suit, skirt trimmed with embroidery and folds, apron drapery and full back; waist trimmed with embroidery to match skirt, ... $12 75 and 14 50

FIG. 64.

No. 78. Combination Suit of plain and striped Chambray; skirt front of plain goods with folds on side edged with embroidery, long front drapery of striped goods, back of striped material and artistically draped, plain basque with striped vest, ... $10 50, 12 75 a꞉d 14 50

FIG. 65.

No. 79. Very pretty Cambric Suit of striped and figured material, skirt of plain goods and trimmed with knife plaiting round bottom. Overdress of figured goods artistically draped, cutaway basque of figured goods with striped vest. Sizes, 34, 36, 38 and .... $4 25 and 5 75

FIG. 66.

No. 80. Stylish Suit of figured or plain sateen trimmed with lace, plaited skirt knife, plaiting round bottom, apron front trimmed with lace, full back drapery, waist as illustrated, ... $6 75, 8 50 and 10 75

FIG. 67.

No. 81. Very Stylish Suit, skirt trimmed with folds and oriental lace, front drapery tucked on side and trimmed with lace, full back and drapery, round basque trimmed with lace, in sateen, ... $12 75 and 15 00

81 a. Lawn..... $8 50 and 10 00

SPECIAL.

No. 82. Figured Colored Lawn Suits, tucked skirt and baby waist, with lace yoke; sizes, 34, 36, 38 and 40 only. .... $2 75 and 3 50

No. 83. Figured Lawn Suit, plaiting on bottom, overdress and waist trimmed with lace; sizes, 34, 36, 38 and 40 only .... $2 65 and 3 75

FIG. 68.   FIG. 69.   FIG. 70.

Fig. 68. No. 84. Very neat Tailor-made Suit of Ladies' Cloth; skirt with narrow knife-plaiting at bottom, two panels on each side trimmed with buttons and stitching: long apron drapery in front and looped at side; basque with revers and trimmed with buttons; all colors,
$11 50, 13 25 and 15 00
No. 85. Tricot in all fashionable shades,
$14 00 and 16 50
No. 86. Homespun all wool, black and colored,
$12 25 and 15 50
No. 87. French all wool Cashmere. all colors,
$12 50 and 15 00
No. 88. English Serge............ $8 50 and 10 50
No. 89. Homespun, cotton mixed. $9 50 and 11 50

Fig. 69. No. 90. Stylish Walking Costume of French all wool Cashmere; skirt with box-plaiting round bottom, headed by double box-plaits with 5 rows of braid between; apron drapery in front; basque Jersey-fitting; all colors
$12 50 and 16 00
No. 91. Flannel, all wool, all colors,
$8 25 and 10 00
No. 92. English Serge, in all the fashionionable colors.............. ....$7 25 and 9 00

Fig. 70. No. 93. Elegant Combination Costume of all wool Homespun and Velvet; kilt-plaited skirt with folds of velvet, kilt-plaiting round bottom; cutaway basque, with velvet collar and cuffs; black and colored.... $15 50 and 18 75
No. 94. Assabet cloth, with Velvet; all colors,
$14 00 and 17 50
No. 95. All wool Cashmere, with Velvet; black and colored.... ... ...$13 50 and 16 50
No. 96. Mixed Homespun, with Velveteen; all colors.........................$10 75 and 13 25

LADIES' TAILOR MADE SUITS.

(NOT ILLUSTRATED.)

No. 97. Box-plaited skirt, apron drapery, full back, round basque with coat back; Ladies' cloth, Tricot or Homespun... .$12 50 and 15 00
No. 98. Same style, of all wool Flannel,
$7 50 and 9 00
No. 99. Same style, of English Cashmere or Serge........ ....$6 50 and 7 50

No. 100. Skirt; long English drapery, tucks in front, full back; round basque with revers; Ladies'cloth,Tricot or Homespun $10 50 and 12 50
No. 101. Same style, Flannel............. $8 75
No. 102. Plain skirt, bound with braid, side panels trimmed with large buttons, puffed back; short basque with coat collar and postillion back; Ladies' cloth or Tricot.... $14 50 and 17 50

No. 103. Same style, all wool Flannel,
$10 75 and 12 50
104. Skirt; fan-plaited front, panel on sides, finished with 2 rows of buttons, apron drapery and full draped back over deep side plaited bottom; basque with vest front and coat back; Ladies' cloth or Tricot....... ....$16 50
No. 105. Same style, all wool Flannel.......12 50

SEPARATE SKIRTS TO BE WORN WITH JERSEYS.

No.106. Same Style as 97. Ladies'cloth,etc.,etc., each................. .....$8 50 and 11 00
No.107. Same Style as 97. Flannel, each,
$5 00 and 6 50

No. 108. Same Style as 100. Ladies' cloth, etc., etc.,each.... .. ..$7 00 and 8 50
No. 109. Same Style as 100. Flannel, each.. $5 75

No. 110. Same Style as 102. Ladies' cloth, etc., etc.,each...... ....$10 00 and 12 00
No. 111. Same Style as 102. Flannel.......$7 50

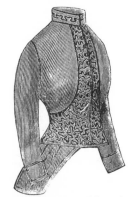

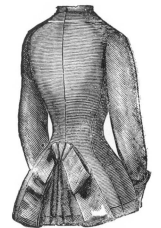

1. All wool Jerseys, coat back, black. 98c, $1 25, 1 50
2. Same style of imported cashmere, black only,
$1 75 2 00, 2 25, 2 65
3. Same style colored,
$2 25, 2 65

No. 4. Elegant Cashmere Jersey, with vest front; can be had in brown, with tan vest trimmed with wooden beads, or black with cardinal vest, trimmed with jet beads................$4 9~

No. 5. Very stylish Cashmere Jersey, short braided front and postillion back, black only...........$2 50

No. 6. All Wool Jersey, with fan back and bow; black only,
$1 15 and 1 30
No. 7. Same, in Cashmere,
$1 50 and 1 75

No. 8. Beatrice; imported Cashmere Jersey, coat front with vest of contrasting color; brown only.......................$5 25

Beaded Jerseys.

No. 18. Beaded Cashmere Jerseys, in a variety of designs,
$4 25 and 5 60

No. 9. Imported Cashmere Jersey with vest front, edged with rosary beads,
$3 75

No. 10. Very nice Cashmere Jersey, coat back with four loops of same material.. $2 75

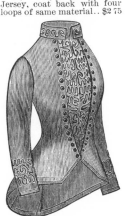

No. 13. All Wool Jersey, with braided front.... .....$1 35
No. 14. Better quality...$1 75
No. 15. Same, of Cashmere,
$2 50 and 3 25

No. 11. Battenberg: imported Cashmere Jersey; can be worn double breasted, buttoned on side or hooked in front, military style as illustrated...............................$3 50

No. 12. Imported Cashmere Jersey, edged with gilt braid buttoned, diagonally coat back.............$3 95

No. 16. Lawn Tennis Jersey, embroidered with lawn tennis designs; in navy blue and garnet......$3 75

No. 17. Braided Jersey, made of all wool jersey cloth, black only.... $2 25 and 2 75

No. 19. Boucle Jersey, postillion back, buttoned diagonally, faced with satin; in black, brown, navy blue and drab,
$3 95

No. 20. Handsome Cashmere Jersey, colored vest trimmed with embroidery; can be had in black and red, or black and white.....$2 65

LADIES' WRAPS, ETC.

No. 22. Handsome soleil Wrap, trimmed with beaded chenille fringe............ ..$5 75 and 7 00

No. 23. Silk Ottoman Wrap, trimmed with beaded chenille fringe............ $9 25 and 12 50
No. 24. Same style, in brocaded velvet....... ....$8 00

No. 21. Very pretty brocaded velvet Wrap, long tabs in front, trimmed with 2 rows of lace headed with beaded gimp,
$12 50 and 15 50

No. 25. Stylish Boucle Jacket, to be hooked diagonally with cord loops, trimmed with velvet, coat back....................$8 75

RIDING HABITS.

No. 29. Very handsome Wrap, (imported) made of Ottoman cloth richly beaded, trimmed with lace; black only $11 50

No.30. Handsome black Brocaded Velvet Wrap, trimmed with beaded gimp and lace, epaulets of beaded gimp $16 50 and 20 00
No. 31. Same, of Grenadine, with colored silk lining,
$19 00, 22 50 and 25 50

No. 26. Ladies' cloth Raglan, double breasted, of twilled cloth, plaited in back, trimmed with braid; in black, brown and blue .. $10 75
No. 27. Single breasted Raglan, of twilled cloth, plaited back; in black and brown $7 00
No. 28. Raglan, made of Bison cloth, in black and brown, double box plaited back, roling collar.................... ..... $8 75 and 11 25

No. 32. Boucle Jacket, with vest of contrasting color, edged with wooden beads.... $5 75 and 7 25

No. 33. All wool Jersey Jacket, double breasted front, coat back,
$3 75, 4 50 and 6 00

No. 34. The above illustration repre sents a Riding Costume, made in navy blue, bottle green, dark garnet, black or seal brown cloth; according to quality...............$16 00, 18 00 and 20 00
35. Same, in flannel $13 50, 15 50 and 18 00

72. **Ladies' Cambric Skirt and Basque,** skirt with two ruffles on bottom and basque with one ruffle $1 60

73. In Calico $1 00, 1 25, 1 35

74. **Very pretty striped Jersey Flannel Wrapper;** shirred back and Princess front, knife plaiting round bottom, with belt of ribbon; all colors . . $7 50
Sizes in stock only 34, 36, 38, 40, 42.

75. **Very handsome Cashmere Wrapper;** Princess style elaborately trimmed with braid in front, on collar, cuffs and pockets; colors, black, navy blue, light blue, brown and pink, $8 75

76. **Very neat Mother Hubbard Wrapper of Flannel,** knife plaiting round bottom; plaited yoke and turned down collar; in brown, navy blue garnet, bottle green, gray and black. $5 00

77. Same, of Cashmere 4 50

77. **Princess Wrapper,** neat patterns, cambric, with two flounces . . . $1 49

78. In Calico $1 25

79. In French Sateen . . . $2 50, 2 75, 3 25

80. **Very pretty Mother Hubbard Wrapper,** in Cambric $1 65

81. In Calico $1 35

82. In White Lawn $2 00, 2 25, 2 50

83. In Sateen, ... $2 25, 2 50, 2 75, 3 00

84. **Cambric Mother Hubbard Wrapper,** with watteau back, . . . $1 85

85. Better quality $2.25

86. **Neat Cambric Wrapper,** princess style, box plaited front and flounce round bottom $1 65

87. Better quality $1 85

Ladies' Wrappers.

58. White lawn wrapper, with yoke of all-over embroidery ; sleeves and pockets trimmed to match; ruffle on bottom, $2 25, 2 75 and 3.75
59. Same style without embroidery, $1 75 and 2 25

No. 60. Very pretty ginham wrapper, trimmed with colored embroidery and plaited yoke, $2 75

61. Elegant white lawn wrapper, deep embroidered ruffle round bottom, embroidery down front, embroidered yoke and sleeve, satin belt . . . . $5 25 and 6 50

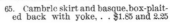

62. Neat Mother Hubbard Wrapper of calico . . . . . 95c and $1 20
63. Same style of cambric . . $1 40
66   "   "   lawn, $150 and 1.75

64. Cambric jersey wrapper, $1.45 and 1.65

65. Cambric skirt and basque, box-plaited back with yoke, . . $1.85 and 2.25

66. Neat cambric wrapper, plaited front, all colors. $65

LINEN DUSTERS AND RAGLANS. CHILDREN'S RUBBER COATS.   LADIES' RUBBER COATS.

37. Mother Hubbard Child's Coat, black only
....$1 10
38. Misses' Circular with hood, black or silver...$1 15
39. Misses' Newport, black or gray......$1 25

40. Ladies' Silver Gray Gossamers, lined with Alpaca, reversible,
$3 25, 4 25, 6 00
41. Silver Gray Circulars, guaranteed water-proof... ....$1 65

42. Same, Newports..$1 98
43. Dolman, new style,
$1 98

33. **Pongee Linen Raglan,** double breasted tucked back................$3 25
34. Linen Ulster, double breasted, back of skirt plaited, rolling collar........$1 25, 1 50
35; Linen Raglan, double breasted, double box plaits in back, dolman sleeves.....$1 75
36' Mohair Raglan, double breasted, double box plaits in back......................$2 98

RUBBER GOODS.

NOT ILLUSTRATED.

44. Servia Circular $1 25
45. Servia Newports.............. $1 50, $2 00
46. Olivette Circular..............................$1 75
47. Newport, with checked lining...........$2 50
48. Circular, with checked lining...........$2 20

Our next number of this Price List will be issued early in the Fall; we will send a copy free of charge to any one applying for it by postal card or letter.

In this Price List we do not give illustrations and prices for Winter goods, but we have always on hand a large assortment suitable for cold climates; and we will cheerfully furnish prices of such articles on application.

All our goods are marked at the lowest prices, which do not include postage. No goods sent by mail, except sufficient money accompanies the order, for postage; otherwise we will reduce orders, and take out part of goods to the amount of postage required.

CHILDREN'S SUITS.

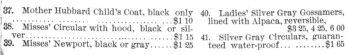

494   495   496   497-498

No. 494. Boys' One Piece Suit, skirt of all wool plaid, waist of plain goods to match; colors, brown, navy blue and gray; age, 2 to 5 years $3 85
No. 495. Boys' Neat Two Piece Suit, of checked cassimere; plaited skirt, trimmed in back and front with tucks, belt of same goods; colors, gray and brown; age, 2 to 5 years $4 95
No. 496. Neat Two Piece Killt Suit, of checked cassimere, trimmed with silk velvet; skirt knife-plaited at sides, waist plaited with velvet vest insertion, and pockets, collar and band of velvet; age 2 to 5 years...$5 10
No. 497. Boys' Neat One Piece Suit, made of flannel, brown, gray and navy blue; age 2 to 5 years $2 75
No. 498. Homespun Cheviot, same colors $4 25

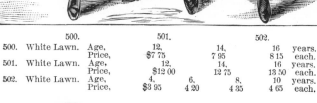

500.	White Lawn.	Age,	12,		14,		16	years.
		Price,	$7 75		7 95		8 15	each.
501.	White Lawn.	Age,	12,		14,		16	years.
		Price,	$12 00		12 75		13 50	each.
502.	White Lawn.	Age,	4,	6,		8,	10	years.
		Price,	$3 95	4 20		4 35	4 65	each.

503.	White Lawn.	Age,	4,	6,	8,	10	years.
		Price	$2 05	2 20	2 35	2 55	each.
504.	White Lawn.	Age,	12,		14,	16	years.
		Price,	$1 80		1 95	2 10	each.
505.	White Lawn.	Age,	12,		14,	16	years.
		Price,	$5 60		5 90	6 20	each.

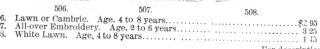

506.	Lawn or Cambric. Age. 4 to 8 years	$2 95
507.	All-over Embroidery. Age, 2 to 6 years	3 25
508.	White Lawn. Age, 4 to 8 years	1 45

509.	Pique, white or cream. Age. 2 to 5 years			$3 95
510.	Pique. Age, 2 to 5 years			4 50
511.	Flannel. Age,	2,	4,	6 years.
	Price,	$3 70	5 95	4 35

For description refer to page 22.

512   513   514

512. Chambray, light blue; age, 2 to 6 years $1 65
513. Checked Chambray; age, 6 to 10 years................................ 1 79
514. Gingham, light blue; age,   10,   12,   14,   16 years.
                    Price $4 75, 5 25, 5 75, 6 25. each.

515   516   517

515. Checked Gingham, blue only; age 2 to 6 years...... .... .95
516. Embroidered Gingham, navy blue and cardinal; age,   2   4   6 years
                          Price, $2 75, 2 95, 3 15, each.
517. Gingham, trimmed with turkey red embroidery;
        Age,   2,   4,   6,   8   years.
        Price, 95c, $1 05, 1 15, 1 25, each.

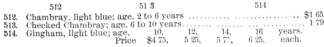

518   519   520

518. Turkey red; age 2 to 5 years...... ....$1 65
519. Chambray, blue or red; age,   4,   6,   8,   10 years.
                Price, $2 60, 2 75, 2 90, 3 05 each.
520. Gingham, with gamp, blue and red; age,   4,   6,   8,   10 years
                    Price, $2 45, 2 60, 2 75 2 90 each

521   522   523

521. Lace, with colored lining; age,   2,   4,   6,   8   years.
                Price, $4 25, 4 60, 4 95, 5 40 each.
522. Embroidered Cashmere, light blue and pink; age,   2,   4,   6 years
                    Price, $3 65, 3 88, 4 15 each
523. Cardinal and navy blue; age,   4,   6,   8,   10,   12 year
                Prices, $3 75, 4 10, 4 45, 4 85, 5 35 each.

For description, see page 22.

524, 525.   526, 527.   528.   529.   530.   531.

524. Gingham, blue and brown, 2 to 6 years 75c
525. 8 to 12 years.................................$1 20
526. Cambric, 4 to 6 years 65c
527. 8 to 12 years.................................70c
528. Seersucker, 4 to 8 years.................................$2 25

529.	Cashmere Jersey cloth.	Age,	2,	4,	6 years
		Price,	$5 40	5 65	5 85 each
530.	Jersey Cloth, navy blue or red.	Age,	2,	4,	6 years
		Price,	$4 50	4 75	5 00 each
531.	Cashmere Jersey cloth, cardinal, blue and brown.	Age,	2,	4,	6 years
		Price,	$5 50	5 75	6 00 each

532, 533.   533.   535.

536.   537.   538.

532.	Tricot, brown, navy blue and garnet.	Age,	10,	12,	14,	16 years
		Price,	$6 50	7 25	8 00	8 75 each
533.	Same style, in Flannel; same colors.	Age,	10,	12,	14,	16 years
		Price,	$5 25	5 75	6 25	6 75 each
534.	Cheviot, navy blue.	Age,	10,	12,	14,	16 years
		Price,	$8 75	9 50	10 25	11 00 each
535.	Flannel, gray and brown.	Age,	6,	8,	10,	12 years
		Price,	$6 25	6 55	6 85	7 15 each

536.	Flannel, brown and blue.	Age,	6,	8,	10,		12 years
		Price,	$3 85	4 20	4 60		4 95 each
537.	Cashmere, navy blue and cardinal.	Age,	2,	3,	4,	5,	6 years
		Price,	$4 20	4 35	4 50	4 75	4 95 each
538.	Twilled Flannel, navy blue only.	Age,	2,	4,	6,	8,	10 years
		Price,	$1 62	1 80	2 05	2 35	2 65 each

For description, see page 22.

CHILDREN'S CLOAKS.

539   540   541   542   543   544

539. Very pretty Misses' Boucle Cloak shirred Skirt, plain vest with belt; silk lined hood; age,

Age,	6,	8,	10,	12	years.
Price,	$4 45	4 85	5 25	5 65	each.

540. Box-plaited Coat of checked material, belt with handsome buckle:

Age,	4,	6,	8,	10,	12	14 years.
Price,	$4 25,	4 75,	5 50,	6 25,	7 00,	7 75 each.

541. Misses' Jacket of fancy material, vest front trimmed with large buttons:

Age,	10,	12,	14	16	years.
Price,	$4 75,	5 50,	6 25,	7 00	each.

No. 542. Very pretty Child's Coat, made of plain Flannel, with silk lined hood, trimmed with ribbon bow; 2 to 5 years. $3 65

No. 543. Striped Flannel Coat, box-plaited front and back, trimmed with very handsome metal buttons; age,

	6,	8,	10	12	years.
Price,	$5 25,	5 75,	6 25,	7 00,	each.

No. 544. Very stylish Child's Coat, made of plain cloth, gathered round waist; and trimmed with colored ribbon hood lined with silk; colors, tan and brown

Age,	2,	4,	6,	8,	10	years.
Price,	$6 50,	7 25,	8 00,	9 25,	10 50	each.

No. 545. Very pretty white Merino Coat, plaits in front and back, trimmed with ribbon embroidered collar and cuffs; in cream, navy blue, tan, garnet and brown...$3 85

No. 546. Child's Walking Coat of striped Jersey Flannel; double box plaited back and front, trimmed with sash and bow; 2 to 6 years, ... $2 95

No. 547. Child's Mother Hubbard Cloak, basket flannel; colors, light blue, cream, cardinal, garnet and navy; sizes, 6 months to 4 years, $3 75

No 548. Elegant Child's Coat of merino, tucked skirt, plaited satin front with stripes of satin across cream only............. $5 65

DESCRIPTION OF SUITS ON PAGES 18, 19 and 20.
MISSES' AND CHILDREN'S SUITS.

500. Very pretty two-piece suit for miss, of white lawn, skirt with tucked front ; side and back knife plaited and trimmed with embroidery ; waist with plaited vest, trimmed with embroidery and satin ribbon bows.

501. Neat Misses' Suit of best quality lawn; skirt trimmed with two deep flounces of fine embroidery; waist trimmed with embroidery, vest insertion; satin, ribbon belt and bow.

502. One piece Misses' Suit of white lawn, richly trimmed with embroidery; tucked yoke and shirred front.

503. White Lawn Suit trimmed with Hamburg embroidery as illustrated.

504. 2 Piece Lawn Suit for miss ; skirt trimmed with 5 tucks, plaited blouse with belt.

505. Misses' 2 piece Suit of white lawn ; skirt trimmed with narrow tucks and 2 rows of handsome embroidery; baby waist with embroidered yoke and belt.

506. Very pretty Suit of white lawn or cambric ; skirt with one row of handsome embroidery headed by 4 tucks ; waist box-plaited front and back with one row of insertion in centre and loose band of embroidery on each side; can be had for children from 4 to 8 years.

507. Elegant suit of all over embroidery and 2 deep flounces of Hamburg edge, wide sash trimmed with edging to correspond; age 2 to 6 years.

508. White Lawn Suit, with 3 narrow tucks round bottom; tucked front, and back with one row of embroidery down each side in front, age 4 to 8 years.

509. Handsome one piece kilt suit of pique, for boys; box-plaited front and back; can be had in white or cream; age 2 to 5 years.

510. Boys' 2 piece kilt suit of pique; plaited skirt; waist with vest insertion; age 2 to 5 years.

511. Boys' 2 piece Sailor Suit of flannel, trimmed with white braid, box plaited skirt; blouse with sailor collar; age 2, 4 and 6 years.

512. Chambray blouse suit with sailor collar, trimmed with striped goods to match; light blue; age 2 to 6 years.

513. Checked Chambray suit, trimmed with turkey red and embroidery; gretchen style ; skirt gathered at waist and tucked bottom; turkey red yoke trimmed with embroidery; age 6 to 10 years.

514. Two piece gingham suit; tucked skirt trimmed with colored embroidery; waist with tucked front and a band of embroidery on each side; can be had in light blue; age 2 to 5 years.

515. Pretty style of checked gingham dress, trimmed with plain goods to match; blue only; age 2 to 6 years.

516. Stylish embroidered gingham suit; to be worn with gamp waist; navy blue and cardinal; age 2 to 6 years.

517. Very neat gingham dress; trimmed with 3 tucks ; edged with turkey red round bottom; waist jacket shape : plaited front, trimmed with turkey red embroidery; age 2, 4, 6 and 8 years.

518. Child's neat turkey red suit, with deep ruffle of embroidery, double box-plaited front and back; embroiderd yoke trimmed with edging; age 2 to 5 years.

519. Child's chambray suit; with deep flounce of embroidery; with baby waist and embroidered yoke; blue and red; age 4, 6, 8 and 10 years.

520. Child's neat suit, with adjusted gamp ; laced; skirt one deep flounce of embroidery; blue and red only; age 4, 6, 8 and 10 years.

521. Very pretty lace suit; with colored lining; trimmed with lace round bottom and ribbon bows for girls from 2 to 8 years of age.

522. Embroidered cashmere dress, laced front with a vest of contrasting color; silk embroidered bottom; headed by 3 tucks ; worsted lace collar; colors, light blue, cardinal and pink ; age 2, 4, 6 and 8 years.

523. Two piece suit of flannel plaited skirt, trimmed with braid ; blouse trimmed to correspond; cardinal and navy blue; age 4, 6, 8, 10 and 12 years.

524 and 525. Very pretty gingham suit, trimmed with striped goods to match; plain goods and striped skirt; can be had in blue or brown; age from 2 to 12 years.

526 and 527. Polka dot cambric dress, with baby waist; age from 4 to 12 years.

528. Striped seersucker suit; skirt with 3 tucks; waist with tucked cambric insertion; 2 embroidered bands across, and trimmed with embroidery and belt; age 4 to 8 years.

529. Imported cashmere jersey dress; knife plaits in front, collar and sides; scalloped and trimmed with jersey cloth of contrasting color; belt and fancy wooden buckles ; age 2, 4 and 6 years.

530. Imported jersey blouse suit, plaited skirt of navy blue or red jersey cloth, with blouse of white or goods to match ; age 2, 4 and 6 years.

531. Imported cashmere jersey dress; trimmed with white hercules braid ; buttoned diagonally; cardinal, blue and brown; age 2, 4 and 6 years.

532 and 533. Two piece tricot suit for miss, skirt plaited at side and back; trimmed with fancy buttons; shawl drapery in front and neatly draped in back; short basque buttoned at side; navy blue, brown and garnet ; age 10, 12, 14 and 16 years; can also be had in flannel in same colors.

534. Misses' stylish combination suit of cheviot; striped skirt; with drapery and waist of plain goods to match; striped vest with revers and fancy buttons; can be had in navy blue; age 10, 12, 14 and 16 years.

535. One piece Misses' suit of flannel; trimmed with velvet in contrasting colors ; plaited skirt and coat shaped waist ; bodice of same material; revers of velvet; colors gray and brown; age 6, 8, 10 and 12 years.

536. Very pretty flannel suit; plaited skirt and loose jacket, trimmed with narrow white hercules braid ; colors blue and brown ; age 6, 8, 10 and 12 years.

537. Elegant sailor suit of cashmere ; double box-plaited skirt ; trimmed with hercules braid and anchors ; blouse trimmed with braid and ribbon bows; navy blue and cardinal; age 2 to 6 years.

538. Sailor suit of twilled flannel ; shirred skirt trimmed with 3 rows of braid ; blouse trimmed to correspond, navy blue only; age 2 to 10 years.

BATHING SUITS, &c.

549. Men's Bathing Suits, as illustrated, M. H. M. blue flannel, all wool $1 50
550. Belvidere A, blue flannel, very heavy . . 2 00
551. Woven Suits, one piece, fancy striped,
                    $1 00, 1 50 and 2 00
552. Bathing Tights, per pair . . . 15, 25 and 35c

553. Boys' Bathing Suits, as illustrated,
| Sizes, | 4, | 6, | 8, | 10, | 12 yrs. |
| Price, | $1 50, | 1 75, | 2 00, | 2 25, | 2.50 each. |

554. Boys' one-piece Bathing Suits, trimmed with worsted braid,
| Sizes, | 4, | 6, | 8, | 10, | 12 yrs. |
| Price, | $1 00, | 1 10, | 1 20, | 1 30, | 1 40 each. |

CANVAS BATHING BELTS.
555. In red, white, blue and black, 2 in. wide, 15c
556. 2½ inch, 2 straps 21c
557. 2½ inch, 3 straps 29c
558. 3-inch, 3 straps 32c

BATHING CAPS, ETC.
559. Oil Silk Bathing Caps, each,
           18, 20, 25, 35 and 50c
560. All styles of Bathing Shoes, per pair.
           75c, $1 00 and 1 25

561. Ladies' Bathing Suits, as illustrated, made of M. H. M. flannel. $3 00
562. Made of Belvidere A. flannel 3 50
563. Made of plain M. H. M. flannel 2 50
564. Misses' Suits, as illustrated above.
| Sizes, | 4, | 6, | 8, | 10, | 12 yrs. |
| Price, | $1 50, | 1 75, | 2 00, | 2 25, | 2 50 each |

565. Misses' Suits, plain,
| Sizes, | 4, | 6, | 8, | 10, | 12 yrs. |
| Prices, | $1 00, | 1 25, | 1 50, | 1 75, | 2 00 each |

Shawls, Etc.

1. Elegant all-wool Cashmere Scarf, can be had plain or with embroidery, all colors; price, plain, $2 75 and $3 50; embroidery, $3 75 4 50, 6 00 and 8 50

2. Hand-knitted Shetland Wool Shawl, in shell or basket stich, in blue, black, white or cardinal.
$1 50, 1 75, 2 00 and 2 50
3. Machine made, Fancy Stich,
75c, $1 00, 1 25, 1 50, 1 75, 2 00 and 2 50
4. Hand made.........$1 50, 1 85, 2 50, 3 00, 3 50 and 4 00
5. Hand made Zephyr Breakfast Shawls..........$1 75

6. Embroidered Cashmere Fichu, all-wool, black only,
$1 75, 2 25, 3 00, 3 50, 4 00, 4 50 and 5 00

Shawls.

(NOT ILLUSTRATED.)

8. Plaid Shawls, with plain centers
$4 50, 5 50, 6 50 and 7 50
9. Single, full size, plain centers,
$1 75, 2 25, 2 75, 3 25 and 4 00
10. Paisley Woven Shawls. $5 00 to 15 00
11. Single Woolen Shawls,
$1 50, 2 00, 2 25, to 5 00
12. Double Woolen Shawls,
13. Black Cashmere Shawls, square,
$2 25 to 5 00
14. Double Chasmere Shawls, square
$3 00 to 15 00
15. Reversible Beaver Shawls, all wool
$4 50, 5 49, 6 85 and 7 95
16. Cashmere Square Shawls, colors cream, cardinal, blue, pink, $1 25, 1 75, 2 25, 3 00

7. Imported Jacquard Shawl, plaid center and broche border.......................$7 50 and 9 00

17. Square Persian Shawls, various colors and designs........$2 00, 3 50, 5 00, 6 00, 8 00 and 10 00

18. Cheched all-wool, Watervliet make,..$3 85
19. Waterloo make................... 4 15
20. Rochester make.................... 4 00
21. Sterling make........................ 3 05

22. Camel's Hair. felled centers..$65 00 to 75 00
23. Imitation, $9 00, 10 50, 12 50, 15 00, 18 00, 12 50, 25 00 to................ ....$30 00

24. French Silk Broche Shawls.
$10 50, 12 50 and 15 0

Ladies' Skirts.

1. Very handsome Skirt of imported Farmer's satin (guaranteed fast black) with two rows deep of box plaits round bottom headed with bands of same material, price... $1 45
2. Same, with one row of box plaits 1 20

3. Very neat Poplin Skirt, with deep knife plaiting, trimmed with five rows of braid........................$1 75

4. Very handsome striped Poplin Skirt, trimmed with box and knife plaits with embroidered band between..$1 35

5. Fancy Striped Seersucker Skirt, deep knife plaiting round bottom and band above................. .... 60c
6. Same, better quality.......... ...75c

7. Neat Poplin Skirt, knife plaiting round bottom headed by two braided bands... ....64c

8. Fancy Striped Chambray Skirt, with two rows of box plaits and two bands $1 95

9. Colored Farmer's Satin Skirt, trimmed with box plaits, red and black stripes between.....................95c

10. Neat Poplin Skirt, trimmed with four rows of piped box plaits and band.................... ...70c
11. Same, with two rows of box plaits............................ 55c

12. Gingham Skirt, knife plaiting round bottom with three rows of handsome embroidery between bands......$1 35

13. Very Pretty Seersucker Skirt, with deep ruffle and fold on bottom, embroidered..........................$1 37

14. Skirt of Seersucker, "Special Bargain"........................ .40c
15. Same, of plain Poplin, with piped band.............. ....28c

16. Gingham Skirt, knife plaits round bottom of striped material to match turned at band as illustrated 98c

17. Lawn Tennis Skirt. in different fancy stripes.................. ....$1 55
18. Same, better quality........... 1 75

19. Very Neat Gingham Skirt, two knife plaitings with border and two bands.................. .....$1 10

20. "Special Bargains." Rich-looking Skirt of striped flannel, trimmed with Farmer's satin.......................95c

21. Black Farmer's Satin Skirt quilted around bottom, as per illustration, with 12 rows of quilting.........85c, $1 00, 1 25 and 1 75

LADIES' UNDERWEAR.

As our Ladies' Underwear is made in our own workrooms, under our own supervision, and as we sell directly to the consumers, we are obliged to use greater care in their manufacture than the wholesale manufacturers, whose goods pass through two or three hands before reaching them; and as there are not more than three or four houses in New York that manufacture their own Underwear, we claim that we are enabled to offer superior goods at minimum prices.

Particular attention is paid to Bridal Sets and Ladies' *trousseaux*, of which we have a large and varied assortment constantly on hand. Extra sizes and special designs can be furnished on short notice at a small advance. In ordering, please give full directions as to style, shape, length and width. For chemises give size around shoulders; for drawers give length, and for gowns give bust measure.

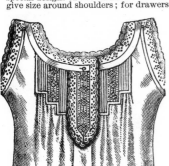

No. 1. Muslin, yoke of Hamburg insertion and tucks, neck and sleeves trimmed with Hamburg edge.....83c

No. 2. Good Muslin Chemise, trimmed with insertion and edging.
45c

No. 3. French Chemises, hand embroidered,
88c, $1.00, 1.25, 1.50, 1.75 and 2.00

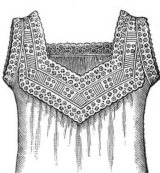

No. 4. Very handsome Pompadour Chemise, fine muslin, yoke of tucks, insertion and edging to match...99c

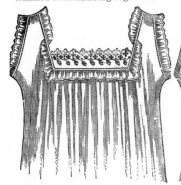

No. 5. Muslin, neck and sleeves trimmed with fine cambric ruffle, band of embroidery across front..40c

No. 6. Corded band, fine muslin.42c
No. 7. Good Muslin Chemise, trimmed with cambric ruffle.........35c

No. 8. Fine Muslin Chemise, bosom with 5 rows of insertion between wide tucks; neck and sleeves trimmed to match.... .... 79c

No.9. Finest Cambric Chemise, yoke of torchon lace and Hamburg insertion, neck and sleeves edged with torchon lace, tucked bottom... $1.25
No. 10. Same style, bottom trimmed with cambric ruffle, edged with lace.........................$1.51

No. 11. Elaborate Cambric Chemise, back and front of all over embroidery, embroidered ruffle on neck and sleeves, tucked bottom,....$1.45

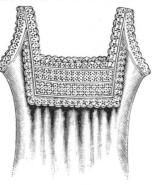

No. 12. Fine Muslin Chemise, square bosom of embroidery, neck and sleeves trimmed to match........71c

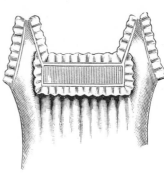

No. 13. Good muslin chemise, pompadour yoke of fine tucking trimmed with cambric ruffle......... ....38c

No. 14. Bosom of solid embroidery and edging to match.............70c

No. 15. Cambric Chemise, bosom of fine embroidery and torchon insertion, finished with torchon lace,98c

No. 16. Fine Muslin, bosom of solid tucking, insertion and needle work edging... ....63c

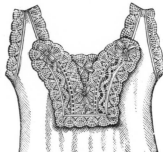

No. 17. Muslin Chemise, bosom of torchon lace, and ribbon drawn through a beading....... ....81c

No. 18. Bosom of tucks and insertion, neck and sleeves edged with embroidery..... .... 48c
No. 19. Same style, much better quality. .... • 65c

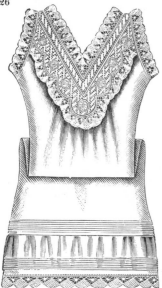 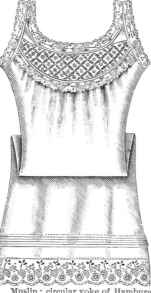 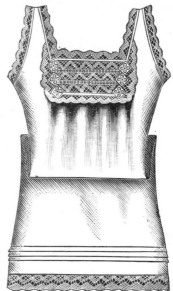 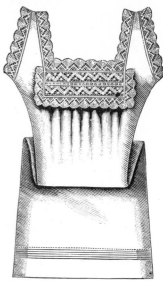

20. Cambric; V shaped yoke of Torchon lace and Hamburg medalions; bottom finished with ruffle, tucked and edged with lace.... ....$1 69

21. Muslin; circular yoke of Hamburg embroidery; bottom handsomely trimmed to match..............$1 15

22. Muslin; square bosom of torchon lace and Medalion; bottom with 3 tucks and wide torchon lace....$1 19

23. Cambric chemise, trimmed with torchon lace and insertion; tucked bottom........................79c.

24. Fine Muslin, 5 tucks on each side of insertion, ruffle of embroidery...................61c.
25. Better quality.........92c.

26. Fine cambric; deep ruffle of Medici lace, and tucks above..................$1 55

27. Very fine muslin drawers, deep ruffle of embroidery, with tucks above.........95c.
28. Same style, with ruffle swiss of embroidery...$1 30

29. Three bands of insertion between tucks, ruffle of embroidery on bottom....$1 25

30. Ruffle of embroidery, French tucking, ...72c.

31. Muslin; two ruffles of embroidery, tucks above..85c.

32. Muslin; 30 fine tucks, deep ruffle of handsome embroidery......................85c.

33. Muslin; ruffle of embroidery on bottom, two clusters of tucks above................ .....63c.

34. Fine muslin drawers; ten fine tucks, two French tucks between...............42c.

35. Fine muslin, trimmed with a cambric ruffle edged with embroidery, tucks above, 39c

36. Hem and 5 tucks.....28c. All these styles can be had open or closed.

37. Ruffle of embroidery, with tucks above......45c.

WHITE SKIRTS.

33. Skirt, with ruffle of handsome em- broidery, two clusters of tucks above.............. ....$1.58

34. Fine Skirt, 2 ruffles of embroidery, headed with fine tucks.......... $1 45
35. Same style, much finer quality $2.35

36. Skirt, with cambric ruffle, band of insertion between tucks, edged with embroidery...$1 19

37. Elegant Skirt, deep ruffle of handsome embroidery, with tucks above......$3.55

38. Very pretty Skirt, deep cambric flounce, trimmed with two ruffles of lace and one of embroidery $1.88

39. Muslin Skirt, cambric ruffle, with wide tucks trimmed with embroidery...............$1.05

40. Cambric ruffle, tucked... 49c

41. Elegant Skirt of muslin, deep flounce of embroidery on bottom, tucks above, $1.23

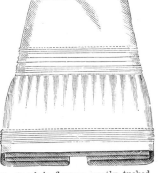

42. Cambric ruffle, with tucks, lace inser- tion and edge..... ....88c
43. Same style, trimmed with real torchon lace....................... ....$1.00

44. Ruffle of fine torchon insertion and tucks, edged with deep lace, $1.68
45. Same style, narrower lace. $1.35

46. Cambric flounce, neatly tucked, two clusters of tucks above ruffle, and two space tucks between...69c

47. Skirt, with two embroidered ruffles, 5 tucks above........$1.00

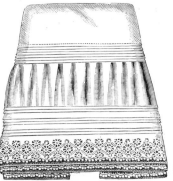

48. Handsome Skirt of muslin, one ruffle of torchon lace, tucks above, and flounce of Hamburg edging.................$1.99

49. Pretty style of Skirt, embroi- dered ruffle, with five tucks above.....................93c

50. Cambric, ruffle, with fancy tucking and deep Hamburg embroidery...$1.29

51. Muslin Skirt, two ruffle of lace, tucks above...................................88c

NIGHT ROBES.

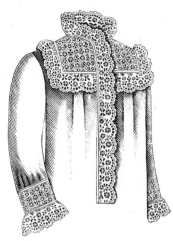

52. Mother Hubbard Gown; double yoke, front and back trimmed with everlasting edge................50c

53. Mother Hubbard Gown; box-plaited yoke, with Hamburg insertion between, neck and sleeves trimmed to match...................87c

54. Yoke of Hamburg insertion and tucking, cambric ruffle on neck and sleeves, edged with embroidery................79c

55. Elegant Muslin Gown; pompadour yoke of solid embroidery, trimmed with deep Hamburg ruffle, sleeves to match............................$1.30

56. Mother Hubbard; very fine muslin, double yoke front and back, rolling collar, trimmed with embroidery..................95c

57. Muslin; square yoke of tucks and insertion, center piece, neck and sleeves trimmed with Hamburg edge.......................79c

58. Very Handsome Mother Hubbard Gown; yoke of fine embroidery and tucks, French sleeves.....$1.21

59. Finest quality Muslin; yoke of large and small tucks, finished with Hamburg ruffle. box-plaited back, $1.05

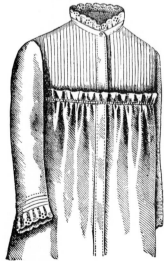

60. Mother Hubbard; tucked yoke, neck and sleeves trimmed with embroidery..................68c

61. Mother Hubbard; yoke of all-over embroidery, neck and sleeves trimmed to match............$1.00

62. Very fine Muslin Robe; bosom of fine tucks and box-plaits, trimmed with embroidery.......$1.09

63. Cambric; yoke and sleeves of fine embroidery and torchon lace, plaited back, $3.25

SHORT GOWNS. (NOT ILLUSTRATED.)

64. Good Muslin, trimmed with cambric ruffle, three tucks down each side 47c
65. Tucked down front, neck and sleeves trimmed with embroidery...58c
66. Pointed bosom of solid embroidery, neck and sleeves trimmed to match..................................$1.20
67. Fine Cambric, yoke of tucks and insertion, neck and sleeves trimmed to match............................1.35

924 TO 928 THIRD AVE., AND 160 TO 164 EAST 56th St., NEW YORK.

29

BRIDAL SETS.

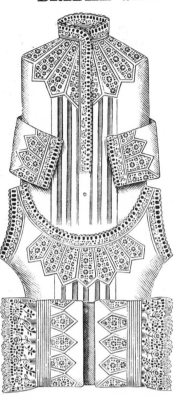

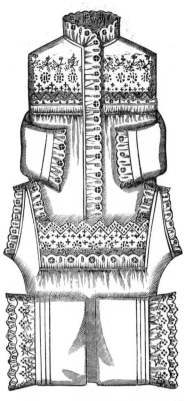

68. Cambric; Gown, with pompadour yoke of fancy tucking timmed with fine torchon lace and ribbon drawn through; Chemise, pompadour shape; Drawers to match.........$5 48
69. Corset Cover to match.................$1 13

70. Elegant Set, of muslin, Gown, with 8 bands of insertion joined together forming handsome yoke; Chemise and Drawers to match....$4 35

71. Fine Muslin; Mother Hubbard Gown, with a yoke of solid embroidery; Pompadour Chemise and Drawers to match...................$2 95

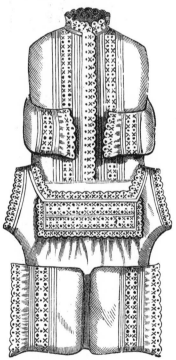

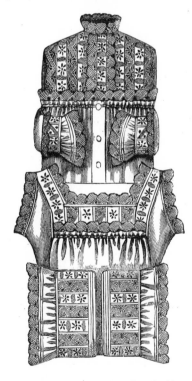

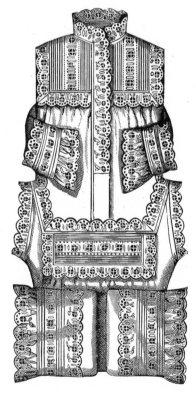

72. Fine Muslin; Gown, trimmed down front to bottom with insertion and tucks: Chemise, pompadour shape; Drawers to match.
Gown...$1 99
Chemise................................ 71
Drawers.................................. 89
Set.. 3 59

73. Cambric; torchon lace and embroidery; a very handsome set.........................$5 21
74. Corset Cover to match, extra........... 1 35

75. Muslin; trimmed with fine embroidery and tucks......................................$4 25

Have your friends send their address and they will receive our Price List. It enables them to buy New York goods at New York prices.
All our goods are marked at the lowest prices, which do not include postage. No goods sent by mail, except sufficient money accompanies the order for postage; otherwise we will reduce orders, and take out part of goods to the amount of postage required.

DRESSING SACQUES.

SIZES FROM 34 TO 46 INCH BUST.

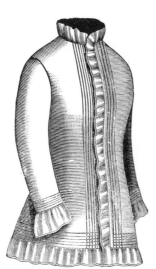

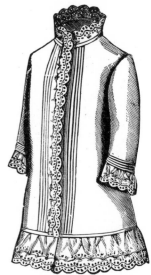

76, Very handsome Sacque of Lawn, richly trimmed with embroidery, ...$2.68.

77. Lawn, trimmed with ruffles of same and tucks.,............72c.

78. Lawn, trimmed with tucks and insertion, ruffles of embroidery on neck, sleeves and round bottom ....$1.95.

79, Lawn, trimmed with tucks and ruffles of embroidery........$1.25

Dressing Sacques—NOT ILLUSTRATED

G. Very Fine Lawn Dressing Sacques trimmed with Nainsook embroidery, ...$2.95
H. Also finer and more elaborate, at $2.95............ ...$3.58 and $4.58

Gamp Waists—NOT ILLUSTRATED

I. Ladies' Gamp Waists with tucked yokes............................98c
J. Gamp Waists with yoke and sleeves of fine embroidery............$2.50

Ladies' Trousseaux.

OUTFIT No. 82, 21 Pieces, $12.40.

1 Chemise with cambric ruffle.	$0.29
1 " trimmed with embroidery.	40
1 " bosom of tucks and embroidery	48
1 Pair Drawers tucked	35
1 " trimmed with embroidery	39
1 " better quality	45
1 Mother Hubbard Gown with edge	50
1 Gown with tucks and insertion.	79
1 " better quality	87
1 Skirt with cambric ruffle, tucked . . .	49
1 " better quality	68
1 " with ruffle of embroidery	93
1 Short underskirt tucked	38
1 " with cambric ruffle	55
1 Bridal Set, 3 pieces	2.98
1 Corset cover, high neck	19
1 " low neck	28
1 Corset	68
1 Dressing Sacque.	72
21 Pieces	$12.40

80. Very handsome striped or plain Flannel Dressing Sacque, with a vest of plain flannel in contrasting colors....... $2.65.

1. Neat Striped or plain Flannel Dressing Sacques all colors, $2.35
Same of striped Jersey cloth $2.65

1 Dressing Sacque,..........................$2.79

31 Pieces... ....$42.68

SHORT UNDERSKIRTS.

A. Good Muslin, hem and five tucks.... 38
B. Same with cambric ruffle............. 48
C. Fine Muslin, with ruffle of embroidery, seven tucks above, ... 75
D. Fine Muslin with tucks, insertion and ruffle of embroidery 98
E. Very fine cambric with three clusters of tucks and deep ruffle of medici lace..$2.25
F. Extra fine quality, with tucks, deep ruffle of medici lace and insertion...$2.88

Have your friends send their address and they will receive our Price List. It enables them to buy New York goods at New York prices.

All our goods are marked at the lowest prices, which do not include postage. No goods sent by mail, except sufficient money accompanies the order for postage; otherwise we will reduce orders and take out part of goods to the amount of postage required.

OUTFIT No. 83, 26 Pieces, $24.52.

1 Muslin Chemise with embroidery,........$0.48
1   "   finer quality   " 65
1   "   bosom of fine   " 71
1 Cambric Chemise, trimmed with lace 79
1 Pair muslin drawers with ruffle of embroidery and tucks.......................49
1 Pair muslin drawers with tucks, insertion and ruffle of embroidery......................60
1 Pair muslin drawers, much finer quality.... 95
1 Mother Hubbard Gown, tucked yoke with cambric ruffle......................59
1 Gown, pointed bosom, tucked and trimmed with embroidery,......................95
1 Mother Hubbard Gown with yoke of tucks, insertion, and ruffle of embroidery, 1.21
1 Gown, pointed yoke with five rows of insertion and tucks..........................1.29
2 Skirts, tucked cambric ruffle, at 49 98
1   "   ruffle of embroidery....................93
1   "   Cambric ruffle, tucked and edged with embroidery.........................1.05
1 Skirt with ruffle of embroidery............1.59
1 Short underskirt with ruffle of embroidery..75
1 Flannel underskirt....................1.75
1 Bridal Set, cambric, 3 pieces................5.18
2 Corset Covers, high neck with embroidery at 29c each.........................58
1 Corset Cover, low neck, finer quality........75
1 Bridal Corset 1.00
1 Dressing Sacque.... ....1.25

26 Pieces, $24.52.

OUTFIT No. 84, 31 Pieces, $42.68.

2 Chemises, fine embroidery and tucks, at 63c. $1.26
1   "   finer quality, at 83c............. 1 66
1 Chemise, bosom fine embroidery.......... 95
1   "   very fine quality lace....... 1.35
2 Pair drawers, ruffles of embroidery and tucks, at 47c. 94
1 Pair   "   deep ruffle of fine embroidery .95
1   "   with fine lace 1.00
2 Gowns, tucked bosom at $1.05 .... 2.10
1   "   square bosom of tucks and embroidery 1.25
1   "   very fine quality................. 1.85
1   "   very fine lace................. 2.35
2 Skirts, fine tucked cambric, ruffle at 68c... 1.36
1   "   ruffle of embroidery............. 1.25
1   "   fine insertion of lace and embroidery 1.99
1   "   very handsome embroidery,..... 3 55
1 very elaborate Bridal Set of lace and embroidery, 3 pieces.................... 6.93
1 Fine flannel underskirt................. 1.75
1 Underskirt, very fine quality, with deep embroidery at bottom................. 2.75
1 Muslin underskirt with tucks, insertion and ruffle of embroidery....................98
2 Corset Covers, high neck, tucked bosom at 49c. 98
1 Corset Cover, low neck with torchon and embroidery....................... 1.19
1 Bridal Corset, fine coutille.............. 1.50

Corset Covers, etc.

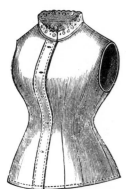

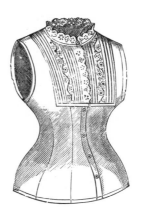

87. Cambric high neck, trimmed with embroidery.........29c
88. Plain Muslin, high or low, 21c

89. Cambric; bosom of fancy-tucking, trimmed with ruffle of embroidery.............50c

90. High neck; bosom of tucks and insertion..............68c

91. Cambric; high neck, yoke of all-over embroidery..$1 15

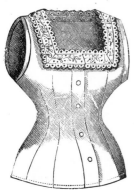

92. Cambric; pompadour front trimmed with embroidery..69c

93. Cambric; bosom of fine torchon and embroidery........$1 19

94. Cambric; square neck, trimmed with wide embroidery 65c

95. Cambric; square neck trimmed with lace and embroidery....78c

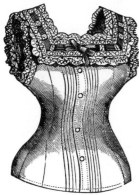

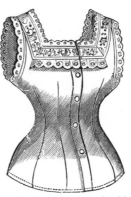

96. Cambric; square neck, trimmed with fine torchon lace, ribbon drawn through........$1 13

97. Cambric; square neck, bosom of tucks and embroidery
..............................71c

98. Square neck, trimmed with embroidery...............65c

99. Cambric; square neck trimmed with embroidery.............75c

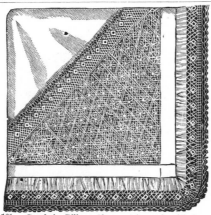

100. Cambric Pillow Shams; ruffle of embroidery and tucks; per pair.... ..$1 98

101. Cambric Pillow Sham; trimmed with lace, per pair...... ....$1 65

102. Elaborate Shams of all-over embroidery, with ruffle of same and tucks between; per pair. $5 25
103. Fine Cambric Shams, with ruffle of the same and 15 tucks; per pair....................$1 50
104. Cambric; ruffle of the same and 5 tucks; per pair. 90c

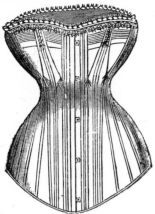

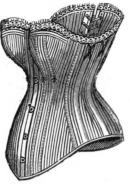

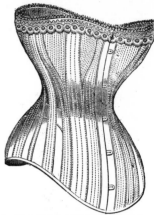

1.   Very good jean corset, white or drab, 18 to 30 inches,...........50c

2.   Extra heavy, double front steels. white or drab, 18 to 30 inches,..$1.00
3.   31 to 36 inches,............... 1.25

4.   American Coutille, hook clasp, linen band inside, 14 three-bone strips outside, boned bosom, edged with everlasting trimming, white drab, 18 to 30 inches,...........$1.00

5.   Heavily boned jean corset, perfect fitting, white or drab, 18 to 30 inches,...........................68c

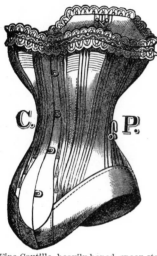

6.   Fine Coutille, heavily boned. spoon steels, broad webbing band around bottom, suitable for stout ladies, white or drab, 20 to 36 inches,............................$3.75

7.   Mme. Clark's Hygeian Corset, double steels, elastic gores, white and drab, 18 to 30 inches, ...$1.25

8.   Roth's Patent Double Bone Corset, whit or drab, 18 to 30 inches, ...$1.2

9.   Nursing Corset made of jean and heavily boned, white or drab, 18 30 inches,...... ....$1.00

10.   Thomson's Abdominable Corset, with elastic gores and side lacing, white or drab, 18 to 30 inches, $1.25.   10 A, 31 to 36, $1.68

11.   Fine French Coutille, perfect fitting, boned bust and spoon steels, white or drab....... .$2.25

12.   American Sateen Corset, with embroidered clasp and silk ribbon, colors white, drab, pink, blue, cardinal, black and old gold, 18 to 30 inches, ...$1.00

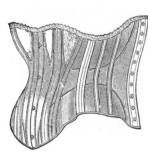

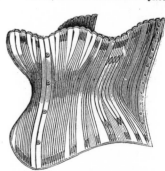

13.   Thomson's "R. H." Corset, extra short, in white or drab, 18 to 30 ihches, ...$1.00

14.   Misses' Hand-made Corset, well boned, white or drab...............63c

15.   Ball's Health Preserving Corset, with wire elastic section, need no "breaking in," guaranteed perfectly satisfactory in every respect, or money refunded after three week's wear, white or drab, 18 to 30 inches...................$1 25

16.   Short French woven corset, 11 inches long, 4 broad bones on each side..............................$1 35

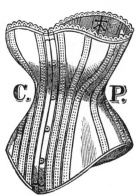
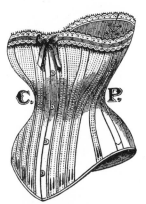
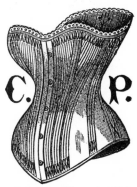

17. "P. D." French Coutille, side steels. white or drab, 18 to 30 inches.................. $1.50

18. "C. P." French Coutille, with side steels, white or drab, 18 to 30 inches...................... $1.50

19. Fine Sateen, trimmed with lace, in black, white, blue, pink cream and red, 18 to 30 inches...... $2.25

20. French Coutille, perfect fitting. boned bust, white or drab, 18 to 30 inches.................. $2.45

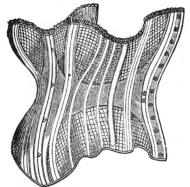

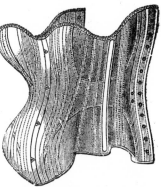

21. Thomson's Ventilating Corset for summer wear, perfect in shape, 98c

22. Fine Satin Bridal Corset, white, gold, black, cream, pink. blue and cardinal, 18 to 30 inches $3.25

23. R. & G. French Sateen Corset, trimmed with Russia lace and silk ribbon, white, drab, pink, blue, cardinal, cream, black and old gold, 18 to 30 inches......... $1.58

24. Thomson's Glove Fitting Corset. quality G, fine coutille, 18 to 32 inches, white or drab....... $1.25
25. 33 to 36 inches $1.50

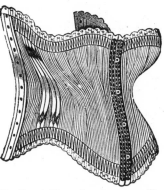

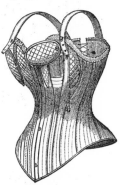
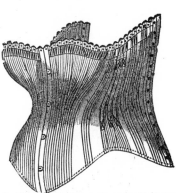

26. French Woven Corset, extra quality, fine bone, scalloped top and bottom, each bone fanned with silk, white or drab, 18 to 30 inches........... $2.00

27. Misses' Fine French Woven Corset........73c
28. Better quality.... $1.00

29. Dr. Warner's Nursing Corset................ $1.35

30. Fine French Woven Corset, extra heavy boned on each side, white or drab, 18 to 30 inches.......................... $1.25
31. Same style, better quality....... $1.62

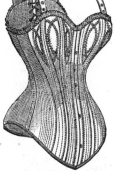

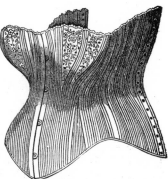

32. French woven corset, embroidered bust, double side bones, white or drab, 18 to 30, $1 00
32a. Same style, extra short,........ $1 00

33. Dr. Warner's Health Corset............ $1.25

34. Dr. Warner's Coraline Corset made throughout of superior material, and is warranted in every respect ; side steels can be removed without injury to the corset in case they are not desired........ $1.00

35. French Woven, with side steels, 18 to 30 inches, white or drab............ 75c

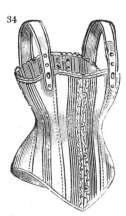

The Pivot Corset.

PAT. MARCH 20, 1883.

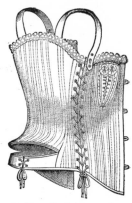

36. Misses' Corset, made of very soft jean, corded and boned, with shoulder straps, 45c.

37. This corset has an expanding hip and bust, yielding to every movement of the wearer, constantly making an easy and elegant fit. It swings on a *pivot* under an underlying extension which preserves the perfect contour of the figure and at the same time separates the elastic from the heat of the body........................98c.

38. Ladies' corset waist, made of fine sateen, buttons in front, laced up the back, cloth covered steels front and back, put in patent pockets and can be instantly removed; 18 to 30 inches, white or drab....$1 50

39. 31 to 36 inches........$1 75

40. Mme. Foy's improved corset, with shoulder straps and skirt supporting attachment..................98c.

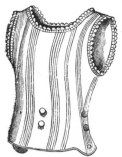

THE LITTLE BEAUTY

TRADE MARK.

41. Child's corded waist, made of extra heavy jean, 55c.

42. Child's corset waist, made of double jean, with clusters of cording.................6c.

43. Shoulder braces for children, youths and adults, white or drab.........79c.

44. Abdominal supporter, supports the abdomen in the most comfortable manner; in ordering give measure around the full part of the abdomen; drab only..................$1 50

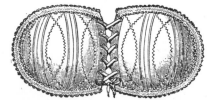

45. Dress Pads made of tampico grass 35c.

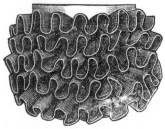

46. The Princess of Wales adjustable bustle; in ordering give waist measure...................69c.

47. Tampico bustle, with 5 rows of box plaiting,........................42c.

48. Ladies' dress forms of hair, with springs........................50c.

49. Alaska down, without wires; one of the most durable bustles made.............39c.

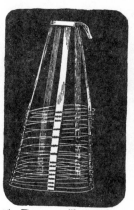

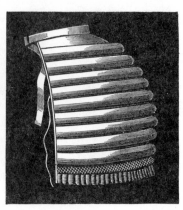

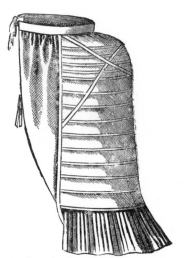

50. Bustle top and tape front, 25 springs.............65c.

51. Hoop, as illustrated, 15 springs.................32c.

52. Alaska down, 9 rolls.............49c.

53. Same, 12 rolls....................68c.

54. Same style in the imitation, with 6 rolls.................25c.

55. Long bustle, made of jean with steels that can be taken out when washed, in white or drab........$1 10

924 TO 928 THIRD AVE., AND 160 TO 164 EAST 56th St., NEW YORK.

35

Misses' Underwear and Worsted Goods.

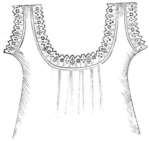

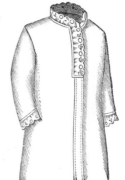

503. Fine Muslin Chemise.
Age, 2 4 6 8 10 12 14 years.
Price, 19 24 26 30 33 35 39 cents.

500. Good Muslin Night Dress, with six tucks on each side of front to waist; neck and sleeves trimmed with ruffle of embroidery.
Age, 2 4 6 8 10 12 14 years.
Price 45 49 55 63 68 75 78 cents.

501. Better quality Night Dress with pointed yoke, three insertions down front between tucks.
Age, 8 10 12 14 years.
Price, 92c 95c $1.00 $1.10

502. Misses' Sacque Chemise of good Muslin, trimmed with ruffle of embroidery.
Age, 2 4 6 8 10 12 14 years.
Price, 29 31 33 35 39 43 45 cents.

504. Good Muslin Night Gowns, trimmed with embroidery.
Age, 2 4 6 8 10 12 14 years.
Price, 42 45 52 56 65 70 75 cents.

506. Very fine Chemise, tucked yoke; trimmed with embroidery.
Age, 2 4 6 8 10 12 14 years.
Price, 39 45 49 55 60 65 70 cents.

507. Fine Muslin Skirt, ruffle of good embroidery, two clusters of tucks above.
Age, 6 8 10 12 14 years.
Price, 51 56 60 65 72 cents,

508. Same quality, with deep hem and two clusters of tucks.
Age, 6 8 10 12 14 years.
Price, 25 27 29 35 40 cents.

505. Child's Muslin Drawers' waist trimmed with embroidery....28c.

510. Fine Muslin Drawers, ruffle of embroidery, tucks above; six button holes in band.
Age, 2 4 6 8 10 12 14 years.
Price, 27 31 33 37 43 47 51 cents.

511. Same style, better quality, with deep embroidery; six buttonholes in band.
Age, 2 4 6 8 10 12 14 years.
Price, 39 44 49 55 58 63 68 cents,

512. Good Muslin Skirt with cluster of 5 tucks and Hamburg edge.
Age 6 mos. to 4 years........28c.

513. Same style, without embroidery ....19c.

514. Plain Muslin Drawers, hem and three tucks with button holes
Age, 2 4 6 8 10 12 14 years.
Price, 13 15 17 20 22 24 26 cents.

509. Children's Muslin Night Gowns.
Age, 2 4 6 years.
Price, 50 55 60 cents.

Misses' Corset Covers.

Cambric; trimmed with Hamburg edge, 42c.
Cambric; trimmed with insertion and Hamburg edge, 59c.

515. Fascinators of Shetland Wool or Crimped Worsted in all colors; to be used as a light head-covering.
518 25c 35c 50c 75c $1.00 $1.50.
c16. Nubias made of worsted with tassels, in black, white and colors.
25c 35c 40c 50c 60c 75c 95c $1.00 $1.25 $1.35 $1.50

517. Infants' Sacque of Split zephyr, hand-knitted in chain stitch, white body, with double scalloped edging of contrasting color, 50c and 75c.

518. Infants' hand made zephyr Sacques, in white, pink and blue................$1.00

519. Others, similar to the above style, 43c. and upward.

520. Worsted Bootees, per pair, 50c.

521. Hand Knit Zephyr Shirts, high or low neck, with either long or short sleeves; knit with the best quality Saxony wool.
48c 60c 75c and $1.00.

Whenever you send us money with an order for goods, and fail to hear from us within ten days after sending the order, please inform us of the fact by letter or postal card, as lost money can be more readily traced when looked after at once. Customers in California or on the Pacific Coast should write within fifteen days after sending.

522. Worsted Bootees, per pair, 25c and 35c.

523. Infants' Satin Shoes and Slippers, embroidery of same color silk...$1.00

524. Cashmere.........1.00

525. Knit Shoes, per pair........ ......15c

526. Finer quality, 23c and upward.

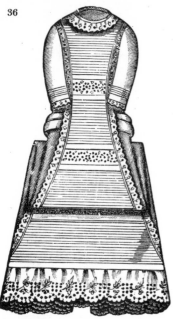

27. Cambric Robe, trimmed down front with 5 rows of Hamburg insertion between clusters of fine tucks, bottom with ruffle of embroidery.........................$1 69

528. Elaborate Robe, entire front of bands of insertion, deep ruffle of embroidery on bottom........................ ....$2 59

529. Cambric, with entire front of alternate rows of wide Hamburg insertion and tucks, deep ruffle of embroidery on bottom, sleeves of the same....... ....$4 48

530. Very fine Cambric Slip, yoke of nainsook embroidery; skirt with 2 rows of Nainsook insertion, between clusters of tucks, ruffle of embroidery at bottom $6 35

531. Elegant Slip of fine Cambric, circular yoke of embroidery, skirt with deep flounce of very fine embroidery, wide insertion, and 2 clusters of tucks on each side.............$4 75

532. Very handsome Slip of Sheer Nainsook, richly trimmed with embroidery, yoke back and front. $4 10

533. Elaborate Slip of fine French lawn, yoke of Valenciennes lace and Swiss insertion; skirt trimmed with two rows of Valenciennes insertion and one of Swiss, also three ruffles of Valenciennes lace..$5 89

534. Fine Cambric, with circular yoke of tucks and insertion, finished with ruffle of embroidery; skirt with ruffle of fine embroidery and two insertions between three clusters of tucks.............$2 75

535. Cambric, square yoke of insertion and tucking, skirt with two rows of insertion between tucks and ruffle of embroidery on bottom $2 31

536. Cambric, square yoke, back and front of solid embroidery, skirt trimmed with deep ruffle of fine embroidery headed by a band of insertion and five fine tucks on each side, sleeves trimmed to match.............$2 48

537. Cambric, yoke back and front of embroidery, bottom with ruffle of the same and two clusters of tucks above $1 99

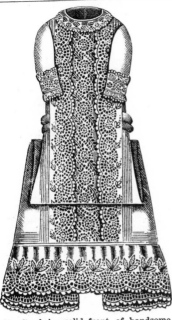

538. Cambric; solid front of handsome embroidery, with tucks on each side, deep ruffle of embroidery on bottom and tucks above......................$2 75

539. Cambric; circular yoke of insertion and tucks, bottom with tucks, insertion and a ruffle of embroidery..............,...$1 75

540. Cambric; square yoke of cluster tucking, skirt trimmed with ruffle of fine embroidery, insertion and tucks.......$1 59

541. Cambric; tucked yoke trimmed with Hamburg edge, neck and sleeves to match, bottom with deep hem................,..........56c.

542. Cambric robe slip; trimmed down front with three box plaits and two rows of insertion, ruffle of embroidery on bottom, sleeves trimmed to match... ....$1 49

543. Fine Cambric slip; yoke of tucks, insertion and ruffle of embroidery; skirt with ruffle of embroidery and two clusters of tucks above........ ....$1 21

544. Cambric; pompadour yoke of tucking trimmed with embroidery; skirt with ruffle of embroidery, one insertion and three wide tucks on each side of it.................$1 05

545. Cambric; handsomely trimmed with insertion between clusters of tucks and a deep ruffle of embroidery...................... $2 75

546. Cambric; square yoke of cluster tucking with one insertion in centre; skirt with ruffle of embroidery and tucks above............81c.

547. Cambric Slip; tucked yoke edged with embroidery, skirt with tucks and ruffle of embroidery, 98c.

548. Cambric Slip; yoke of embroidery, bottom with deep hem and cluster of tucks above......................63c.

549. Muslin, neatly trimmed with embroidery, tucked bottom......................38c.

CHILDREN'S SHORT DRESSES.   Sizes 18, 20 and 22 inches long.

550. Very handsome "Greenaway" dress, yoke front and back of solid nainsook embroidery, entire skirt an elegant ruffle of the same embroidery, $5.15.

551. Very elaborate "Gretchen" dress waist of tucks and nainsook embroidery, skirt one deep flounce of embroidery to match, $4.25.

552. Gamp dress, tucked yoke, waist, skirt and sleeves of fine embroidery, $4.20.

553. Elaborate low neck dress, waist tucked and trimmed with nainsook embroidery; skirt one deep flounce of elegant nainsook embroidery, $3.50.

554. Mother Hubbard slip, one deep ruffle of solid embroidery; neck, yoke and sleeves to match, $2.75.

555. Cambric, square yoke of solid embroidery, skirt with deep flounce of embroidery, headed by 3 clusters of tucks $2.53.

556. Cambric, yoke with 3 bands of insertion; skirt trimmed with ruffle of embroidery and one insertion between two wide tucks, 85c.

557. Cambric, pompadour yoke of tucks, insertion and hamburg edge; skirt with 2 insertions between 3 clusters of tucks and a ruffle of fine embroidery, $2.58.

558. Lawn yoke of Hamburg embroidery skirt trimmed with embroidery, two rows of insertion and tucks between; wide sash in back, $2.35.

559. "Gretchen" dress, waist with two rows of fine insertion between 3 box plaits; skirt trimmed with deep embroidery headed by 3 French tucks, $1.95.

560. Greenaway dress, waist with square yoke of tucks and insertion. waist band of insertion; skirt one deep flounce of Hamburg embroidery, $1.79.

561. Cambric, square yoke of solid embroidery; bottom trimmed with one row of insertion between two clusters of tucks and a ruffle of embroidery, $1.85.

562. Handsome Child's Dress, yoke front and back of embroidery, same as flounce, 5 box plaits down front and back................ $1.69

563. Cambric slip, trimmed with fine embroidery and tucks.........$1.69

564. Cambric, yoke front and back of tucks and embroidery, deep ruffle of embroidery on skirt, with tucks above................ $1.59

565. Mother Hubbard Dress of Victoria lawn, yoke back and front of ½ in. tucks, bottom with tucks to match, and trimming of deep embroidery, $1.58

566. French Lawn. waist with 3 rows of insertion, skirt with deep hem and tucks above............................... $1.25

567. Cambric "Gretchen" Dress, waist tucked, back and front with ruffle of embroidery at neck, skirt tucked to match, 73c

568. Cambric, square yoke of solid embroidery, waisband of insertion, skirt tucked, $1.10

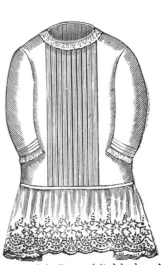

569. Cambric Dress, plaited back and front, deep ruffle of embroidery on bottom, neck and sleeves trimmed with Hamburg edge............$1.15

571. Infants' Merino Sacques, hand embroidered.....98c, $1.10 and $1.25
572. Flannel Sacque, with three rows of chain stitching all around in red, white or blue............ ....50c

573. Cambric, tucked back and front, trimmed with Hamburg edge....38c
574. Same, with 3 rows of insertion and tucks................... ....60c
575. Yoke of solid embroidery 85c

570. Greenaway Dress, cross-bar muslin, neck and sleeves trimmed with ruffle of the same, skirt with wide hem.......63c

576. Child's Gamp Waist of cambric, yoke of embroidery 85c
577. Same in very fine quality ...$1.49

578. Child's Gamp Waist of cambric, yoke tucked back and front, sleeves tucked and trimmed with embroidery; age 2 to 6 years.............69c
579. 8 to 12 years...................79c

580. Box plaited front and back, two insertions down front.............36c
581. Same style, with embroidery on ruffle............. 65c

INFANTS' WEAR.

Of Infants' Wear we have a large assortment constantly on hand, including all qualities and styles—plain as well as most elaborate—all equally well made and nicely finished.   Every article can be obtained singly, although we would recommend those customers who require a complete outfit to order the whole set, as each of these includes all the necessary articles, and nothing is forgotten.   These outfits consist of infants' long clothes, are well selected, and prove very popular.

INFANTS' OUTFITS.

575.
Infants' Outfit A.
26 PIECES, $14.64.

1 Robe, front tucked and embroidered.......$1.69
1 Day Slip, trimmed with embroidery........ 38
1   "   "   "   "   81
1   "   "   "   " 1.49
4 Night Slips at 25c............. 1.00
4 Cambric Shirts at 12c........... 48
2 Flannel Shirts at 88c........... 1.76
1 Embroidered Flannel Shirt......... 1.75
3 Bands at 18c 54
2 Barrow Coats at 60c........... 1.20
1 Muslin Skirt, tucked............ 33
1 Cambric   "   "   58
1 Flannel Shawl, hand embroidered..... 98
2 Pair Bootees at 15c........... 30
1 Piece Linen Diaper............. 1.35
                                    ———
26 Pieces $14.64

576.
Infants' Outfit B.
33 PIECES, $28.60.

1 Robe $2.98
1 Day Slip 63
1   " 1.21
1   " 1.59
1   " 2.00
4 Night Slips at 33c 1.32
2 Plain Flannel Skirts at 88c 1.76
1 Embroidered Flannel Skirt 2.25
2 Barrow Coats at 79c 1.58
4 Bands at 25c 1.00
1 Flannel Shawl, hand embroidered . . . 1.50
6 Linen Shirts, trimmed with lace, at 25c. . . 1.50
1 Piece Linen Diaper 1.75
2 Pair Bootees at 25c 50
1 Cambric Skirt 58
1   "   "   trimmed with embroidery..|. 1.10
1   "   "   more elaborite 1.35
1 Infants' Basket 3.75
1 Rubber Diaper 25
                                    ———
33 Pieces. $28.60

577.
Infants' Outfit C.
51 PIECES, $50.86.

1 Very Elaborate Robe $4.50
1 Day Slip. 1.05
1   " 1.49
1   " 1.50
1   " 2.00
1   " 2.48
6 Night Slips, cambric, at 39c 2.75
2 Flannel Skirts at $1.20 . . . . 2.34
1 Embroidered Flannel Skirt 2.40
1 Very Handsome "   " 1.98
4 Barrow Coats at 79c 3.98
6 Flannel Bands at 25c 3.16
1 Flannel Shawl, hand embroidered. . . 1.50
6 Linen Shirts,trimmed with torchon lace,35c 1.79
1 Piece Linen Diaper. 2.10
3 Pair Bootees at 30c 2.25
2 Cambric Skirts at 58c 90
1   "   "   with embroidery 1.16
1 Handsome Cambric Skirt 1.10
1 Infants' Basket.. . . . . 1.75
1 Rubber Diaper 4.50
1 Flannel Wrapper 53
6 Bibs at 15c 2.75
                                    90
                                    ———
51 Pieces. $50.86

Long Cambric Skirts.

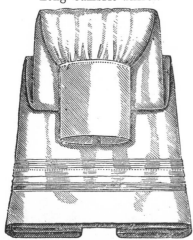

578. Infants' Cambric Skirt with fancy tucking,58c
579. Muslin. deep hem and cluster of tucks above,
579. A. Muslin trimmed with tucks and Hamburg
edge 63c

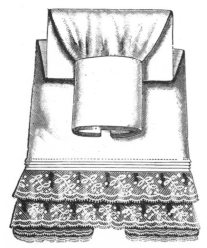

585. Muslin Skirt, with two ruffles of Valenciennes lace 88c

Baby Basket.

580. Infants' Basket, covered with Swiss over
colored Selisia, trimmed with ribbon and lace,
pocket and cushions . . . . $3.75, 4.50 and 5.50
581.   Articles necessary for child's toilet, as illustrated in basket above, $1.00 to $2.00, according
to quality.

Short Flannel Skirts.

586. Infants' Short Skirts of Gilbert flannel, with
feather stitching 65c
587. Short Skirts of Gilbert flannel, with plain
hem 55c
588. Short Skirts of Gilbert Flannel, embroidered
with silk, age 6 mos. to 4 years, as illustrated
above,. $1.33
589. Other styles, made of Gilbert flannel, embroidered in silk, various designs, 85c, 95c, $1.25
and $1.75.

Barrow Coats.

590. Infants' Flannel Barrow Coats, 60c, 69c, 79c

Long Cambric Skirts.

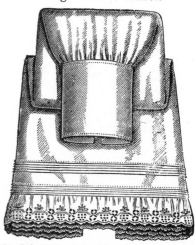

582. Infants' Cambric Skirt, with ruffle of embroidery and two clusters of tucks . . . 98c
583. Same style, better quality and finer embroidery. $1.19
584. Same style, with one insertion $1.05

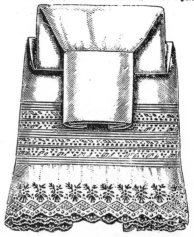

591. Cambric, two insertions between tucks, ruffle
of fine embroidery $1.75
592. Finer quality $2.50
593. Same style, with one insertion $1.48

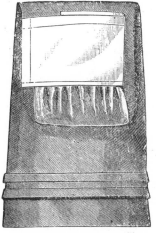

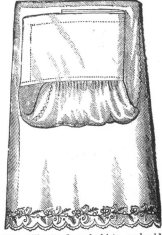

594. Infants' skirts, made of Gilbert's flannel, richly embroidered with silk, various designs, $2.75, $2.88, $3.00, $3.25 and $3.75.

595. Infants' skirt, made of Gilbert's flannel with hem and two tucks, $1 19
596. Infants' flannel skirts, 69c. 88c. and $1 00.

597. Gilbert's flannel skirts, embroidered in silk...... ....$1 75
598. Flannel skirts embroidered in silk, various neat designs...$1 25 and $1 49

Infants' Shirts.

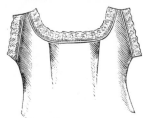

599. Infants' cambric shirts, trimmed with valenciennes lace.................12c.
600. Cambric, with needlework edges....16c.
901. Linen, with valenciennes lace.......25c.
602. Linen, with fine torchon lace..........35c.

Flannel Wrappers.

608. Infants' wrapper of striped or plain flannel, neatly trimmed with torchon lace and finished with satin ribbon bow............$2 25
609. Same style without lace or ribbon..........................$1 75
609 A. Finer quality wrappers. $2 95, $3 25 and $3 98

Infants' Shirts.

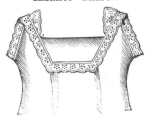

603. Linen, with valenciennes lace... .....25c
604. Linen, with torchon lace..............47c
605. Finer quality.......................55c

Infants' Diapers.

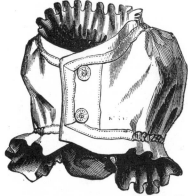

606. Mme. Hughes' diapers, sizes 2, 3, 4,...53c.
607. Mme. Hughes' diapers, sizes 5 and 6, 63c.

Flannel Shawls.

612. Gilbert's flannel shawls, hand embroidered in silk...... ....$1 12
613. Gilbert's flannel shawls, scalloped and embroidered on corner........ ....98c

614. Infants' flannel wrappers, $1 29
615. Soft Flannel wrappers, white or blue, pearl buttons down front, collar and cuffs bound with satin ribbon.................$1 42

Infant's Diapers.

610. Goodyear diapers, sizes 2, 3 and 4.....25c
611. Goodyear diapers, sizes 5 and 6........29c

Flannel Shawls.

616. Infants' shawls of Gilbert's flannel, 34 inches square, hand embroidered with the best Saddler's silk twist........................$1 75, $2 25 and $2 75
617. Extra fine quality...............$3 50 and $3 75

INFANTS' SHORT SKIRTS.

621. Lansdale Cambric, deep ruffle of embroidery..................$1.18

619. Cambric, trimmed with embroidery, 65c.

620. Cambric, with tucks, insertion and ruffle of embroidery..................93c.

618. Muslin, hem and tucks. 33c.

INFANTS' BIBS.

622. 20c. and 25c.

623. 8c, 12c and 15c.

624. 35c.

625. 45c.

626. 59c.

Nurses' and Waitresses' Caps. and Aprons.

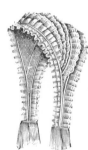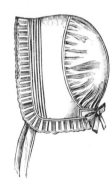

627. 35c.

628. 35c.

629. 23c.

630. 23c

631. Night Cap, 31c.

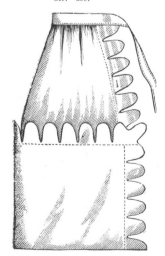

632. Muslin, extra wide scalloped all round..................33c.
633. Muslin, with hem and 5 tucks, one width..................24c.
634. Same style, extra wide.....31c

635. Extra wide Muslin, apron embroidered bottom with tucks and insertion above, wide sash trimmed with embroidery.....70c
636. Same style, Cambric ...,...85c

637. Muslin, extra wide, with 5 one-inch tucks..................33c.
638. Cambric, extra wide, with 3 three-inch tucks..............45c.

639. Muslin, extra wide, embroidered bottom with tucks above..................56c.
640. Cambric, same style..,61c

Ladies' Aprons.

 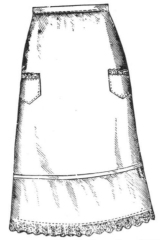 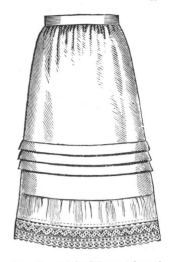

641. Lawn, box plaited ruffle, trimmed with lace and insertion......28c
642. Cross Bar, with pockets and ruffle on bottom........13c and 19c

643. Cross Bar Ruffle and pockets trimmed with embroidery.......23c

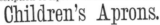
(For description of Aprons not illustrated see Page 44.)

644. Fancy Striped Lawn, trimmed with a ruffle, edged with Irish lace; 3 French tucks above.....

Children's Aprons.

645. Box Plaited Gingham Apron, collar and sleeves trimmed with embroidery. Age, 2, 4, 6, 8 years. Price, 35, 35, 39, 45 cents.

646. Mother Hubbard Apron of gingham, collar and sleeves, trimmed with embroidery. Age, 2, 4, 6 years. Price, 35, 35, 38 cents.

647. Mother Hubbard Apron of cross-bar muslin, shirred back and front, and tied on shoulders. Age, 2, 4, 6, 8, 10, 12 yrs. Price, 28, 30, 33, 35, 39, 45 cts.

648. Checked Nainsook, yoke back and front of Hamburg net. Age, 4, 6, 8, 10 years. Price, 60, 65, 70, 75 cents.

649. Checked Nainsook, yoke back and front, collar and sleeve trimmed with embroidery. Age, 2, 4, 6, 8 years. Price, 43, 48, 52, 55 cents.

650. Fine Checked Nainsook with gamp waist, neck and sleeves, trimmed with embroidery. Age, 3, 5, 7, 9 years. Price, 68, 73, 78, 85 cents.

651. Cross-bar, trimmed with embroidery. Age, 3, 5, 7, 9, 11 yrs. Price, 39, 43, 48, 51, 56 cts.

652. Cambric, yoke back and front, trimmed with embroidery. Age, 3, 5, 7, 9, 11 yrs. Price, 36, 39, 43, 46, 51 cts.

653. Checked Nainsook, trimmed with cambric ruffles. Age, 4, 6, 8, 10, 12 yrs. Price, 42, 48, 55, 58, 65 cts.

655. Very Fine Checked Nainsook, yoke of insertion, trimmed with embroidery. Age, 2, 4, 6, 8 years. Price, 50, 55, 60, 65 cents.

LADIES' APRONS.

656. Ladies' kitchen aprons of Amoskeag gingham, 1½ widths........................20c
657. Same as above,,with 2 widths...........25c
658. Ladies' white lawn aprons with hem and five tucks................................29c
659. Same as above, trimmed with embroidery, 50c
659 A. Very pretty Swiss aprons, trimmed with lace; 55c 75c and $1 10 each.

LADIES' FRENCH UNDERWEAR.

660. Chemise, with bosom handsomely embroidered between clusters of fine tucks $1 11 and $1 63.
661. Chemise, sacque shape, bosom handsomely hand embroidered $1 39 and $1 65.
662. Gowns with tucked bosoms and made throughout by hand; collar front piece and sleeves hand embroidered. $1 20 $1 27 $1 35 and $1 50.
663. Finer and more elaborately embroidered, $2 25 and $2 75.

FRENCH SHAMS.

664. Linen, hand embroidered all around, and each corner very handsomely embroidered, $4 85 and $5 00 per pair

FLANNEL SKIRTS.

665. Skirt of very fine Gilbert's flannel, with hem and tuck, made on a yoke...........$1 69
666. Skirt of Ballard Vale flannel, very nicely embroidered with silk, made on a yoke. ..$2 35
667. Very fine Gilbert's flannel, with scallop and dot, seams herring boned with silk, made on a yoke...................................$2 45
668. Finer quality, $3 35 and $3 50.

Infants' Cashmere and Pique Cloaks.

669. Mother Hubbard Cashmere Cloak, plaited waist; bottom handsomely embroidered with silk; collar and sleeves embroidered to match, finished at side with satin ribbon bow; colors, cream, light blue, tan, garnet and cardinal $7 89

670. Very pretty Mother Hubbard Cloak of basket cloth, collar edged with satin cording and finished at neck with satin ribbon bow, cream only...........$2 55

671. Mother Hubbard Cloak of Cashmere, embroidered with silk; colors, cream, light blue, tan, cardinal and garnet.........................$5 10

672. Handsome Mother Hubbard Cloak of Cashmere, embroidered collar, trimmed with satin ribbon; colors, cream, light blue, tan, garnet and cardinal.........$4 50

673. Pique Cloak, trimmed with insertion, and a ruffle of embroidery...........$3 98
674. Pique Cloaks, upper capes trimmed with ruffle of embroidery...........$1 35
675. Better quality Pique, both capes trimmed with ruffles of embroidery..$2 88

676. Cashmere trimmed with quilting; all white or white with blue quilting; all drab or drab with blue quilting.........$2 75

677. White Cashmere, hand embroidered....................$5 00

678. Cashmere, hand embroidered, white only...............$4 00

HANDKERCHIEFS.

1000. Men's all linen, colored and mourning border, hem-stitched, each, 25 and 31c; per dozen, $2.75 and $3.60.

1001. Men's all linen, colored border, hem-stitched handkerchiefs, each, 20, 25 and 33c; per doz, $2.25 2.75 and 3.75.

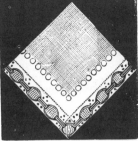

1002. Men's all linen, fancy colored border, hem-stitched, each, 25c; per dozen, $2.75.

1003. Men's all linen, mourning, solid border, hem-stitched, each, 33 and 47c; per dozen, $3.75 and 5.35.

1004. Men's all linen, colored border, hem-stitched, each, 33, 39 and 45c. per dozen, $3.75, 4.50 and 5.00.

1005. Men's all linen, fancy colored border, hem-stitched, each. 25 and 29c; per dozen, $2.75 and 3.25.

1006. Men's all linen, colored border hem-stitched handkerchiefs, each, 35, 43 and 49c; per doz. $4.00, 5.00, 5.75

1007. Children's all linen, colored border handkerchiefs, hemmed, each, 7c; per dozen, 75c.

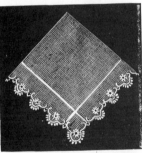

1008. Ladies' Sheer Linen Handkerchiefs, scalloped edge, embroidered in white or colors, each, 43c., 55, 69, 71, 89, 93, $1.19, 1.29, 1.42 and 1.69.

1009. Heavy brocade silk handkerchiefs, black, white and solid colors, each, 88c, $1.19, 1.39, 1.65, 1.92 and 2.25.

1010. Gents' heavy twilled, silk handkerchiefs, white and solid colors, also colored centres, with borders of contrasting colors, each, 50c, 69, 75, $1.00, 1.35 and 1.75.

1011. Ladies' white embroidered handkerchiefs, scalioped edges, all linen, each, 50, 69, 88, 95c and $1.39.

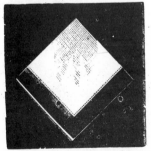

1012. Ladies' all linen, mourning, solid border, hem-stitched, each, 20, 25 and 33c; per doz. $2.25, 2.75 and 3.75.

1013. Ladies' fancy mourning hem-stitched, each, 20, 25 and 33c; per dozen, $2.25, 2.75 and 3.75.

1014. Ladies' all linen, fancy colored border, hem-stitched, each, 16c; per dozen, $1.85.

1015. Ladies' all linen, colored border, hem-stitched, each, 12½c; per dozen, $1.42.

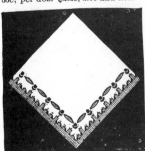

1016. Ladies' all linen, colored border hem-stitched, each, 13c; per dozen, $1.50.

1017. Ladies' all linen, colored border, hem-stitched handkerchiefs, each, 25c; per dozen, $2.75.

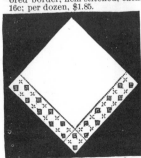

1018. Ladies' all linen, colored border, hem-stitched, each, 20c; 25.

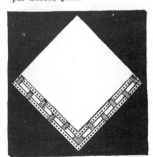

1019. Ladies' all linen, colored border, hem-stitched, each, 10c; per dozen, $1.15.

Ladies' and Children's Collars and Cuffs.

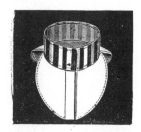

1020.   Black and White Striped Linen Collars.............15c
1021.   Cuffs to match, per pair 16c

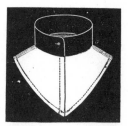

1022.   All Black Linen.. 16c
1023.   Cuffs, to match, per pair... ....22c

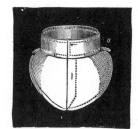

1024.   All Linen ; very high, 15c

BLACK & WHITE STRIPED EDGE

1025.   Linen Collars, Black and White striped edge...16c
1026.   Cuffs to match, per pair 22c

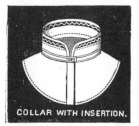

COLLAR WITH INSERTION.

1027.   Collars with insertion 10c

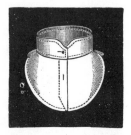

1028.   New Collars, very high..................15c

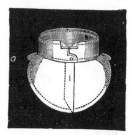

1029.   All Linen, entirely new...... ....20c

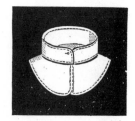

1030.   Ladies' all Linen standing Collars.......10c and 15c

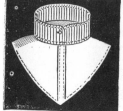

1031.   Ladies' Collars and Cuffs with black, pink or blue stripes, per set....25c

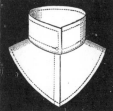

1032.   Latest style, extra fine Linen....... ....18c

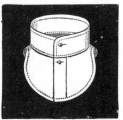

1033.   Children's Linen Collars, sizes 10, 10½, 11, each...11c
1034.   Ladies' sizes 15c

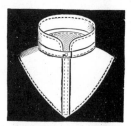

1035.   Very fine Linen, entirely new and very high...16c

1036.   Boys' Linen Collars. round or square corners, 13c 15c and 18c.

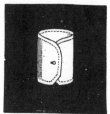

1037.   All Linen Cuffs, per pair.................15c

1038.   All Linen reversible Cuffs, per pair.........18c

1039.   Plain Linen Cuffs, per pair.............15c

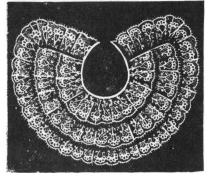

1040.   Child's Collar, 3 rows of Oriental Lace, 50c

1041.   Child's Collar of Hamburg Embroidery. 25c 39c 50c and 75c.

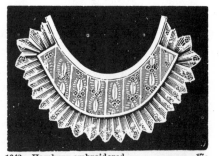

1042.   Hamburg embroidered................17c

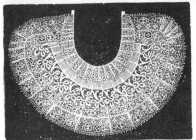

1043.   Child's Collar of Maltese Lace and Irish Point embroidery....... 59c

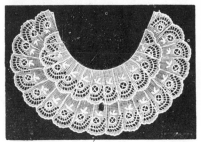

1044.   Child's Collar, double row of Swiss embroidery 35c

1045.   Child's Collar, Swiss medallion, cream color lace 25c

RUCHINGS.

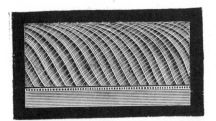

1046. Crepe Lisse Fedora Ruching; per yd., 20c.
1047. Black Crepe Lisse " " 50c.

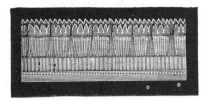

1048. Cream or White Mull edged with lace; per yd., 25c.

1049. Crepe Lisse, double shell, silk stitched; per yd., 33c.

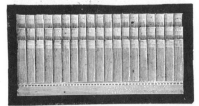

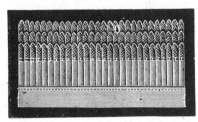

1050. Two-fold Cream Bunting; per yd. 8c.

1051. Crepe Lisse, with 3 rows, side plaited; per yd., 35c.

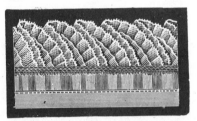

1052. Crepe Lisse, 3 rows side plaits; per yd., 31c.

1053. Crepe Lisse, fancy plaits silk stitched; per yd., 33c.

1054. Crepe Lisse, lace edge, 6 yards in box; per box, 69c.

1055. Crepe Lisse, shell pattern, Valenciennes lace edge; per yd., 55c.

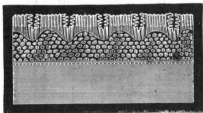

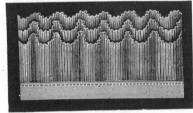

1056. Fine Silk Mull, cream, pink, blue, cardinal and orange; per yd., 45c.

1057. Fine Crepe Lisse, silver or gilt tinsel, white or black; per yd., 42c.

1058. 3 rows Fine Plaited Crepe Lisse, in black or white; per yd., 55c.

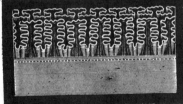

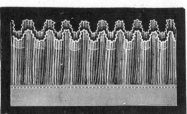

1059. Fine Black Crepe Lisse, with black, white, orange or cardinal ribbon edge, new and handsome; per yd., 65c.

1060. 2 row Fine Plaited Crepe Lisse; per yd., 39c.

1061. Fancy Plaited Crepe Lisse, with pearl beads; per yd., 45c.

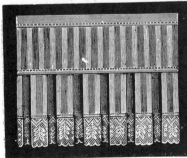

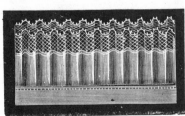

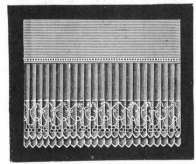

1062. Organdie Skirt Plaiting, box plaits; per yd., 18c.

1063. 2 row Valenciennes, lace edge or fine mull; per yd., 23c.

1064. Organdie Skirt, 2 row valenciennes edge, per yd., 25c.

BEADED FRONTS.

1065.   Black Beaded Fronts, for ladies' dresses, beautifully beaded on net, $1 49, 1 98, 2 25, 3 00, 3 75, 4 50, 5 50, 6 75 and 8 75.
1066.   White Beaded Fronts, $4 50, 5 00, 6 00, 6 75, 8 00 and 9 00.

RUCHINGS.

(NOT ILLUSTRATED).

1067.	Two folds fine Bunting	per yard, 8c
1068.	Tricotine Fedora, all shades	" 20c
1069.	Tourists' Ruffling, with plain or colored dot, 6 yards for	15c
1070.	Tourists' Ruffling, lace edge, 6 yards for	25, 35 and 50c
1071.	Fifty different designs Organdie or Crepe Lisse Ruffling, per yard, 25c	
1072.	Two folds fine Bunting, orange, cardinal or black dot,	18c
1073.	Fifty new and beautiful designs in Beaded Rufflings; colors, orange pink, blue, cardinal, cream, etc., etc.	per yard, 75, 89c, and $1 00
1074.	Black Crepe Ruchings, trimmed with mourning beads, per yd, 75c, $1 00	
1075.	Jet Ruchings, full assortment, per yard, 75c, $1 00, 1 10, 1 25 and 1 69	

LACE PILLOW SHAMS, TIDIES, Etc.

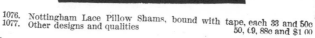

1076.   Nottingham Lace Pillow Shams, bound with tape, each 33 and 50c
1077.   Other designs and qualities   50, 69, 88c and $1 00

BLACK CRAPE VEILS.

1078.	32x34 inch	....	$1 75
1079.	32x38 "	....	2 00
1080.	38x42 "	....	3 00
1081.	34x50 "	....	3 50
1082.	38x52 "	....	4 00
1083.	42x52 "	....	4 50
1084.	42x52 "dble. cr.		5 00
1085.	42x62 "		6 00

and upwards to $10 00.

1086.   Nottingham Lace Tidies, 9 inch square, 9c; 13½ inch square, 14c; 18 inch square, 25c; 23 inch square, 36c ; 27 inch square, 45c.
1087.   Same style as Nottingham Curtains, ¼ yard square, 8c ; ½ yard square, 13c ; ¾ yard square, 30 and 35c ; ⅞ yard square, handsome patterns, 45 and 50c ; 1 yard square, finer, 65, 75 and 88c; ⅜ of a yard long and ¼ of a yard wide, 13c; ⅞ yard long and ½ yard wide, 35 ; 1¾ yards long and 1 yard wide.....................$1 00

1088.   Point Applique Tidy, ecru or white, 9 inches square, 31c ; 13½ inches, 56c ; 18 inches, 71c.

1089.   Imitation Russian Lace Tidy, 8½ inches square, 13c; 11½ inches, 23c; 16 inches, 31c; 22 inches, 55c; 27 inches, 63c; 36 inches, $1 15.

1090.   Lace Bureau Covers, 22 inches wide and 45 inches long, each 59c.
1091.   Lace Bureau Covers, 27 inches wide, and 50 inches long (as illustrated), each 69c.

1092.   Antique Lace Tidies, ¼ yard square, finished tidies, each 9, 13, 18, 23, 29, 33c ; ⅜ yard square, each, 19, 23, 27, 31, 45, 59c; ½ yard square, each, 33, 42, 50, 69, 75c ; ¾ yard square, each, 75, 89, 98c, $1 25, 1 49, 1 75.
1093.   Antique Lace Tidies, oblong, ½ yard wide and ¾ yard long, each, 75, 89c, $1 00 ; ⅝ yard wide and 1 yard long, each, $1 49. $1 69, $2 15.
1094.   Antique Lace Pillow Shams, each $1 50, 1 98, 2 25.
1095.   Antique Squares to join with ribbon, each 3, 4, 6, 9, 12, 15, 18 and 21c.

1096.   Russian Lace Bureau Covers, 27 inches wide, and 45 inches long, each $1 15.
1097.   Other designs, qualities and sizes, each 65, 88c, $1 00 and 1 25.

HAMBURG EMBROIDERIES.

The prices quoted are for the widths of the Embroidery only. We do not guarantee to furnish exact patterns illustrated, when order is received if all sold, but claim the privilege of substitution in such cases.

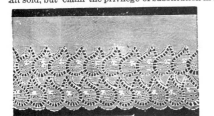

1098. Cambric edge, 3 inches wide, per yard, 25c.
1099.   "   "   5½ "   "   "   " 37c.
1100.   "   "   9   "   "   "   " 59c.

01. Cambric edge, 4½ inches wide, per yard 29c, 33c, 39c and 45c.

1102. Cambric edge, 2 inches wide, per yard, 11c.
1103.   "   "   4   "   "   "   " 17c.
1104.   "   "   6   "   "   "   " 25c.

1108. Cambric or Swiss edge, 1⅞ inches wide, per yard, 13c.
1109. Cambric or Swiss edge, 3⅛ inches wide, per yard, 19c.
1110. Cambric or Swiss edge, 4½ inches wide, per yard, 27c.
1111. Cambric or Swiss edge, 6¾ inches wide, per yard, 42c.

1105. Cambric or Swiss edge, 2 inches wide, per yard, 16c.
1106.   "   "   "   4 "   "   "   " 25c.
1107.   "   "   "   6 "   "   "   " 39c.

1117. Cambric edge, 6 inches wide, per yard, 46c, 58c and 69c.

1112. Cambric edge, ½ inches wide, per yard, 05c.
1113.   "   "   1⅞ "   "   "   " 09c.
1114.   "   "   3   "   "   "   " 13c.
1115.   "   "   4¾ "   "   "   " 16c.
1116.   "   "   7   "   "   "   " 25c.

1118. Cambric edge, 1 inch wide, 10c.
1119.   "   "   2 inches wide, 14c.
1120.   "   "   3½ "   "   19c.
1121.   "   "   5   "   "   29c, 33c and 39c.

1122. Cambric edge, 2 inches wide, per yard, 12c and 15c.
1123.   "   "   3 "   "   "   " 19c and 23c.
1124.   "   "   5 "   "   "   " 27c and 33c.

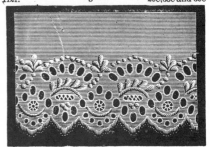

1125. Cambric edge, 2½ inches wide, per yard, 14c.
1126.   "   "   3½ "   "   "   " 21c.
1127.   "   "   5   "   "   "   " 27c, 31c and 35c.

1128. Cambric edge, 3 inches wide, per yard, 20c.
1129.   "   "   4   "   "   "   " 27c.
1130.   "   "   6   "   "   "   " 35c.
1131.   "   "   7½ "   "   "   " 42c.

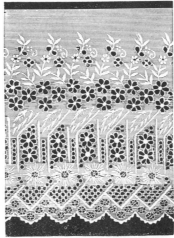

1132. Cambric flouncing, 10½ inches wide, per yard, 59c.
1133. Cambric flouncing, 15 inches wide, per yard, 79c.
1134. Cambric flouncing, 27 inches wide, per yard, $1.50, $1.98 and $2.25.

Above prices are for widths of Embroideries only; with the margins, they are 10 inches wider.

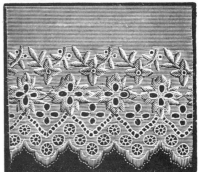

1135. Cambric edge, 3½ inches wide, per yard, 19c, 21c and 25c.
1136. Cambric edge, 5 inches wide, per yard, 29c, 33c and 37c.
1137. Cambric edge, 7½ inches wide, per yard, 45c, 59c and 63c.

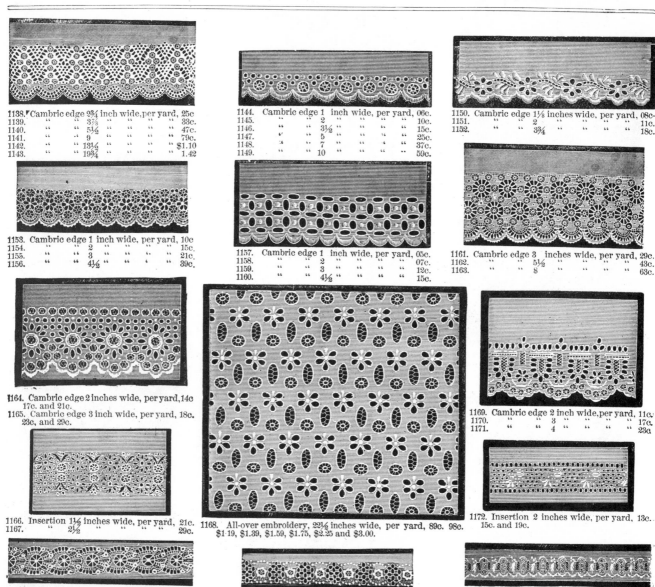

1138. Cambric edge 2¾ inch wide, per yard, 25c
1139.   "   3⅞   "   "   "   "   33c.
1140.   "   5½   "   "   "   "   47c.
1141.   "   9   "   "   "   "   79c.
1142.   "   13½   "   "   "   " $1.10
1143.   "   19¾   "   "   "   "   1.42

1144. Cambric edge 1 inch wide, per yard, 06c.
1145.   "   2   "   "   "   "   10c.
1146.   "   3½   "   "   "   "   15c.
1147.   "   5   "   "   "   "   25c.
1148.   "   7   "   "   "   "   37c.
1149.   "   10   "   "   "   "   59c.

1150. Cambric edge 1⅛ inches wide, per yard, 08c.
1151.   "   2   "   "   "   "   11c.
1152.   "   3¾   "   "   "   "   18c.

1153. Cambric edge 1 inch wide, per yard, 10c
1154.   "   2   "   "   "   "   15c.
1155.   "   3   "   "   "   "   21c.
1156.   "   4½   "   "   "   "   39c.

1157. Cambric edge 1 inch wide, per yard, 05c.
1158.   "   2   "   "   "   "   07c.
1159.   "   3   "   "   "   "   12c.
1160.   "   4½   "   "   "   "   15c.

1161. Cambric edge 3 inches wide, per yard, 29c.
1162.   "   5½   "   "   "   "   43c.
1163.   "   8   "   "   "   "   63c.

1164. Cambric edge 2 inches wide, per yard, 14c
     17c. and 21c.
1165. Cambric edge 3 inch wide, per yard, 18c.
     23c. and 29c.

1168. All-over embroidery, 22½ inches wide, per yard, 89c. 98c.
     $1·19, $1.39, $1.59, $1.75, $2.25 and $3.00.

1169. Cambric edge 2 inch wide, per yard, 11c.
1170.   "   3   "   "   "   "   17c.
1171.   "   4   "   "   "   "   23c

1166. Insertion 1½ inches wide, per yard, 21c.
1167.   "   2½   "   "   "   "   29c.

1172. Insertion 2 inches wide, per yard, 13c.
     15c. and 19c.

1173. Insertion 1 inch wide, per yard, 15c.
1174.   "   2   "   "   "   "   25c.

1175. Insertion ¾ inches wide, per yard, 09c.
1176.   "   1½   "   "   "   "   14c.

1177. Insertion 1¼ inches wide, per yard, 10c
1178.   "   1¾   "   "   "   "   17c.
1179.   "   2½   "   "   "   "   22c.

1180. Insertion 1 to 2 inches wide, per yard,
     8c. 10c. 12c. and 14c.

1181. Insertion 2 inches wide, per yard, 15c.

1182. Insertion 1½ inches wide, per yard, 10c.
     13c. and 15c.

IRISH POINT EMBROIDERY.

1183. 2½ inch wide per yard, ... 47c.
1184. 3½   "   "   "   .... 63c.
1185. 6   "   "   "   ...$1.10

1186. 6 inches wide, per yard, 89c.
     $1.10 and $1.25.
1187. 9 inches wide, per yard, $1.50
     and $1.75.

1188. 5 inches wide, per yard, 50c.
     65c. 79c. and 88c.

1189. 3 inches wide, per yard,
     30c. 47c. and 55c.
1190. 5 inches wide, per yard,
     75c. and $1.00.

IRISH POINT INSERTION,—1191. Insertion of Irish point embroidery, 2 inches wide, per yard, 27c. 39c. 45c. and 57c.

CAMBRIC TRIMMINGS.

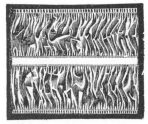

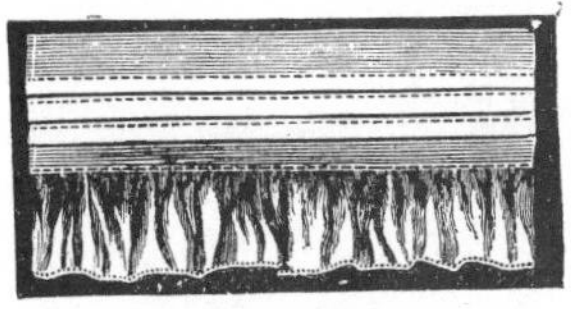

1191. Width, 1⅛ inches, per yard........7c

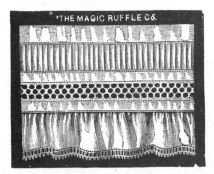

1192. Plaiting with everlasting insertion and ruffle edged with lace, 3¼ inches wide, per yard...18c

1193. Tucks, with puffing and lace edge, 4½ inches wide, per yard................................22c

1194. Bias tucking between narrow puffing and ruffle edged lace, 4¾ inches wide, per yard...24c

Colored Embroideries.

Red embroidered in white ; navy-blue embroidered in red ; red embroidered in navy-blue ; navy-blue embroidered in white.

1195.	1 inch wide, per yard		...........8c and 10c
1196.	2¼	"	"	...........10c " 13c
1197.	3	"	"	...........15c " 19c
1198.	5	"	"	...........25c " 29c
1199.	9	"	"	...........33c " 39c
1200.	13½	"	"	...........59c " 75c
1201.	18	"	"	...........98c "$1 39
1202.	27	"	"	...........$1 75 " 2 00

Black, embroidered in white.

1204.	1½ inch wide, per yard		......15c
1205.	2½	"	"	......21c
1206.	4	"	"	......33c

IRISH EDGINGS.

1207.	I.	Per piece........ ....13c
1208.	II.	"..............16c and 18c
1209.	III.	"..............20c " 27c

Sold by the piece only.

Everlasting Insertion and Edging.

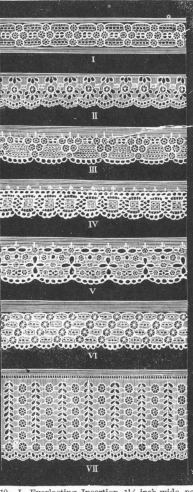

1210. I. Everlasting Insertion, 1¼ inch wide, per yard, 5c, 7 and 9c; per dozen, 55c, 75c and $1 00
1211. II. Everlasting Edging, 1 inch wide, per yard, 8c.; per dozen........................90c

1212.		2 inches wide, per yard, 11c; per doz...$1 25
1213.		3	"	16c;	"	1 80
1214.		4½	"	21c;	"	2 40
1215.	III.	1 inch wide, per yd, 5c;	"	55
1216.		1⅞	"	"	8c;	"	85
1217.	IV.	1	"	"	9c;	"	1 00
1218.		1¾	"	"	11c;	"	1 25
1219.	V.	1⅛	"	"	10c;	"	1 15
1220.		2	"	"	12c;	"	1 35
1221.	VI.	1	"	"	9c;	"	1 00
1222.		2	"	"	12c;	"	1 35

1223. VII. Indian Trimming, 1 inch wide, per yard, 5c; per dozen........................50c

1224.		2 inches wide, per yard, 7c; per doz......75c
1225.		3⅛	"	"	10c;	"	...$1 10
1226.		3⅞	"	"	13c;	"	1 45

SWISS EMBROIDERY.

1227.	¾ inches wide, per yard................	7c
1228.	1⅛	"	"	9c
1229.	2	"	"	15c
1230.	3	"	"	21c
1231.	4½	"	"	29c
1232.	6	"	"	39c
1233.	7½	"	"	47c
1234.	9	"	"	59c
1235.	13	"	"	79c
1236.	18	"	"	$1 19

The above are for widths of the embroidery only. The embroidery marked 18 inches wide, is, including the margin, 32 inches wide.

CAMBRIC TRIMMINGS.

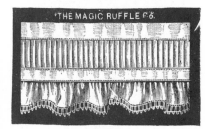

1237. Width, 1¾ inches, per yard..........9c

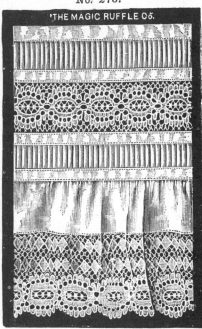

1238. Plaiting, with ruffle edged with lace, 2¼ inches wide, per yard........................10c

No. 273.

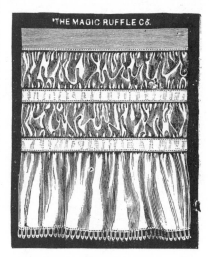

1239. Plaiting, with insertion and ruffle edged with lace, 7 inches wide, per yard.............63c

1240. Two rows of puffing between two tucks and ruffle, with lace edge, 5½ ins. wide, per yd..17c

Lace Department.

Having our Lace Goods selected by our own buyers in Europe, we are enabled to offer one of the most extensive assortments that can be found anywhere, AT THE VERY LOWEST PRICES. as we avoid the importer's profit by our own direct importations.

Our stock is replete with the latest and most fashionable designs in Oriental, Egyptian, Spanish. Spanish Guipure, Wool, Fedora, Platte Val. and **Point** Gauze Laces, of which we illustrate the most desirable. When ordering, kindly designate a second choice, as the first selection may be sold out when the order reaches us, otherwise we claim the privilege of substituting.

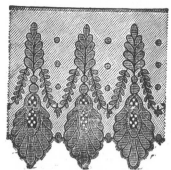

1241. French Laces, 2 inches wide, all silk, per
   yard................................ 8, 10c
1242. 3½ inches wide, per yard... ......11, 15c
1243. 4½ inches wide, per yard... ......17, 23c

1245. Spanish Guipure, black or cream. 2⅛ inches
   wide, per yard.....................................20c
1246. 3⅜ inches wide, per yard................25c
1247. 3¾ inches wide, per yard................31c
1248. 4¾ inches wide, per yard................45c
1249. 6 inches wide, per yard................57c
1250. 9½ inches wide, per yard............ .. 75c

1251. Escurial Lace, all silk, 2 ins. wide, per yd.23c
1252. 4 inches wide, per yard.. ....27c
1253. 5 inches wide, per yard... ....33c
1254. 7 inches wide, per yard... ....47c

                        PER YARD.
1255. All Silk Chantilly Lace, black, 4 ins. wide, 85c
1256. 6 inches wide, per yard....................$1 15
1257. 8 inches wide, per yard................... 1 49

1258. French Lace, 1 inch wide, all silk, per yard... 9   11c
1259. 2½ inches wide, all silk, per yard.............19   23c
1260. 3½ inches wide, all silk, per yard............27   31c

1261. Black All Silk Spanish Lace Flouncing, 18 inches
   wide, per yard.............. ....$1 49
1262. 27 inches wide, per yard... .... 1 98
1263. 36 inches wide, per yard 2 49

1264. French Laces, 1 inch wide, all silk, per
   yard............................... 6, 8c
1265. 2½ inch wide, per yard............11, 14c
1266. 3¾ inch wide, per yard.. ......21, 25c
1266a 4½ inch wide, per yard..........29, 31c

1267. Escurial. 3 inches wide, per yard.. .....42c
1268. 3¾ inches wide, per yard. 55c
1269. 5½ inches wide, per yard................75c

1270. Black Silk Spanish Lace, 1½ inches wide,
   per yard........................... ....10c
1271. 3 inches wide, per yard..............16c
1272. 5½ inches wide, per yard.....   ....25c
1273. 7 inches wide, per yard.............. ....33c

1274. Black Silk Chantilly Lace Flouncing. 12
   inches wide, per yard.......... ... .79c
1275. 18 inches wide, per yard...... ...$1 25
1276. 27 inches wide, per yard 1 75
1277. 36 inches wide, per yard... .. .. 2 10

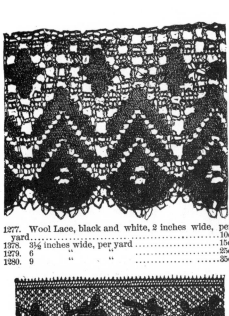

1286. Black Beaded Lace, 4½ ins. wide, per yd. 75c

1277. Wool Lace, black and white, 2 inches wide, per
    yard..10c
1378. 3½ inches wide, per yard 15c
1279. 6   "   " 25c
1280. 9   "   " 35c

1296. Black Silk Spanish Guipure Lace, 2 inches wide,
    per yard..................................13c
1297. 3½ inches wide, per yard 19c
1298. 4½   "   " 25c
1299. 6   "   " 33c
1300. 9   "   " 47c

1281. Spanish Guipure, 3 inches wide, per yard......39c
1282.   "   "   3¾   "   " 47c
1283.   "   "   4½   "   " 55c

1287. Black Beaded Lace, 3½ ins. wide, per yd. 35c

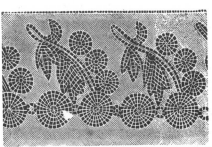

1288. 2 inches wide, black or cream,
    per yard 21c
1289. 3 inches wide, per yard.....25c
1290. 3½   "   "   " 33c
1291. 4½   "   "   " 37c
1292. 5   "   "   " 49c
1293. 6   "   "   " 39c

1301. Black Beaded Lace, 4 inches wide, per yard..40c

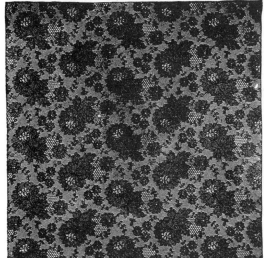

1294. Escurial, 6 inches wide, per yd.,
    $1 35, 150, 1 75
1295. 3½ inches wide, per yard,
    69, 75 and 89c

1284. Black all-silk Chantilly Net, 27 inches wide, per yard,
    $1 75, 2 25 and 2 75

1285. All Silk Spanish Netting, black or white, 27 inches wide, per yard........ . ...$2 25 and 2 75

1302. Black All-Silk Escurial Lace Flouncing, 3½ inches
    wide, per yard..........................25c
1303. 5 inches wide, per yard.....   ....35c
1304. 7½   "   "   " 45c
1305. 13   "   "   " $1 25
1306. 21   "   "   " 1 75

WHITE LACES.

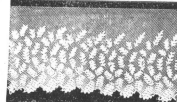

1334. Fine White Mauresque Laces, 3 inches wide 33c

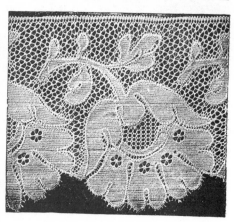

1318. White Spanish Guipure Lace, 2½ inches wide, per yard..19c
1319. 4 inches wide, per yard.....................28c
1320. 7 " " 39c
1321. 11 " " 59c

1335. Mauresque, 3 inch wide, per yard, 49c

1339. All Silk Escurial Lace, 1¾ in. wide, per yd. 21c
1340. 3 inches wide, per yard.....................29c
1341. 5 " " 39c

ORIENTAL.

1322. Oriental Lace, 2½ inches wide, per yard, 11c
1323. " " 3¾ " " 16c
1324. " " 5 " " 23c
1325. " " 7 " " 31c
1326. " " 9 " " 39c

ORIENTAL.

1342. Fine White Oriental Lace, with loop edge, 2½ inches wide, per yard..........25c
1343. Fine White Oriental Lace, with loop edge, 4¼ inches wide, per yard..........37c
1344. Fine White Oriental Lace, with loop edge, 5¾ inches wide, per yard..........47c

1327. Oriental Lace, 2½ in. wide, per yd. 10c
1328. " " 4½ " " 19c
1329. " " 5¾ " " 23c
1330. " " 7¼ " " 29c

1336. White Oriental Netting, 27 inches wide, per yard, 65c, 75c, 98c, $1 35, 1 49, 1 98, 2 25
1337. Same in ecru, per yard $1 39, 1 75, 1 98, 2 10

1345. Oriental Lace, 2½ inches wide, per yd 13c
1346. " " 4 " " 17c
1347. " " 6 " " 23c

1331. Oriental Lace, white or ecru, 4 inches wide, per yard.................21c
1332. Oriental Lace, white or ecru, 6 inches wide, per yard.................35c
1333. Oriental Lace, white or ecru, 13½ inches wide, per yard.................55c

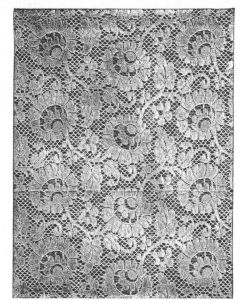

1338. All Silk Spanish Guipure Netting, black or cream, 27 inches wide, per yard.................$1 90 and 2 50

1348. Oriental Lace, 2½ inches wide, per yd., 25c
1349. " " 4½ " " 49c
1350. " " 7 " " 65c
1351. " " 11 " " 93c

EGYPTIAN LACES.

1358. Egyptian Lace, white and ecru, 4 inche wide, per yard...........................18c
1359. Egyptian Lace, white and ecru, 6 inches wide, per yard................................29c
1360. Egyptian Lace, white and ecru, 9 inches wide, per yard................................39c
1361. Egyptian Lace, white and ecru, 15 inches wide, per yard................................63c

1362. Egyptian Lace, white and ecru, 4 inches wide, per yard..........................19c
1363. Egyptian Lace, white and ecru, 5½ inches wide, per yard..........................29c
1364. Egyptian Lace, white and ecru, 7 inches wide, per yard..........................35c
1365. Egyptian Lace, white and ecru, 9½ inches wide, per yard..........................47c

1366. Egyptian Lace, white and ecru, 4 inches wide, per yard............................15c
1367. Egyptian Lace, white and ecru, 5 inches wide, per yard............................25c
1368. Egyptian Lace, white and ecru, 9 inches wide, per yard............................39c
1369. Egyptian Lace, white and ecru, 13 inches wide, per yard............................49c

WOOL LACES.

1370. Wool Lace, in black, navy blue, cream, garnet, myrtle green, olive, brown, medium and seal brown, 3 inches wide, per yard.19c
1371. 4 " " " " 25c
1372. 6½ " " " " 39c

1373. Wool Angora Lace, in black, cream, navy blue, garnet, myrtle, olive brown, medium and seal brown, 2½ inches wide, per yard....................21c
1374. 3½ " " " " 25c
1375. 6 " " " " 35c
1376. 9½ " " " " 59c

FEDORA LACES.

1377. Fedora Lace, white, 3 inches wide, per yard.....45c
1378. " " 6¾ " " " 95c

1380. Fedora Lace, white, 3⅝ inches wide per yard 50c
1381. Fedora Lace, white, 4⅞ inches wide. per yard 75c
1382. Fedora Lace, white, 6 inches wide, per yard 98c

1379. Fedora Lace netting, white, 27 inches wide, per yard...........................$3.95

We will send this Catalogue, free of charge, to any one applying for it by letter or postal card.
Do not cut or mutilate this book ; by simply referring to the number of the page and article you desire, your order will be understood.

WOOL LACES.

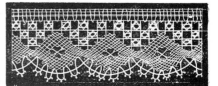

PLATTE VAL. LACES.

1383. Platte Val. Lace, 1⅞ inches wide, per yard...................................15c
1384. 2⅞ inches wide, per yard.... ....25c
1385. 3½ " " " " 33c
1386. 5½ " " " " 41c
1387. 7¼ " " " " 49c
1388. 15½ " " " " 79c
1389. 27 " " " " $1 10
1390. 36 " " " " $1 39 and $1 45
1391. Netting, 27 inches wide, per yard, $1.59, $1.75, $1.98 and $2.25.

1392. Platte Val. Lace, 15 inches wide, per yard...........................79c
1393. 27 inches wide, per yard..........$1.15
1394. 36 " " " " $1.98
1395. 42 " " " " $2.49
1396. All over Netting to match, 27 inches wide, per yard..........$1.39, 1.75 and $2.25.

1397.	1½ inches wide, per yard	6c
1398.	2½ " "	9c
1399.	3½ " "	13c
1400.	5 " "	15c

1401. Torchon insertion, 1½ inches wide, per yard 11, 13, 17c
1402. 2¼ inches wide, per yard 15, 21, 23c
1403. 3¾ " " 25, 33c

MEDICI.

1404.	1 inch wide, per yard	12c
1405.	2½ inches wide, per yard	18c
1406.	3½ " "	23c
1407.	5 " "	31c

1408. 1 inch wide, per yard 12, 18, 21c
1409. 2½ inches wide, per yard 25, 27, 29c
1410. 3½ " " 31, 35, 39c

Black and Colored Satin Ribbon.

Warranted pure Silk.

No.	Width	per yd.	Piece of 10 yds
1437.	2,	½ inch 7c	60c
1438.	3,	¾ " 8c	75c
1439.	4,	⅞ " 10c	95c
1440.	5,	1 " 12c	$1 15
1441.	7,	1¼ " 14c	1 35
1442.	9,	1½ " 17c	1 65
1443.	12,	2 " 22c	2 15
1444.	16,	2½ " 26c	2 55
1445.	22,	3 " 33c	3 25

Colored Satin Ribbon.

Cotton back, for looping up curtains, etc.

No.	Width	per yd.	Piece of 10 yds
1446.	7,	1¼ inch 7c	65c
1447.	9,	1½ " 9c	85c
1448.	12,	2 " 11c	$1 05
1449.	16,	2½ " 14c	1 35

Colored Gros Grain Ribbons.

Best quality, all colors.

No.	Width	per yd.	Piece of 10 yds
1451.	4,	⅞ inch 9c	85c
1452.	5,	1 " 12c	$1 15
1453.	7,	1¼ " 13c	1 25
1454.	9,	1½ " 15c	1 45
1455.	12,	2 " 20c	1 95

Black Ottoman Ribbon.

Warranted Pure Silk.

No.	Width	per yd.	Piece of 10 yds
1456.	5,	1 inch 13c	$1 25
1457.	7,	1¼ " 16c	1 50
1458.	9,	1½ " 22c	2 15
1459.	12,	2 " 26c	2 55
1460.	16,	2½ " 31c	3 05

TORCHON LACES.

1411. 1 inch wide, per yard 3, 5, 7c
1412. 2 inches wide, per yard 6, 8, 11, 14c
1413. 3 " " 18, 23, 27, 31c

LACE NETTINGS.

1414. Cotton Illusion, 1 yard wide, per yard ..20c
1415. Wash Blonde, cream and white, per yard, 20, 25, 31 and 38c
1416. Dotted Cotton Blonde, 27 inches wide, per yard ....25, 31 and 38c
1417. Bobbinet, for darning and run work, suitable for pillow shams and bed spreads, 1 yard wide, per yard, 20c; 3 yards wide........49c
1418. Snowflake, cream white, black and colored nets. This net is covered with fine bright spots, suitable for veiling or neckwear. 27 inches wide, per yard....................30c
1419. White Silk Illusion, 1 yard wide, per yd.30c
1420. White Silk Illusion, 2 yards wide, for bridal veiling, per yard........ ....58 and 80c
1421. Tissue Veiling, 15 inches wide, all colors, per yard....................30c
1422. Tissue Veiling, 27 inches wide, all colors, per yard....................45c
1423. Barege Veilings, 15 inches wide........25c
1424. " " 27 " 35c
1425. Sewing Silk Veiling, all colors, 15 inches wide, per yard..........................37c

Ribbons.

Black Velvet and Satin Ribbon.

No.	Width	Per yd.	Piece of 10 yds
1461.	7,	1¼ inch 19c	$1 85
1462.	9,	1½ " 27c	2 65
1463.	12,	2 " 33c	3 25
1464.	16,	2½ " 42c	4 15

Black Velvet Ribbon.

No.	Per yard.	Per piece.
1465.	1 ....2c	15c
1466.	1⅛ 3c	18c
1467.	1¼ 2c	21c
1468.	1 1-3 ....3c	23c
1469.	1½ 3c	25c
1470.	1¾ 4c	27c
1471.	2 ....4c	29c
1472.	2¼ 4c	33c
1473.	2½ 5c	35c
1474.	3 ....5c	39c
1475.	3¼ 6c	41c
1476.	3½ 6c	49c
1477.	4 ....7c	59c
1478.	4½ 7c	63c
1479.	5 ....9c	69c
1480.	5½ 9c	71c
1481.	6 ....10c	79c
1482.	6½ 11c	89c
1483.	7 ....12c	98c
1484.	8 ....15c	$1 29
1485.	9 ....16c	1 35
1486.	10 ....17c	1 45
1487.	11 ....18c	1 59
1488.	12 ....19c	1 69

Colored Velvet Ribbons.

No.	Per yard.	Per piece.
1489.	3 ....5c	49c
1490.	4 ....7c	59c
1491.	5 ....8c	69c
1492.	7 ....11c	98c
1493.	9 ....15c	$1 39

Scale for Black Velvet Ribbons.

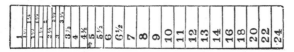

1426. 3 inches wide, per yard 35c
1427. 5 " " 59c

1428. 1 inch wide, per yard .. ....4, 7, 10 and 12c
1429. 2 " " ....15. 18 and 23

ANTIQUE LACES.

1430.	2 inches wide, per yard	10c
1431.	3¼ " "	14c
1432.	4 " "	21c
1433.	6 " "	33c

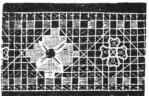

1434. Insertion. 3 inches wide, per yard.....15c
1435. " 4½ " " 21c
1436. " 5¾ " " 33c

Feather Edge Ribbons.

All Colors and Widths.

1494. No. 12 Satin Picot, per yard..............32c
1495. " 16 " " 39c
1496. " 12 Gros grain Picot, per yard.....29c
1497. " 16 " " 39c
1498. " 12 Moire " " 32c
1499. " 16 " " 39c

Black Gros Grain Ribbon.

No.	Width	Per yd.	Piece of 10 yds
1500.	5,	1 inch........12c	$1 35
1501.	7,	1¼ " 15c	1 75
1502.	9,	1½ " 20c	1 95
1503.	12,	2 " 25c	2 45
1504.	16,	2½ " 35c	3 45
1505.	22,	3 " 42c	4 15

Sash Ribbon.

1506. Colored gros grain Sash Ribbon, pure silk, 6 inches wide, per yard....................60c
1507. Colored gros grain Sash Ribbon, pure silk, 7 inches wide, per yard...................71c
1508. Colored Satin Sash Ribbon, pure silk, 7 inches wide, per yard...................90c
1509. Colored Satin Sash Ribbon, pure silk, 9 inches wide, per yard...................$1 50
1510. Moire or watered Sash Ribbon, all colors, 9 inches wide, per yard...................$1 50
1511. Blocked Sash Ribbon, 7 in. wide, yer yd.75c

We can also furnish any articles not in our Catalogue from other cuts or descriptions furnished us. Our patrons will, however, avoid mistakes by describing explicitly what they wish.

Our next number of this Price List will be issued early in the Fall. We will send a copy, free of charge, to any one applying for it by postal card or letter.

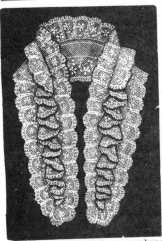

1512. Fichus of Oriental Lace, very handsome... ....75c, $1 00, 1 25 and 1 50

1513. Fedora Vest of Oriental net and lace, $1.00, 1.25, 1.50, 1.75.

1514. Byron Standing Collar, $3 75
1514a. Byron Turndown Collar, $3 75

1515. Collarette of Oriental Lace, 75c and $1 00

1516. Black or Cream Spanish Lace Fichus all silk; 75c, $1.00, 1.25, 1.75, 2 00, 2 25, 3 00, 4 00 and upward.

1517. Zouave Jacket of Vermacilli net, $4.49.
1517a.   "   "   Octagon net.....$6.59.
When ordering please state bust measure.

1518. Black or Cream Spanish Lace Scarfs, all silk........50c, 75c and $1 00

1519. Belt and Bodice of Vermacilii net, $2 98
1519a.   "   "   Octagon net... 3 58
When ordering state waist measure.

1520. Collarette and Jabot of Oriental lace and colored satin ribbon bow, $1 50

1521. Collarette and Jabot of cream lace and colored satin ribbon loops......50c, 75c. $1 00

1522. Beaded Plastron with Pendant and Fringe........................$3 95
1522a. Beaded Plastron without Fringe, $3.29

1523. Mull Handkerchief, trimmed with lace, 15c, 18c. 25c, 35c

Child's Collar of Linen Flax

1524. Child's Collar of Linen Flax..$1.10, 1.25, 1.35

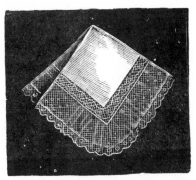

1525. Mull Handkerchief, trimmed with fine lace.............. ....50c, 75c, $1 00, 1 35

HOSIERY DEPARTMENT.---Ladies' Hosiery.

Owing to the large increase of sales in our Hosiery Department, we have been obliged to double our facilities, and are therefore in a position to offer a larger and more varied assortment of these goods than ever before. For this season we have, through our European buyer, imported very largely all the leading styles, including those of English and French manufacturers. Fancy combinations and vertical stripes are in vogue, also all the new shades in plain colors, such as tan, modes, bronze, navy blue, seal brown, garnet, cardinal, etc., etc. An examination of figures is invited, as we claim that we cannot be undersold; our standard being low prices for quality of goods furnished, we mean to keep our reputation.

In silk hosiery we defy competition, this being one of our specialties. The Brilliant Lisle Hose, with the improved Maco feet, are considered the best goods imported.

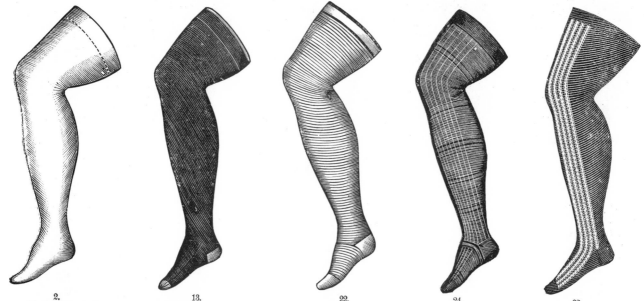

2.　　　　　　　　13.　　　　　　　　22.　　　　　　　　24.　　　　　　　　62.

Unbleached Balbriggan Hose.

1. Ladies' Unbleached Hose, patent seams, per pair, 10c; per dozen...................$1 00
2. Full regular made, per pair, 19c; per dozen, see illustration.....................$2 00
3. Extra fine quality, silk clocked. per pair, 25c; per dozen..................................$2 90
4. Extra heavy quality, silk clocked, per pair, 25c; per dozen......................$2 90
5. Better quality per pair, 35c; per dozen..$4 00
6. Best quality, per pair, 45c; per dozen....$5 20
7. Ladies' Unbleached Hose, extra fine quality, Opera length, per pair, 50c; per dozen....$5 75
8. Ladies' Unbleached Hose, fine quality, double heels and toes, per pair, 50c; per dozen...$5 85
9. French Hose, extra heavy thread, per pair. 75c; per dozen......................$8 75
We can also furnish any of the above in white.

Solid Colored Cotton Hose.

Colors, Navy Blue, Seal Brown, Garnet, Wine, Cardinal, Mode, Tan and Black.
10. Solid Colored Cotton Hose, per pair, 10c; per dozen..............................$1 00
11. Better quality, with patent seams, per pair, 12½c; per dozen.....................$1 25
12. Finer quality, regular made, per pair, 19c; dozen.........................$2 00
13. Same ingrain, colors, per pair, 21c; per dozen, see cut...........................$2 45
14. Same ingrain, with unbleached soles, per pair, 25c; per dozen..................$2 90
15. Finer quality, ingrain colors, with Schoppers' unbleached soles, per pair, 35c; per dozen..$4 00
16. Finer quality, English goods, ingrain colors with unbleached soles, per pair, 50c; per dozen...........................$5 85
17. Finest quality, English goods with unbleached feet, per pair, 65c; per dozen....$7 60
18. Fine Derby Ribbed Hose, full regular made, can only be had in black with unbleached soles, fast colors per pair, 35c; per dozen......$4 00
19. Ladies' English Derby Ribbed Hose in black and colors with unbleached soles, per pair, 69c; per dozen..........................$8 00

Ladies' Fancy Cotton Hose.

20. Ladies' Fancy Cotton Hose, patent seams, per pair, 10c; per dozen.............$1 00
21. Better quality, per pair, 12½c; per dozen.$1 25
22. Fancy Striped Hose, full regular made, unbleached grounds with wide or narrow stripes, in navy blue, seal brown, garnet or cardinal, see cut, per pair, 19c; per dozen.............$2 25
23. Better quality, per pair, 25c; per dozen.$2 90
24. Finer quality, in narrow and wide stripes in a handsome combination of colors, see cut, per pair, 35c; per dozen.................$4 00
25. Finest quality, very handsome, extra fine drop stitch, 40 gauge, in alternate stripes and bars very choice patterns, per pair, 43c; per dozen...........................$5 00

26. Unbleached Hose, in 25 choice designs, such as black and white blocks running vertical, in circles, cresents, etc., etc., these styles are predominate, per pair 25c; per dozen....$2 90
27. Finer quality, per pair, 35c; per dozen..$4 00
28. Best quality, French goods per pair, 50c; per dozen..........................$5 85
29. Full Regular Made Fancy Hose, dark tan or mode grounds with cardinal, navy, light blue, or old gold stripes across, per pair, 25c; per dozen..............................$2 90
30. Finer quality, elegant combination of colors, per pair, 35c; per dozen.................$4 00
31. Finer quality in tans, modes and dark colors, with stripes running vertically and across, in newest shades, per pair, 45c; per dozen...$5 20
32. Best quality, English goods, light and dark grounds, with plain stripes, very substantial, per pair, 58c; per dozen...................$6 75

Ladies' Outsize Hose.

33. Unbleached Cotton Outsize Hose, full regular made, per pair, 29c; per dozen........$3 25
34. Extra wide, unbleached, finer quality, per pair, 35c; per dozen....................$4 00
35. Fine quality, balbriggan, silk clocked, extra wide, per pair, 45c; per dozen........$5 20
36. Extra quality unbleached lisle hose, extra wide, per pair, 75c; per dozen.........$8 75
37. Outsize Hose in black and the following colors, navy blue, seal brown, garnet, cardinal, tan and mode, per pair, 35c; per dozen......$4 00
38. Finer quality, with unbleached soles, per pair, 50c; per dozen....................$5 85
39. Best quality, English goods, same shades as above with unbleached soles, per pair, 75c; per dozen..........................$8 75
40. Ladies' extra quality, lisle thread outsize hose in all shades with unbleached soles, per pair, 75c; per dozen.....................$8 75

Ladies' Knit Hose.

41. German Knit Hose, brown and blue mixed, per pair, 25c; per dozen..................$2 90
42. Plain white, per pair, 25c; per dozen...$2 90
43. Cardinal grounds with white stripes, suitable for hard ware, per pair, 35c; per dozen...$4 00
44. Oxford Mixed Hose, per pair, 25c per dozen............................$2 90
45. Better quality, per pair. 35c; per dozen.$4 00
46. Best quality English goods with unbleached soles, per pair, 45c; per dozen...........$5 20

Ladies' Opera Length Hose.

47. Cotton, in light pink, blue, salmon and flesh colors, per pair, 75c; per dozen..........$8 50
48. Lisle in light colors, such as pink, blue, salmon and flesh colors, per pair, $1.00; per dozen...........................$11 50
49. Spun silk, per pair, $1.68, per dozen...$19 00
The above can also be furnished in black and dark colors.

50. Ladies' Opera Length Hose, fancy lisle thread, with large and small blocks covering full length of stocking, elegant combination of colors, per pair...................$2 25

Ladies' Plain Lisle Hose.

51. Colors, navy. seal garnet, cardinal, tan, mode brown, pink, sky blue. bronze, and myrtle green, per pair, 39c; per dozen....$4 50
52. Better quality, same colors, unbleached soles, per pair, 50c; per dozen.........$5 85
53. Finer quality, 4 thread lisle with unbleached soles, per pair, 63c; per dozen......$7 20
54. Finest quality, French lisle with unbleached lisle soles, per pair, 98c; per dozen......$11 20
55. Extra quality, "Richelieu" ribbed hose, all colors, per pair, 65c; per dozen.........$7 75
56. Extra quality, narrow, ribbed lisle hose, all colors, per pair, 59c; per dozen..........$7 00
57. Extra quality, Lisle Hose, instep embroidered with silk in black and following colors, viz.: old gold and sky blue, per pair 98c; per dozen...........................$11 50

Ladies' Fancy Lisle Hose.

58. Brilliant Lisle Hose, handsome patterns in dark grounds with fine stripes, elegant combinations, per pair, 59c; per dozen........$7 00
59. Fancy Lisle Hose, with open worked instep, all colors, per pair, 75c; per dozen....$8 75
60. Fancy Lisle Hose, black and navy blue ground, with old gold and light blue narrow and wide stripes, extending half length of the hose, per pair, 56c; per dozen..........$6 10
61. Fancy Lisle Hose, unbleached top with solid colored instep in navy blue, black, seal brown, tan and mode, per pair, 58c; per dozen....$6 75
62. Vertical Striped Lisle Hose, black grounds with light blue, white and old gold stripes; light grounds such as lavender, sky blue and pink with vertical stripes, elegant combination, see illustration, per pair.................$1 09
63. Fancy Lisle Hose, dark grounds with light zig-zag silk stripes running vertical, these goods can be had in elegant combination and have some handsome designs, per pair....$1 09
64. French Lisle Hose, black grounds with white, old gold or sky blue blocks running half length of hose, very handsome, per pair.........$1 19

Ladies' Silk Hose.

65. Spun Silk Hose, in light or dark colors, per pair, 89c; per dozen.........$10 50
66. Better quality, spun silk with white spun silk feet, per pair, $1 09; per dozen......$12 50
67. All Silk Hose, in all shades, per pair, $1 68; per dozen.............................$20 00
68. All Silk Hose. much heavier, per pair..$2 25
69. All Silk Hose, extra heavy, per pair....$2 75
70. All Silk Hose, rich ribbed. per pair.....$3 25
We can furnish the above in navy, seal, cardinal, garnet, black, myrtle, gray, old gold, white and cream.

MISSES' AND BOYS' HOSE.

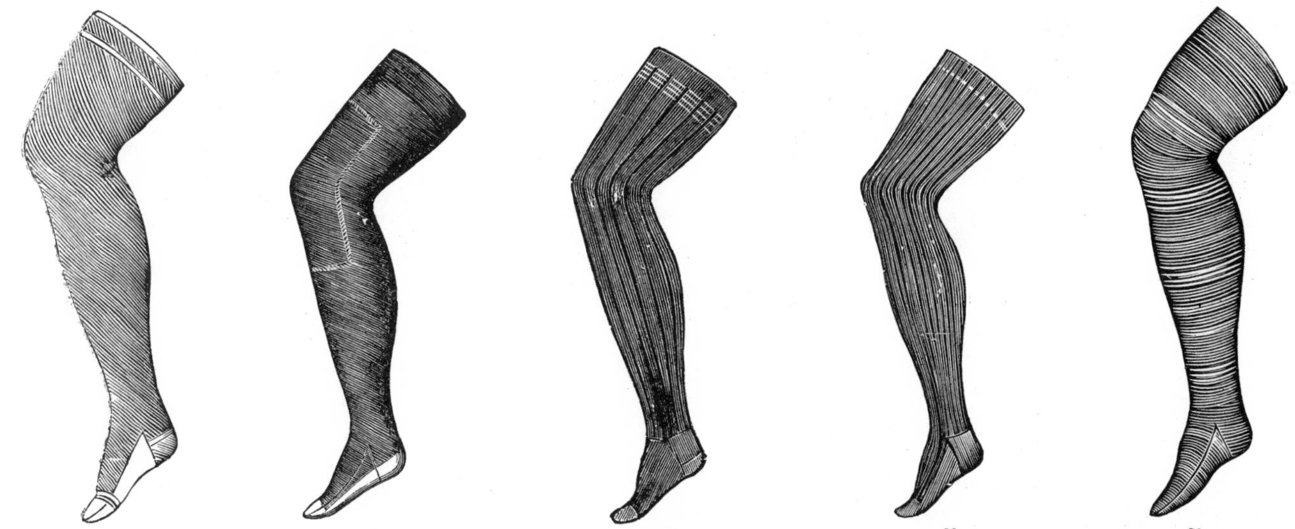

72 74 81 83 89

Children's Hosiery.

Scale of Sizes for Misses', Boys' and Infants' Hose.

Children of 2 years......................5 inch.
" " 3 " ....5½ "
" " 4 " ....6 "
" " 5 " ....6 to 6½ "
" " 6 " ....6½ to 7 "
" " 7 " ....7 "
" " 8 " ....7½ "

Solid Colored Cotton Hose.

71. Children's Solid Colored Hose, patent seams, black, navy, seal, garnet and cardinal, per pair, 12c; per dozen..............................$1 25
72. Full regular made, unbleached soles,(see cut) all colors,
Sizes 5, 5½, 6, 6½, 7, 7½, 8, 8½
Prices 18c, 21c, 25c
73. Better quality,
Sizes, 6, 5½, 6, 6½, 7, 7½, 8, 8½
Prices, 25c, 29c, 35c
74. Same with double knees, (see cut),
Sizes, 5, 5½, 6, 6½, 7. 7½ 8, 8½
Prices. 28c, 30c, 33c, 35c, 38c, 41c, 43c, 45c
75. Best quality English goods with unbleached soles,
Sizes, 5, 5½, 6, 6½, 7, 7½, 8, 8½
Prices, 40c, 43c, 45c, 48c, 50c, 53c, 55c, 58c
76. Same with double knee,
Sizes, 5, 5½, 6, 6½, 7, 7½, 8, 8½
prices, 45c, 48c, 53c, 55c, 58c, 60c, 63c, 65c
77. Children's full regular made hose, colors, tan and mode,
Sizes, 5, 5½, 6, 6½, 7, 7½, 8, 8½
Prices, 25c, 29c, 35c
78. Best quality, English goods with unbleached feet,
Sizes, 5, 5½, 6, 6¼, 7, 7½. 8. 8½
Prices, 30c, 33c, 35c, 38c, 40c, 43c, 45c,48c

Children's Solid Colored Ribbed Hose.

79. Solid colored ribbed hose with patent seams, navy, seal, blue and garnet,
Sizes, 6, 6½, 7, 7½, 8, 8½
Prices, 12c, 15c, per pair
80. Full regular made wide or narrow ribbed hose with white heels and toes, navy, seal, garnet or black,
Sizes, 5½, 6, 6½, 7, 7½, 8, 8½
Prices, 20c, 25c, 29c, per pair
81. Children's full regular made, French narrow or wide ribbed hose with unbleached soles,
Sizes, 5½, 6, 6½, 7, 7½, 8, 8½, 9
Prices, 30c, 35c, 40c, 45c, 50c, 55c, 60c, 65c, per pair
82. Better quality, double knee, with unbleached soles,
Sizes, 5½, 6, 6½, 7, 7½, 8, 8½, 9
Prices,40c, 45c, 50c, 55c, 60c, 65c, 70c, 75c, per pair
83. Best quality, wide or narrow ribbed, like cut
Sizes, 5½, 6, 6½, 7, 7½, 8, 8½, 9,
Prices, 50c, 55c, 60c, 65c, 70c, 75c, 80c, 85c, per pair
84. Solid colored English hose, with unbleached soles, wide or narrow ribbed,
Sizes, 5½, 6, 6½, 7 7½, 8, 8½, 9
Prices, 25c, 29c, 33c, 35c, per pair
85. Finer and heavier quality, with double knee, all colors with unbleached soles,
Sizes, 5½, 6, 6½, 7, 7½, 8, 8½, 9
Prices, 33c, 37c, 40c, per pair
86. English Derby Ribbed Hose, assorted colors with unbleached soles, (as illustrated)
Sizes, 5, 5½ 6, 6½, 7, 7½, 8, 8½,
Prices, 28c, 31c, 35c, per pair
87. Finer quality, English derby ribbed hose, assorted colors with unbleached soles,
Sizes, 5, 5½, 6, 6½, 7, 7½, 8, 8½,
Prices, 33c, 35c, 38c, 41c, 43c, 45c, 48c, 50c, per pair
88. Best quality with double knee,
Sizes, 5, 5½, 6, 6½, 7, 7½, 8, 8½
Prices, 48c, 50c, 53c, 55c, 58c, 60c, 63c, 65c, pair

Children's Fancy Cotton Hose.

89. Children's fancy hose full regular made, light grounds with narrow or wide cardinal, garnet or seal stripes, (like cut),
Sizes, 5, 5½, 6, 6½, 7, 7½, 8, 8½
Prices, 20c, 25c, 29c
90. Better quality, finer gauge in wide or narrow stripes,
Sizes, 5, 5½, 6, 6½, 7, 7½, 8, 8½
Prices, 25c, 28c, 30c, 33c, 35c, 38c, 41c, 43c
91. Children's fancy striped hose full regular made dark grounds with novelty stripes in 20 different styles,
Sizes, 5, 5½, 6, 6½, 7, 7½ 8, 8½
Prices, 29c, 31c, 33c, 35c, 38c, 40c, 43c, 45c
92. Better quality, English goods new combination of colors,
Sizes, 5, 5½, 6, 6½, 7, 7½, 8, 8½
Prices, 35c, 38c, 41c, 43c, 45c, 48c, 50c, 55c
93. Full regular made hose blocked patterns with unbleached grounds,
Sizes, 5, 5½, 6, 6½, 7 7½, 8, 8½
Prices, 29c, 35c, 39c
94. Better quality, new designs dark or light grounds with blocks extending half the length of stocking,
Sizes. 5, 5½, 6, 6½, 7, 7½, 8, 8½
Prices, 39c, 45c, 50c

Children's Plain and Ribbed Lisle Hose.

94. Plain, brilliant Lisle thread hose in all colors,
Sizes, 5, 5½, 6, 6½, 7, 7½, 8, 8½
Prices, 28c, 30c, 33c, 35c, 38c, 41c, 43c, 45c, per pair
96. Better quality, English goods all colors.
Sizes, 5, 5½, 6, 6½, 7, 7½, 8, 8½
Prices, 35c, 38c, 40c, 43c, 45c, 48c. 50c, 53c, per pair
97. Best quality, with unbleaceed feet,
Sizes, 5, 5½, 6, 6½, 7, 7½, 8, 8½
Prices, 43c 45c, 48c 50c, 53c 55, 58c, 60c, per pair
98. French lisle, wide or narrow ribbed, all colors,
Sizes, 5, 5½, 6, 6½, 7, 7½, 8, 8½
Prices, 50c, 54c, 58c, 62c, 66c, 70c, 74c, 78c, per pair
99. Better quality, with fine white lisle feet,
Sizes, 5, 5½, 6, 6½, 7, 7½, 8, 8½
Prices, 58c, 63c, 68c, 75c, 83c, 90c, 98c, $1 05 per pair
100. French open work lisle hose different designs, all colors,
Sizes, 5½, 6, 6½, 7, 7½, 8, 8½
Prices, 58c, 60c, 63c, 68c, 70c, 73c, 75c, per pair

Children's Fancy Lisle Hose.

101. Children's fancy lisle hose, mode and tan grounds with fine combination of light and dark stripes, very neat and handsome designs,
Sizes, 5, 5½, 6, 6½, 7, 7½, 8, 8½
Prices, 43c, 45c, 48c, 50c, 53c, 55c, 58c, 60c, per pair
102. Children's lisle hose, dark grounds with white, old gold, cardinal and light blue and vertical stripes,
Sizes, 6, 6½, 7 7½, 8, 8½
Prices, 65c, 70c, 75c, 80c, 85c, 90c, per pair
103. Children's blocked lisle hose, in 25 different colors,
Sizes, 6, 6½, 7, 7½, 8, 8½,
Prices, 65c. 70c, 75c, 80c, 85c, 90c, per pair
104. Children's Lisle Hose,narrow ribbed,running vertical, peacock blue, bronze, navy and black grounds, with stripes to match, elegant combinations.
Sizes, 5, 5½, 6, 6½, 7, 7½, 8, 8½
Prices, 35c, 38c, 40c, 42c, 45c, 48c, 50c, 55c, per pair

Children's Silk Hose.

105. Children's Spun Silk Hose, assorted colors,
Sizes, 5½, 6, 6½, 7, 7½, 8, 8½
Prices, 53c, 60c, 68c. 75c, 83c, 90c, 98c
106. Pure Silk, $1 38, 1 50, 1 63, 1 75, 1 88, 2 00, 2 25
107. Children's Pure Silk French Ribbed Hose,
Sizes, 6, 6½, 7, 7½, 8, 8½
Prices, $1 80, 2 00, 2 15, 2 35, 2 55, 2 75

Infants Hosiery.

108. Infants' ¾ Hose, light grounds, with fine blue, cardinal or brown stripes, full regular made; sizes, 4 to 6, per pair, 18c; per dozen, $2 00.
109. Better quality, in light or dark stripes; sizes, 4 to 6; per pair, 25c; per dozen..........$2 90.
110. Children's Plain Colored ¾ Hose, assorted colors; sizes, 4 to 5; per pair, 25c; per dozen, $2 90.
111. Better quality Colored ¾ Hose,
Sizes, 4¼, 4½, 5, 5½, 6 and 6½
Prices, 28c, 31c, 33c, 36c, 37c and 39c. per pair,
112. Children's ¾ Hose, light pink and blue; sizes, 4 to 5½; per pair....................25c
113. Much finer, silk clocked, ¾ Hose; sizes, 4 to 6½; per pair..............................35c
114. Children's ½ Socks, full regular made, light grounds, with hair-line stripes of brown, red or blue; sizes, 4 to 5½; per pair...............18c
115. Better quality, striped, fast colors; sizes, 4 to 5½; per pair..............................25c
116. Best English goods, dark or light stripes.
Sizes, 4, 4½, 5, 5½, 6, 6½ and 7
Per pair, 25c, 28c, 31c, 33c, 35c, 38c and 41c
We furnish the above gaods at the same prices in solid colors in black, garnet, cardinal, navy blue, seal, light pink and blue.
117. Children's White ½ Socks, full regular made; sizes, 4 to 6; per pair...............15c
118. Better quality; sizes, 4 to 7; per pair....25c
119. Children's ¾ White Hose; 4 to 6; per pair,15c
120. Finer quality; 4 to 7; per pair...........25c
121. Children's ¾ and ½ Socks, fancy Lisle thread; sizes, 4 to 6; per pair..............35c
122. Infants' Ribbed Wool Hose; sizes, 4 to 5; per pair...................................25c
123. Infants' Plain Cashmere, white and colored, per pair......................33c, 39c, 45c

Men's Half Hose.

SIZES, 9 to 11.

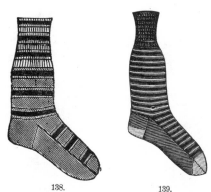

138.　　　　139.　　　　142.　　　　145.　　　　146.　　　　150.

Men's Half Hose.

UNBLEACHED HALF HOSE.

127. Unbleached Half Hose, per pair. 10c ; per dozen.....................................$1 00
128. Full regular made, French feet, per pair, 17c ; per dozen....................$2 00
129. British, full regular made, double heels and toes, per pair, 19c ; per dozen............$2 25
130. Cotton. fine lisle finish, per pair, 19c ; per dozen....................................$2 25
131. Best British,goods extra heavy and gussetted, per pair, 25c; per dozen..................2 90
132. Full regular made,Balbriggan, exta quality, French feet, silk clocked, per pair, 25c ; per dozen....................................$2 90
133. Much finer gauge, silk clocked, per pair, 35c ; per dozen........................$4 00
134. Unbleached Lisle Half Hose, good weight, per pair, 35c ; per dozen.................$4 00
135. Much heavier, 4 thread Lisle. extra quality, per pair, 50c ; per dozen....................$5 85

Men's Fancy Half Hose.

136. Men's Fancy Half Hose, per pair, 10c ; per dozen..$1 00
137. Better quality, brown mixed, per pair, 12½c ; per dozen.........................$1 25

138. Fancy Half Hose, light grounds, with fancy stripes or tans and modes, with handsome combination of colors, full regular made (see cut), per pair, 19c ; per dozen..........$2 25
139. Better quality, English modes, tans, light and dark stripes, full regular made goods, with double heels and toes (like illustration), per pair, 25c ; perdozen $2 90
140. Better quality, English, tans in modes and dark colors, with fine silk stripes. per pair, 35c ; per dozen...................................$4 00
141. Best quality, English half hose, all shades, with silk stripes, per pair, 50c ; per dozen, $5 85
142. Solid Colored Half Hose, white heels and toes, full regular made (same as cut), per pair, 19c ; per dozen..........................$2 25
143. Men's Solid Colored Half Hose, English goods. silk clocked. black. tan, mode, seal, navy, wine, garnet, per pair, 35c ; per dozen $4 00
144. Best quality, English half hose, same colors, silk clocked, per pair, 50c ; per dozen......$5 85
145. Men's Solid Colored Half Hose. modes, tans, cardinal, navy, seal, garnet, with unbleached feet, double heels and toes, (see cut), colors warranted; per pair, 25c; per dozen. $2 90

Men's Summer Merino Half Hose.

146. Fine Summer Merino Half Hose, full regular made, tans and modes (like cut), per pair. 35c ; per dozen........................$4 00

147. Better quality, very soft and fine, per pair, 45c ; per dozen........................$5 20

Men's Lisle Half Hose.

148. Men's Fine Brilliant Lisle Half Hose, navy, seal, garnet, black. cardinal, tan and mode, per pair, 35c : per dozen....................$4 00
149. French Brilliant Lisle Hose. same colors, with white heels and toes, per pair, 45c ; per dozen..$5 20
150. Extra Fine Ribbed. Brilliant Lisle hose (refer to cut), per pair, pair, 56c ; per dozen..$6 80
151. Fine Brilliant Lisle Hose, unbleached soles, per pair, 50c ; per dozen....................$5 85
152. Fancy Lisle Hose, modes. tans and dark colors. with stripes of contrasting colors, elegant combinations. per pair, 50c ; per dozen $5 85
153. Extra Fine French Lisle Hose,dark grounds, with silk stripes, per pair, 75c; per dozen, $8 75

Men's Silk Half Hose.

154. Men's Silk Plaited Half Hose, black, navy, seal, cardinal and garnet, per pair, 68c ; per dozen..$8 00
155. Same, in dark grounds, with old gold and dark stripes, elegant patterns, per pair, 75c ; per dozen $8 75
156. English Spun Silk Hose, black. per pair, 98c

Ladies' Underwear.

Ladies' Vests.

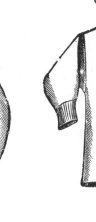

Children's Vests.

Ladies' Drawers.

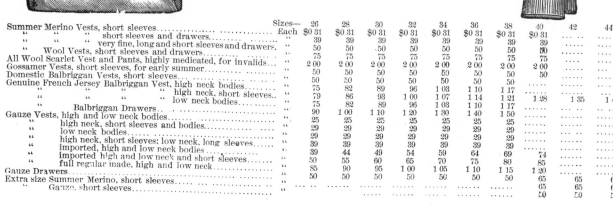

	Sizes—	26	28	30	32	34	36	38	40	42	44
157. Summer Merino Vests, short sleeves.	Each	$0 31	$0 31	$0 31	$0 31	$0 31	$0 31	$0 31	$0 31		
158. " " short sleeves and drawers.	"	39	39	39	39	39	39	39	39		
159. " " " very fine, long and short sleeves and drawers.	"	50	50	50	50	50	50	50	50		
160. " Wool Vests, short sleeves and drawers.	"	75	75	75	50	75	75	75	50		
161. All Wool Scarlet Vest and Pants, highly medicated, for invalids.	"	2 00	2 00	2 00	2 00	2 00	2 00	2 00	2 00		
162. Gossamer Vests, short sleeves, for early summer.	"	50	50	50	50	50	50	50	50		
163. Domestic Balbriggan Vests, short sleeves.	"	50	50	50	50	50	50	50			
164. Genuine French Jersey Balbriggan Vest, high neck bodies.	"	75	82	89	96	1 03	1 10	1 17			
165. " " " " " high neck, short sleeves..	"	79	86	93	1 00	1 07	1 14	1 21	1 28	1 35	1 42
166. " " " " " low neck bodies.	"	75	82	89	96	1 03	1 10	1 17			
167. " Balbriggan Drawers.	"	90	1 00	1 10	1 20	1 30	1 40	1 50			
168. Gauze Vests, high and low neck bodies.	"	25	25	25	25	25	25	25			
169. " high neck, short sleeves and bodies.	"	29	29	29	29	29	29	29			
170. " low neck bodies.	"	29	29	29	29	29	29	29			
171. " high neck, short sleeves; low neck, long sleeves.	"	39	39	39	39	39	39	39			
172. " imported, high and low neck bodies.	"	39	44	49	54	59	64	69	74		
173. " imported high and low neck and short sleeves.	"	50	55	60	65	70	75	80			
174. " full regular made, high and low neck.	"	85	90	95	1 00	1 05	1 10	1 15	1 20		
175. Gauze Drawers.	"	50	50	50	50	50	50	50	65	65	65
176. Extra size Summer Merino, short sleeves.	"								65	65	65
177. " Gauze, short sleeves.	"								50	50	50

MEN'S UNDERWEAR.

SHIRTS FROM 34 TO 46.   DRAWERS FROM 28 TO 44.

No.	Description	30	32	34	36	38	40	42	44	46	48	50
178.	Summer merino shirts, bound with silk .... Each,			$0 31	$0 31	$0 31	$0 31	$0 31	$0 31			
179.	" " drawers	$0 31	$0 31	31	31	31	31	31	31			
180.	Summer merino shirt, bound with silk			39	39	39	39	39	39	39		
181.	" " drawers	39	39	39	39	39	39	39	39			
182.	Summer merino shirts, pearl buttons			50	50	50	50	50	50			
183.	" " drawers, English band	50	50	50	50	50	50	50	50			
184.	Half-wool light weight shirts			75	75	75	75	75	75	75	75	
185.	" " drawers			75	75	75	75	75	75	75	75	
186.	All-wool light weight shirts	1 00	1 00	1 00	1 00	1 00	1 00	1 00	1 00			
187.	" " drawers			1 00	1 00	1 00	1 00	1 00	1 00			
188.	Summer merino Bismarck brown and cadet blue shirts	1 00	1 00	1 00	1 00	1 00	1 00	1 00				
189.	" drawers, same colors	1 00	1 00	1 00	1 00	1 00						
190.	Scotch gray half-wool shirts			50	50	50	50	50	50			
191.	" " drawers	50	50	50	50	50	50					
192.	French balbriggan shirts, long and short sleeves			75	75	75	75	75	1 00	1 10	1 20	1 30
193.	" " drawers	75	75	75	75	75	75	1 00	1 10	1 20		
194.	French balbriggan shirts, very fine, long sleeves			1 00	1 00	1 00	1 00	1 00	1 00	1 25	1 35	1 45
195.	" " drawers	1 00	1 00	1 00	1 00	1 00	1 00					
196.	Fancy balbriggan shirts, four colors, stripes	1 00	1 00	1 00	1 00	1 00	1 00					
197.	Drawers to match	1 00	1 00	1 00	1 00							
198.	Gauze shirts, short sleeves			29	29	29	29	29	29			
199.	" " " finer			35	35	35	35	35	35	35		
200.	" " " very fine			50	50	50	50	59	50			
201.	" " " full regular			75	75	75	75	75	75	85	95	1 05
202.	Jean Drawers, 28, 30 and 32 inch inseam	50	50	50	50	50	50	50	50			
203.	" 28, 30 and 32 inch inseam	75	75	75	75	75	75	75	75			
204.	All Linen Drawers, 28 and 30 inch inseam	1 25	1 25	1 25	1 25	1 25	1 25	1 25	1 25			
205.	Gauze Drawers	50	50	50	50	59	50	50	50			

CHILDREN'S SUMMER MERINO AND GAUZE UNDERWEAR.

BLOOMINGDALE BROS.' SCALE FOR CHILDREN'S UNDERWEAR.

Vests.		Pantalettes.	
SIZES FOR AGE.		**SIZES FOR AGE.**	
16 inches.......1 year and under.	26 inches.......6 to 8 years.	16 inches.........1 to 1½ years.	26 inches.............8 to 10 years.
18 " ....1 to 1½ years.	28 " ....8 to 10 years.	18 " ....1½ to 2 years.	28 " ....10 to 12 years.
20 " ....1½ to 2 years.	30 " ....10 to 12 years.	20 " ....2 to 4 yaars.	30 " ....12 years.
22 " ....2 to 4 years.	32 " ....12 to 13 years.	22 " ....4 to 6 years.	32 " ....13 years.
24 " ....4 to 6 years.	34 " ....13 to 14 years.	24 " ....6 to 8 years.	34 " ....14 years.

At 15 years, suitable sizes can be found in Ladies' and Men's Goods.

No.	Description	16	18	20	22	24	26	28	30	32	34
205a.	Boys' and Misses' Summer Merino Vests, bound with silk, pearl buttons, embroidered neck, long and short sleeves....Each	$0 19	$0 21	$0 23	$0 25	$0 27	$0 29	$0 31	$0 33	$0 35	$0 37
206.	Boys' and Misses' All Wool Vests, silk bound, long and short sleeves	31	36	41	46	51	56	61	66	71	76
207.	Boys' and Misses' balbriggan gossamer Vests, silk bound, short sleeves	19	21	23	25	27	29	31	33	35	37
208.	Boys' and Misses' Gauze Vests, high and low neck, short sleeves	12	14	16	18	20	22	24	26	28	30
209.	" " " "	19	21	23	25	27	29	31	33	35	37
210.	Boys' and Misses' English Vests	28	32	36	40	44	48	52	56	60	64
211.	Boys' and Misses' Vests, high and low neck, short sleeves	50	55	60	65	70	75	80	85	90	95
212.	Boys' and Misses' Vests, Cartwright & Warner's high neck and S. S.	80	90	1 00	1 10	1 20	1 30	1 40	1 50	1 60	1 70

MISSES' PANTALETTES.

No.	Description	16	18	20	22	24	26	28	30	32	34
213.	Summer Merino.....Each	19	21	23	25	27	29	31	33	35	37
214.	Gauze	28	30	32	34	36	38	40	42	44	46
215.	Jean Pantalettes	39	39	39	39	39	39	39	39	39	39

BOYS' DRAWERS.

No.	Description	16	18	20	22	24	26	28	30	32	34
216.	Summer Merino.....Each				25	27	29	31	33	35	37
217.	Gauze Drawers	28	30	32	34	36	38	40	42	44	46
218.	Boys' Jean Drawers	45	45	45	45	45	45	45	45	45	45
219.	Boys' Jean Drawers, to the knee, for short pants	39	39	39	39	39	39	39	39	39	39

GLOVE DEPARTMENT.

Being the sole importers of the Celebrated Prince Baudoin High Lustre Real Kid Gloves, which are specially manufactured to suit the requirements of our best trade. In style, finish and fit, we can recommend them as the most perfect and reliable medium price gloves ever offered in this market.

TRADE PRINCE BAUDOUIN MARK.   B.B 85

REAL KID   HIGH LUSTRE.

GLACÉ.
(Sizes, 5½ to 7½.)

220. 3-Button, Scallop Top, black only, per pair.....................$1 00
221. 5 " " " black and all colors, per pair............1 25
222. 7 " " " " 1 50
223. 4 " Pique embroidered back, per pair...................1 25

MISSES' PRINCE BAUDOUIN.
(Sizes, 4½ to 6½.)

224. 3-Button Scallop Top, tan and brown, per pair................ 75
225. 5 " " " 1 00

SUEDE.
(Sizes, 5½ to 7.)

232. 4-Button Undressed, black, tan and brown, shades, per pair.......$1 00
233. 6-Button " " " 1 25
235. 8-Button Mousquetaire, black, tan and brown, per pair.......... 1 50
236. 16-Button Undressed, white and tan operas, per pair.............. 2 00
237. 20-Button " " 2 75

OUR NAPOLEON.

A first quality real kid glove, hand sewed and equal to any glove made at any price; colors, tan, slate, brown, green and black.

238. 3-button, scalloped top, sizes, 5½ to 8 ....$1 50
239. 5-button, " " 5½ to 7½ 1 75
240. 7-button, " " 5½ to 7¼ 2 00

HOOK GLOVES.

The celebrated "Foster" lacing gloves, first quality, all colors.

226. 5-hook, per pair..$2 00
227. 7-hook, " 2 25
228. 10-hook, " 2 75
229. 15-hook, " 3 25

Second quality.

230. 7-hook, per pair..$1 25
231. 10-hook, " 1 50

GLOVE DEPARTMENT.
(CONTINUED.)

Ladies' Suede Mousquetaire.
EXTRA LONG FOR EVENING WEAR.

23C.	12-button, in tan, opera and white, per pair			$2 00
233.	16-button	"	"	2 50
234.	20-button	"	"	3 00
235.	24-button	"	"	3 50
236.	36-button	"	"	4 50

Lace Top Suede..

The latest Parisian fashon for balls and evening wear, these are 4-button Suede gloves with heavy escurial lace tops.

237.	24 inches long, per pair....	$2 75
238.	36 inche4 long, "	4 00

Genuine Zavier Jouvin Gloves.

Fifteen medals and grand diploma of honor were awarded to the manufacturers of these gloves at all the European exhibitions for rich variety, quality, perfect cut, superior taste and workmanship.

Richelieu Quality.

239.	3-button, black only; per pair	$1 60
240.	4-button, black and street shades; per pair	1.75
241.	6-button, " "	2 00
242.	4-button, " " embroidered back; per pair	1 85
243.	6-button, " " "	2 10

Petite Jouvin Suede Gloves.

244.	4-button, all colors; per pair	$1 50
245.	6-button, "	1 75
246.	8-button, Mousquetaire; per pair	2 00
247.	4-button, embroidered back; per pair	1 68
248.	6-button "	1 90
249.	8-button, Mousuuetaire, embroidered back; per pair	2 15

Bargains in Kid Gloves.

250.	5-button, scalloped top, tan only; per pair	$0 59
251.	6-button, Welt, real kid, black only; per pair	0 75
252.	5-button, scalloped top, real kid, tan and brown; per pair	1 00
253.	4-button, Pique, embroidered back; per pair	0 75

Gentlemen's Gloves.
Sizes, 6¾ to 8¾.

254.	2-button, Premier, Dog Skin	$1 60
255.	2-button, broad embroidery	1 50
256.	2-button, Fisk, Clark & Flagg	2 00
257.	2-button, Castor, embroidered back	1 35
258.	2-button, Dent's Deerskin, driving	1 75
259.	2-button, Walking Kid Richelieu brand	1 54
260.	2-button, Driving	1 50
261.	2-button, Suede Pique, Richelieu "	2 00

Boys' Kid Gloves.

262.	2-button, embroidered back	$1 50

Fabric Gloves.
LISLE THREAD JERSEY GLOVES.

263.	6-button Venetian Lisle, black and tan	19c
264.	6-button Brilliant Lisle, " "	35c

Taffeta (Silk and Linen) Jersey Gloves.

265.	4-button, black and tan	29c
266.	6-button, " "	39c
267.	8-button, " "	49c
268.	6-button, " " sublime quality	50c
269.	8-button, " "	60c

All Silk Jersey Gloves.

270.   6-button length, very fine, black and colors   50c

We call special attention to our stock of English, Milanese Silk Gloves, which for perfection of fit and beauty of finish cannot be excelled.

271.	6-button, black and colors.	$0 75
272.	8-button, " "	1 00
273.	4-button, extra heavy, black and colors	1 00
274.	6-button " " "	1 25

Misses' Gloves.

275.	6-button, Jersey Lisle	25c
276.	6-button, Jersey Taffeta	35c
277.	6-button, Jersey Silk	50c

Lace Mits.
BLACK AND ALL COLORS.

278.	12 inches	25c

279.	14 inches	35c

281.	12 inches	50c

282.	12 inches	65c

283.	14 inches	75c

284.	14 inches	75c

285.	Misses' 10 inches	25c

286.	14 inches long, per pair	50c

287.	16 inches long, per pair.	65c

288.	16 inches long, per pair.	75c

Jersey Mits.

Black, tans, gold ecru, fawn, pink, cream, pale blue and white.

290.	12 inches long		$0 39
291.	14 "		0 50
292.	14 "	Milanese	0 75
293.	16 "		1 00
294.	14 "	extra heavy	1 00
295.	16 "		1 25
296.	20 "		1 00
297.	24 "		1 25
298.	30 "		1 75
299.	36 "		2 50
300.	24 "	lace tops, in operas only	2 00

Gentlemen's Furnishing Department.

CUSTOM SHIRT DEPARTMENT.

We are making better Shirts to order at the remarkably low price of **SIX FOR SIX DOLLARS**, than can be produced by any other house; the fit is guaranteed; they are of the best Muslin, best Linen, and very best workmanship.

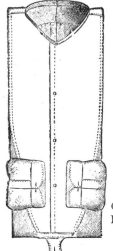

⅜ inch Plain Welt.

SIX { FINELY FINISHED CUSTOM SHIRTS (OPEN BEHIND.) } for **$6.00**

Made from the best brands of Muslin, with 3-ply Linen Bosoms, Neck and Wrist Bands or Cuffs.

These Shirts are fully re-inforced, have French Plaquetted Sleeves, Initial on Tab, and

ARE UNEQUALED AT THE PRICE.

Open front, six for......$6 50.   With collars attached, $7 50
Pleated bosom, six for....8 00.   "   "   9 00
Laundried with the finest finish, $1 50 extra per half doz.

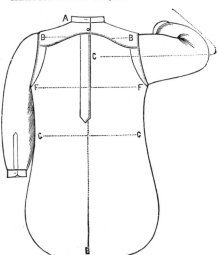

MEASUREMENTS REQUIRED FOR SHIRTS.

A. Around the Neck . . . . inches
     Size of Collar worn . . . .   "
B. Length of Yoke . . . .   "
C. Length of Sleeve . . . .   "
     Centre of Back
     to end of Wrist) . . . .   "
E. Length of Shirt . . . .   "
F. Round the Breast . . . .   "
G. Round the Waist . . . .   "

Men's Unlaundried Shirts.

300. Our stock shirts, which are always on hand, sizes 13½ to 17½, of first-class muslin, 1900 linen, well made..............each, 50c
301 A. Wamsutta Muslin, 2000 all-linen bosom, hand-made, buttonholes throughout....75c
302 X. Utica Nonpareil Muslin, Richardson's all-linen 2200 bosom, re-inforced in front and back, French plackets on sleeves and back, double stitched throughout, consti-tuting the best shirt that can be had at any price. Each $1 00

Men's Laundried Shirts.

303 P. Shirt 75c
304 A.   " $1 00
305 AA. " 1 25
306 X. Full Dress Shirt 1 50
307 XX. Pleated Front 1 75

Blue Flannel Shirts.

Men's Double Breasted Blue Flannel Work-ing shirts. As we manufacture these goods we guarantee them to prove excellent value.

308. Good Flannel . . . . . . $1.00 and 1.25
309. Extra Heavy $1.50
310. Double Backed 2.00
311.   "   Front and Back 2.50

Laundried or Unlaundried, open Back or Front.

Neck. { High, Low or Medium. Button or Stud in Front. Button or Stud in Back. Collar attached or Band.

Bosom. { Length . . . . . inches from Yoke to Band at bottom of Bosom.
Style . . . .
Buttons, Studs or Eyelets.

Wrist. { Wrist Bands or Cuffs, Buttons or Studs. Size of Bands . . . . . .
Cuffs . . . .
(Mentioning any peculiarity of figure.)

Tourists' and Bicycle Shirts.

SCHNEER'S PAT. FEB. 28TH & APRIL 25TH 1882.

The above cut represents our patent Electric Lacing Shirt. It is so arranged that it can be worn with a collar, or the collar may be turned in (forming a yoke to the shirt) and a white collar put on. The advantage of this patent is too apparent to need an explanation.

Another improvement on this shirt is our patent fly front, enabling the wearer to put on and take off without the trouble of lacing and unlacing.

312. Men's navy blue, electric blue, gray, brown, green, etc., $2 25
313. Extra fine, in fancy colors 2 65
314. Boys,' in all shades 2 00

Men's Plaited Flannel Shirts.

315. Best quality flannel, plain colors . . . . . $2.00 and 2.25
316. Fancy striped   "   . . . . . . 2.25 and 2.50

Boys' and Youths' Unlaundried Shirts.

317 B. Same as B men's, sizes 12 to 13½ . .49c
318 A. Same as A men's, sizes 12 to 13½. . 60c
3 9 AA. Same as AA men's, sizes 12 to 13½ 85c

Laundried, 25c extra.

Tourists' and Bycicle Shirts.

320. Men's Navy Blue Tourists Shirts . . . . . $1.00, 1.25, 1.50 and 2.00
321. Men's Colored Flannel Shirts; colors, green, fawn, brown and gray $1.50
322. Cocheca Flannel; colors, green, gray light and dark brown, garnet, ox blood, white etc . . . . $2.00 and 2.50
323. Fancy Striped . . . . . . 2.00 and 2.50
324. Boys' Shirts; colors, blue, brown and gray . . . . $1.00, 1.25 and 1.50

Percale Shirts.

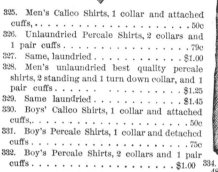

325. Men's Calico Shirts, 1 collar and attached cuffs, ... 50c
326. Unlaundried Percale Shirts, 2 collars and 1 pair cuffs 79c
327. Same, laundried $1.00
328. Men's unlaundried best quality percale shirts, 2 standing and 1 turn down collar, and 1 pair cuffs $1.25
329. Same laundried $1.45
330. Boys' Calico Shirts, 1 collar and attached cuffs, ... 50c
331. Boy's Percale Shirts, 1 collar and detached cuffs 75c
332. Boy's Percale Shirts, 2 collars and 1 pair cuffs $1.00

Night Shirts.

333. Men's fancy night shirts, Wamsutta Muslin, 50 inches long, sizes 14 to 18 inches $1.00

334. Night shirts, plain good muslin, 48 inches long 50c
335. Heavy Muslin, 50 inches long 75c
336. Wamsutta muslin, 52 inches long, ... $1.00
337. Fancy bordered night shirts of Wamsutta muslin, 50 inches long, ... 75c

Robes de Chambre.

338. Fine Cloth Robes de Chambre, with deep facing of quilted cloth and fine silk girdle, lined with sateen, each $11.50
339. Same garments made of cloth, with deep facing of quilted satin, as illustrated; lined with sateen to match the stitching of quilted satin facing ; in seal brown, faced with cardinal satin, stitched and lined with cardinal; green mixture, and faced with dark green satin, stitched and lined with gold; green mixture, faced with garnet satin, stitched and lined with gold ; garnet mixure, faced with garnet satin, stitched and lined with gold; navy blue, faced with navy blue satin, stitched and lined with navy blue ; brown mixture, faced with seal brown satin, stitched and lined with seal brown; gray mixture, faced with royal blue satin, stitched and lined with royal blue $15.00.
340. Extra fine quality cloth Robes de Chambre, with deep facing of quilted satin, and fine silk girdle; lined with quilted satin, each $19.00.

Suspenders.

346. Velocipede Shoulder Braces, a suspender and shoulder brace combined, has side and back pieces. Excellent for growing boys inclined to stoop 75c
347. French Suspenders, white or colored 45, 50c

Supsenders.

341. Very good quality Suspender, with web ends, white or colored 25, 50, 60, 70c
342. Fine Elastic Suspender, with heavy twisted silk ends, 50, 75, 85c, $1.00, 1.25, 1.50, 2.00.
343. All-silk Suspenders, blue or cardinal, $1.00, 1.50, 2.00
344. Boys' Suspenders 18, 20, 25, 30, 50c

Suspenders.

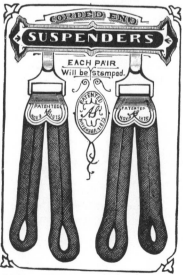

CORDED END
SUSPENDERS
EACH PAIR
Will be stamped.
PATENTED NOV 3 1875

345. Special 100 dozen celebrated National silk, corded ends per pair 39c

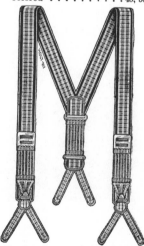

348. Armstrong spiral spring suspenders, per pair . . . 65 and 85c

Our Waist Department is one of the most important in the House, we manufacture these goods on the premises; the patterns are all imported by us direct, and we control them exclusively.

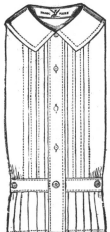

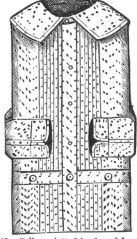

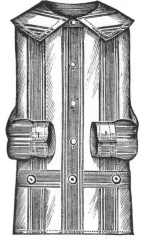

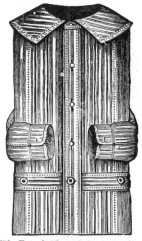

349. White, pleated back and front, muslin collars and cuffs, unlaundried......................45c
350. White, pleated back and front, linen collars and cuffs, unlaundried..................58c
351. White, all linen, pleated back and front, unlaundried $1.00
352. White, with neck-band for attaching, standing or turn-down collar, unlaundried...........58c
Any of the above laundried,17c extra

353. Calico, plaited back and front, 25c
354. Cambric, plaited back and front 35c
355. American Percale, plaited back and front, hand-made button holes 58c
356. Genuine French Percale, our own patterns, consisting of dogs' heads, lions' heads, horses' heads, etc............................75c
Any of the above laundried,17c extra

357. American Percale, in a large variety of checks and stripes, very stylish and perfect fitting......58c
    Laundried,.................17c extra

359. French Flannel, in mode color, stripes and checks, new this season and very nobby.........$1.75

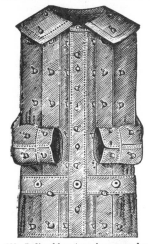

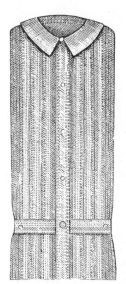

360. Indigo blue, American percales, in a large variety of checks, plaids, stripes and figures unlaundried,71c
361. Indigo blue, French Percales, $1.00

MEN'S RUBBER COATS.

363. American Percale, in a beautiful variety of heads, birds, figures, etc., very stylish and striking effects......................58c
364. Very stylish Waists, in solid red and blue bodies, with collars and cuffs of contrasting colors ; new this season.... ....85c
Any of the above laundried,17c extra

SMOKING JACKETS.

365. Flannel, navy blue, green, gray and brown......................79c
366. Better quality Flannel, myrtle green, brown and blue... ....98c
367. Best quality Flannel, pleated front and back (as illustrated), colors, gray, blue, brown, green and tan, each................$1.50
368. Gilbert's Flannel, in all colors; knife-pleated in front and box-pleated in back, each.........$1.75

White Vests and Bar Coats.

366 a. Striped Seersucker, best goods, ...71c
367 a. Laundried, 17c extra.

MEN'S RUBBER COATS.

368. Men's Gossamer Coats, sizes 34 to 50 in., each.......$1.75, 2.00, 2.50
369. Men's Reversible Checked back coats, dull finish, sizes 34 to 50 in., each..................$2.50 and 3.50
370. Men's dull finished, with old gold backs, each...........$2.98
371. SPECIAL—10,000 Men's Checked back rubber coats, all sizes, real value, $2.00; each $1.27

372. Extra fine quality Cloth Smoking Jackets, with deep facing of quilted satin; quilted satin cuffs and pockets; lined with quilted satin... ... $10.00, 12.00 and 15.75

BAR COATS.
373. Gentlemen's White Vests, sizes 34 to 44 inches, breast measure, Marseilles,each, 75c, $1.00, 1.25,1.50
374. White Cotton Duck..75c, $1 00
375. White Linen Duck..$2.00, 2 50
376. Fancy Marseilles....$2.00, 2.50
BAR COATS.
377. White Duck....$1.00, 1.25, 1.50
378. White Linen Duck..$2.00, 2.50

379. Men's Perfection Storm Coats extra heavy, with side pockets, storm welts, etc.; best coat made for stormy weather, each....$5.00
380. Men's dull finish ventilated back coats, with lace backs, newly patented, each...................$5.00
381. Boys' Gossamer Rubber Coats, sizes 5 to 13 years, each. $1.25, 1.75
382. Boys' Dull Finished Coats,with checked back, each.........$2.50

Men's and Boys' Collars, Cuffs and Neckwear.

ANCHOR BRAND.

THE BURNABY.
383.   Each, 15c ; per dozen....$1 75

ANCHOR BRAND.

ELCOME.
384.   Each, 15c ; per dozen....$1 75

ANCHOR BRAND.

AJAX.
385.   Each, 10c and 15c, 2 for 25c ;
per dozen........$1 00 and $1 50

ANCHOR BRAND.

PENCLIF.
386.   Each, 15c ; per dozen....$1 75

FLORENCE.

387.   Florence, 15c each ; per dozen,
$1 75

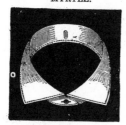

MYRTLE.

388.   Myrtle, 15c each ; per dozen,
$1 75

JASMINE.

389.   Jasmine, 15c each ; per dozen,
$1 75

ARBUTUS.

390.   Arbutus, 15c each ; per dozen,
$1 75

BOYS' CLIFTON.
BOYS SPACE

391.   Boys' Clifton, 13c each ; per
dozen....................$1 25

BOYS' HERO CLUB.
ROUND & SQUARE   BOYS STANDING

392.   Boys' Hero Club, 13c each ; per
dozen....................$1 25

BOYS' BONA.

393.   Boys' Bona, 13c each ; per
dozen....................$1 50

SOUTHWICK.

394.   Southwick, 3 for 25c ; per
dozen....................$1 00

LILAC.

395.   Lilac, 15c each ; per dozen,
$1 75

SPEEDWELL.

396.   Speedwell, 25c per pair ; per
dozen....................$2 90

DAHLIA CUFF.
WIDTH 4¼ INCH

397.   Dahlia, 25c per pair ; per
dozen.................. $2 90
398.   Dahlia, 19c per pair ; per
dozen.................. $2 25

NATION.

399.   Nation, Link Cuffs, 25c
per pair ; per dozen.....$2 90

Men's Neckwear.

"ANCHOR BRAND."
ANCHOR BRAND
FRONT 2 IN   BACK 1½ IN.

MIKADO.
400.   Each, 15c ; per doz..$1 75

PLAIN AND COLORED STRING TIES.
402.   Plain colored, such as brown,
blue and garnet and cardinal.
each............................25c
403.   Fancy Figured Satin, embrac-
ing polka dots, figures, stripes,
etc., each.........25c, 35c and 50c
404.   White Satin and Silk Ties, for
evening and full dress wear, folded 1 inch wide, each,..25c and 35c
405.   Folded, 1⅛ inches wide, each,
35c and 50c

BLACK, WHITE AND COLORED BOWS.

406.   White Satin Band Bows, each,
19c
407.   White Satin Band Bows, with
fancy figures, each..............25c
408.   White Lawn Band Bows, each
5c, 10c and 15c
409.   Black Satin Band Bows, each,
25c
410.   Black Silk Band Bows, each.
25c
411.   Fancy Satin Band Bows, each,
25c

DE JOINVILLE SCARFS.
412.   All the newest styles in these
popular Scarfs, in plain and fancy
patterns,each 25c,50,75,$1.00 to 2.00
413.   Black Satin.................75c

BLACK AND COLORED BOWS.

414.   Black Silk or Satin Bows,each,
19c 25c to 42c
415.   Fancy Satin Bows, each,
18c 25c and 39c

BLACK SILK NECKWEAR.
FOLDED TIES.
416.   ¾x30 in....... 24c, 34c, 44c, 59c
417.   ⅞x31 in....... 28c, 39c, 49c, 68c
418.   1 x32 in....... 29c, 44c, 54c, 74c
419.   1⅛x34 in....... 33c, 53c, 63c, 84c
420.   1¼x36 in....... 34c, 59c, 69c, 94c
421.   Fringe End Ties, 1¼ in., 35c ; 1½
in., 49c.
422.   Black Silk and Satin Bows, 10c
to 44c.

WHITE PUFF SCARFS.
423.   White Satin, each 50c and 75c
424.   White grounds, with fancy figures and stripes, worn very much,
each.............50c, 75c and $1 00

"ANCHOR BRAND."
HEIGHT 2 INCHES   LAPS IN FRONT
IMPROVED CURVE

SOCIETY.
401.   Each, 15c ; per dozen,
$1 75

LAWN AND CAMBRIC NECKWEAR.
425.   Col'd Cambric Ties, per dozen,
15c, 19c and 25c
426.   White Lawn Ties, per dozen,
8c, 9c, 13c, 18c and 19c
427.   White Lawn Bows, per dozen,
20c, 25 and 50c

RUGBY.

428. Dark grounds, with fancy
stripes, checks and figures,
39c, 50c, 75c
429. White satin............ 50c, 75c

THE "WINDSOR."

436. For Boys; silk or satin, all colors, each............... 25c, 35c
437. Black Silk Windsors, each..69c
438. White Silk Windsors, each, 75c

CLAUDENT.

430. Black silk or satin, 50c, 75c, $1.00
431. Colored, fancy patterns, each,
50c, 75c, $1.00

AVONDALE.

439. Dark grounds, fancy stripes
and checks............ 50c, 75c

LA PETITE.

432. Dark grounds, fancy stripes,
checks, etc...........35c, 50c, 75c
433. White and light grounds,50c, 75c

MELTON.

440. Dark grounds..... 19c, 25c, 39c
441. White satin, with figures,
19c, 25c

NO. 546.

434. Dark grounds, fancy checks
stripes and figures.....39c, 50c 75c
435. Light grounds 50c, 75c

GLENDALE.

442. Dark grounds, with fancy
checks, stripes and figures,
39c, 50c, 75c
443. White grounds, with figures,
50c, 75c

Perfumery and Toilet Articles. Zylonite Toilet Articles.

These goods can be had in white or amber.   They are much prettier and more durable than horn or rubber.   The white has the appearance of ivory, while the amber color that of genuine amber.

444. Nail Polishers, 3½ inches long, each...59c

445. Nail Brushes, each.. . ... 69c

446. Hair Brushes, each $1 19

447. Tooth Brushes, each............... 49c

448. Infants' Brushes, each........69c

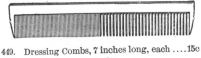

449. Dressing Combs, 7 inches long, each 15c

450. Pocket Folding Combs, each 18c

451. Pocket Combs, 3½ inches long,
each....... ....7c

452. Fine Zylonite
Mirrors, French
plate, 4⅜x9⅜ in.
each....... $1.29

453. Children's Round Combs,
5c

454. Soap Boxes, 3½ inches long. 1¾
inches high and 2½ inches wide....49c

455. Cloth Brushes.................$1.19

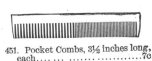

456. Hat Brushes, each.............79c

457. Button Hooks, each............. ....18c

POWDER PUFFS.

458. Powder Puffs............8, 15, 19, 25, 30, 49c

COMBS.
RAW HORN.

459. Very best make and finish raw horn combs, coarse and fine teeth, 5½ inches long 5c
460. 6 inches long 7c
461. 6½ inches long 9c
462. 7 inches long..............................11c
463. 7½ inches long 13c

BUFFALO HORN.

464. Buffalo Horn Comb, 6 inches long.... ..29c
465. 6½ inches long.............................35c
466. 7½ inches long............................49c
467. Horn Pocket Comb with mirror.........13c
468. Pocket Buffalo Horn Combs, in case 10, .15c

RUBBER.

469. Extra heavy Rubber Comb, with coarse and fine teeth 25c
470. Children's Rubber Round Combs.
    5, 8, 9, 10, 12c
471. Pocket Folding Combs, rubber.... 8, 15, 25c
472. Rubber Combs, fine and coarse teeth, folding together 13c
473. Other Rubber Combs........9, 15, 19, 35, 49c

MISCELLANEOUS COMBS.

474. Zylonite Combs, white, red and amber..10c
475. Celluloid Combs......13, 15, 25, 45, 63, 69, 75c
476. Fine Combs, celluloid.....................8c
477. Fine Combs, ivory...............29, 39, 49c

SOAP BOXES.

478. Metal Soap Boxes.............25, 49, 59, 63c

TOILET ARTICLES.

479. Sponges....................10, 15, 25, 50, 75c
480. Chamois Skin........ 10, 15, 25, 50, 75c, $1.00
481. Nail Sets, with brush, file, polisher and powder in box, for the care of finger nails, in leather boxes.................25, 45, 75, $1.25
482. In plush boxes $1.50, 2.00, 3.00
483. Fancy boxes, with scented sachet and two bottles of perfume........ 25, 50, 69c, $1.00, 1.25

SOAPS.

484. Soap, glycerine balls, each, 5c; per doz., 55c
485. Soap, honey, brown Windsor, per cake,
    5, 8, 12c
486. Soap, Castile, white or mottled, per cake,
    5c; per dozen, 55c
487. Soap, Palm, per cake... 10c ; per doz., $1.00
488. Soap, Low's Genuine English Brown Windsor, per cake, 6c; per package of 3 cakes... 17c
489. Soap, Cashmere Bouquet, per cake.....21c
490. Soap, Lubin's, per cake..................26c
491. Soap, pure glycerine....................10c
492. Soap, Glenn's Sulphur, per cake........14c
493. Soap, Constantine's Tar 15c

ATOMIZERS.

494. Atomizers, each 25, 39, 49. 69, 97c

GENTLEMEN'S COMPANIONS.

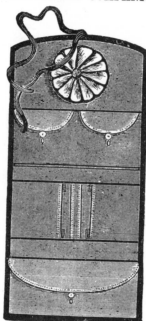

495. Men's Companions, rubber, with pockets for sponge, hair comb, tooth and nail brush, and soap...................................97c
496. Same, in leather 49, 63c
497. Same, in canvas....................93c
498. Rubber, with above complete $2.75
499. Leather,   "   "   " 2.25
500. Canvas,   "   "   " 2.50

SHAVING BRUSHES.

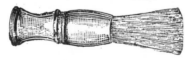

501. Shaving Brushes.................6, 10, 25, 47c

WHISK BROOMS.

502. Whisk Brooms............................10c
503. Whisk Brooms, with ivory handle, each,
    29, 30, 36, 41, 43, 49c

TOILET WATERS.

504. Florida Water (Bazaar)...................25c
505. Bay Rum, pint bottles 25c
506. " quart " 50c
507. " imported, extra 90c
508. Lavender and Violet Water, per bottle,
    53, 59, 71c
509. Murray & Lanman's Florida Water......42c
510. Lubin's Lavender Water, per bottle.....53c
511. Coudray's Lavender Water, per bot..39, 49c
512. Oakley's Violet Water, per bottle........69c
513. Oakley's Bay Rum, per bottle 49c
514. Colgate's " 62c
515. Colgate's Violet Water, small, per bottle, 35c ; large, per bottle......................71c
516. Ammoniated Bay Rum, for dry shampooing. Preyents dandruff and gives fresh effect,
    25, 49c

PUFF BOXES.

517. Plain White Metal Puff Boxes, each,12, 15, 25c
518. Same, with hand-painted decorations, colors pink and blue, each 50, 75c, $1.00
519. Same, porcelain......... 75c, $1.00, 1.50, 2.00

BRUSHES.

520. English Hair Brushes of fine white bristles, black backs, wire drawn 39c

521. Metallic Hair Brushes; made of the best steel. soft, durable and uninjurious, plain, 15c
522. Hand-painted, each....................19, 25c

523. Hair Brushes, plain and fancy backs,
    25, 50, 75c, $1.00, 1.75, 2.00
524. English Hair Brushes, wood backs,
    $1.00, 1.39, 1.69, 1.98
525. Fancy inlaid backs... . 94c, $1.00, 1.25, 1.49

526. Tooth Brushes 10, 15, 25, 40c
527. BLOOMINGDALE's Wire Drawn English Tooth Brush, made of finest white bristles ; every one is warranted 25c
528. Hand brushes.............10, 25, 35, 37, 49c
529. Clothes Brushes....... 25, 50, 75c, $1.00, 2.00

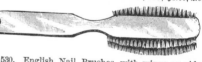

530. English Nail Brushes, with wings on side,
    5 rows......... ....15c
531. 6 rows.................................19c
532. 8 rows.................................25c

MIRRORS, ETC.

533. Plain Square Mirrors, gilt frames, French plate, to hang....................12, 18 to 31c
534. Leather backs, French plate....... 25 to 83c
535. Black backs.................63, 79c, $1.19
536. Celluloid, French plate, to match brushes,
    98c. $1.25, 1.50
537. Leather, on stands, French plate,
    44, 75, 98c, $1.19
538. Nickel-plated Patent Standing Mirrors, French plate.......$1.25, 1.49, 1.95, 2.79, 3.39
539. Traveling Glasses, in canvas, fancy designs,
    50, 75, 95c, $1.33
540. Leather and Plush, French plate,
    89c, 95c, $1.15, 1.49
(For other Mirrors, refer to Index.)

PILLS.

541. Ayer's, per box 13c
542. Brandreth's, per box 9c
543. Carter's Liver, per box 13c
544. Warner's Safe, " 13c
545. Dr. Schenck's, " 13c
546. Jayne's, " 62c
547. Carter's Iron Pills, " 15c
548. Castor Oil Pills, " 34c
549. Hood's Pills " 17c
550. Pinkham's Pills, " 17c
And all others at proportionately low prices.

Patent Medicines.

In Patent Medicines, we have in stock every article to be had, at one-half the price they are sold for at the drug stores.

549. Ayer's Sarsaparilla, per bottle.........64c
550. " Cherry Pectoral, per bottle.......64c
551. " Hair Vigor, "...............64c
552. Appolinaris Water, "...........12c
553. Allcock's Porous Plasters, each.........9c
554. Brown's Troches, per box.............18c
555. Brown's Iron Bitters, per bottle.......73c
556. " Essence of Ginger.............33c
557. Beef, Iron and Wine...................43c
558. Burnett's Cocoaine...................65c
559. Barry's Tricopherous.................29c
560. Calisaya Bark and Iron...............93c
561. Camphor, Ice and Cold Cream........11,13c
562. Chevalier's Life for the Hair............58c
563. Citrate of Magnesia, per bottle.........15c
564. Cuticura Resolvent....................13c
565. Caswell, Hazard & Co.'s Cod Liver Oil..59c
566. Corn Plasters, per box.................7c
567. Cuticura Salve.......................34c
568. Castoria..............................27c
569. Dr. Bull's Cough Syrup, per bottle 18c
570. Dr. Schenck's Syrup, per bottle........73c
571. Dr. Kennedy's Favorite Remedy,per bot..73c
572. Dalley's Pain Extractor................18c
573. Ely's Cream Balm.....................85c
574. Fellow's Hypophosphites, per bottle....97c
575. Green's August Flower................47c
576. German Corn Remover.................13c
577. Hartshorn, in pint bottles, for Toilet,
Kitchen and Laundry, per bottle........10, 15c
578. Horsford's Acid Phosphate, per bottle. .36c
579. Hill's Hair Dye, per bottle.............34c
580. Hamburger Tea, per package............18c
581. Hawley's Pepsine, per bottle...........49c
582. Hall's Hair Renewer, per bottle........56c
583. Hood's Sarsaparilla, per bottle.........69c
584. Hostetter's Bitters, "...........73c
585. Hop Bitters, "...........69c
586. Hoff's Malt Extract "...........29c
587. Hunyadi Water........................23c
588. Husband's Calcined Magnesia.........27c
589. Hale's Honey, Horehound and Tar,per bot.33c
590. Jayne's Expectorant, per bottle........67c
591. Lydia E.Pinkham's Compound,per bottle,65c
592. Liebig's Extract of Meat...............39c
593. " Cocoa Beef Tonic.........73c

594. Magic Depilator, for removing superfluous hair from the skin.......................25c
595. McArthur's Hypophosphites.............79c
596. Murdock's Liquid Food 43c
597. Monell's Teething Cordial...............16c
598. Moller's Norwegian Cod Liver Oil.......55c
509. Nestle's Food........................39c
600. Pond's Extract.......................30c
601. Platt's Chlorides......................36c
602. Perry Davis' Pain Killer................19c
603. Radway's Resolvent...................69c
604. Radway's Ready Relief.................33c
605. Scott's Emulsion of Cod Liver Oil.......68c
606. St. Jacob's Oil........................33c
607. Siedlitz Powders, per box..............23c
608. Schenck's Tonic.......................73c
609. Schenck's Pulmonic...................73c
610. Shaker's Extract......................43c
611. Squibb's Carbolic Acid................23c
612. Swift's Specific.......................73c
613. Tarrant's Seltzer Aperient.............70c
614. Trommer's Malt 65c
615. Tamar Indien........................53c
616. Valentine's Meat Extract..............75c
617. Warner's Rheumatic Cure..............83c
618. Witch Hazel, per bottle. 15c
619. Wei de Meyer's Catarrh Cure, per box...75c
620. Wyeth's Beef, Iron and Wine, per bottle..57c
621. Winslow's Soothing Syrup.............18c
622. Warner's Kidney Cure.................83c
623. Wolff's Schiedam Schnapps.............47c

Tooth and Face Powders and Pastes.

624. Pinaud's Violette de Parma, per bot..69, 96c
625. Pinaud's Eau de Quinine, per bottle. 37, 73c
626. Pinaud's Extract, per bottle.............96c
627. Brilliantine, per bottle...........26, 34, 53c
628. Sozodont Tooth Wash, per bottle......48c
629. Thurston's Tooth Powder, per bottle....14c
630. Calder's Dentine, per bottle.............14c
631. Lyon's Tooth Powder, per box...........15c
632. " " Tablets, ".............29c
633. Jewsbury and Brown's Tooth Powder,
per box................................35c
634. Thompson's Tooth Soap, per cake.......15c
635. Lubin's Sachet Powder, per box.........43c
636. Riker's Face Powder, per box............14c
637. Dorin's Face Powder, per box...........15c
638. Colgate's Sachet Powder, per package...21c

639. Colgate's Cashmere Powder,per package,14c
640. Lubin's Toilet Powder, per package......15c
641. Saunder's Face Powder, white, per box..21c
642. Satina Face Powder, in three shades,
tinted for blondes, tinted for brunettes, and
plain white, an elegant preparation, price
per box................................19c
642a. Magnolia Balm.......................44c
643. Oriental Cream........................88c
644. Laird's Bloom of Youth................44c
645. Coudray's Bandoline, per bottle.........10c
646. Bazaar Quinceline, per bottle. 8c
647. Colgate's Bandoline....................11c
648. Fancy box, with scented sachet and two
bottles of perfume......................69c, $1.25
649. Fancy Box, with one cake of soap, one
box lilly white, two bottles cologne........50c
650. Fancy Box, larger and finer............75c
651. Colgate's Vaseline, for hair, per bottle...11c
652. Colgate's Vaseline, pure, per bottle. 8c
653. Coudray's Quinine, for the hair, per bot..39c
654. Coudray's Brilliantine, per bottle........29c
655. Coudray's Hair Oil, per bottle...........15c
656. Coudray's Cosmetic, per cake...........12c
657. Glove Powder.........................3c

Extracts and Colognes.

All the Bazaar Perfumes and Extracts are manufactured in our laboratory, and have become widely known as the best in the market. The prices are unusually low for the high quality of the extracts.

658. Oakley's Extracts, small................23c
660. Lundborg's Extracts, per bottle.......33, 47c
661. Low, Son & Hayden's Extracts,per bot...23c
662. Piesse & Lubin's Extracts. per bottle....57c
663. Colgate's Extracts. all odors, "....43c
664. Bazaar Perfume, 1 oz...................25c
665. Lubin's Perfume, per bottle............54c
666. German Cologne, per bottle.............18c
667. Farina Cologne, per bottle...........25, 49c
668. "Sweet Bye-and-Bye" Cologne, per bot..16c

The above is simply a schedule of prices of the most popular Patent Medicines, Extracts, Toilet Waters, etc., etc., of which we have a complete stock of both foreign and domestic manufacture constantly on hand, and which are sold far below the prices of drug stores. Special Patent Medicine Catalogues furnished on application.

NOTIONS.

Serpentine Braid.

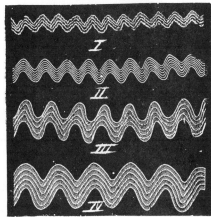

669. Sepentine, No. 9,per doz. pieces of 1½ yds.ea. 3c
670. I. No. 13, " " " " 4c
671. II. No. 17, " " " " 5c
672. III. No. 21, " " " " 7c
673. IV. No. 25, " " " " 8c
674. Linen-Serpentine, No. 13, per dozen pieces of
1½ yards each 9c
675. Linen-Serpentine, No. 17, per dozen piecss of
1½ yards each 12c
676. Linen-Serpentine, No 21, per dozen pieces of
1½ yards each 15c
677. Linen-Serpentine, No. 25, per dozen pieces of
1½ yards each 21c
678. Super-Serpentine Braid, Extra Heavy,
No. 17, per box of 48 yards 27c
679. Same, No.21, " 32c
680. " No.25, " 41c

Braids.

681. Wave Serpentine Braid, in 18 yard pieces,
No. 21, 25, 29, 33, 37, 41, 45, 49, 53
Per doz. 13, 15, 17, 19, 21, 23, 25, 27, 31c
682. Scarlet Worsted Rick Rack Braid, in 1½ yard
pieces, No. 17 per doz 19c
683. Loop Rick Rack, per dozen pieces of 1½ yards
each,
Nos. 13, 17, 21, 25, 29,
Per doz. 8, 10, 13, 17, 21c
For Dress Braids refer to Trimmings.

Novelty Braids.

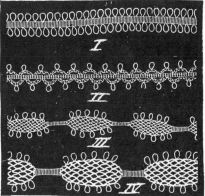

684. Article I. Feather Edge Braid; original 2099.
685. No. 0. Per doz.pieces of 4 yds. each . . 23c
686. No. 1. " 4 " . .24c
687. No. 2, " ' 4 " . .26c
688. No. 3, " " 4 " . .28c
689. No. 4, " " 4 " . .30c
690. Article II, Tubular Braids, per doz. pieces
of 3 yards each 65c
691. Article, III, Medalion Braids, per dozen
pieces of 3 yards, each 68c
692. Article IV, Medalion Braids: per dozen
pieces of 3 yards each 75c

Bindings.

693. Furniture Binding, all colors, 18 yard
pieces, ⅝ inch wide, per piece 22c
694. Carpet Binding :
No. 1, per piece of 10 yards, 15c; per yard . . 2c
No. 2. " 10 " 25c; " . . 3c
No. 3, " 10 " 28c; " . . 3c
695. Tick Binding, blue and white or red and
white striped, per piece of 12 yards 10c
696. Flannel Binding, silk, white, in 12 yard
pieces, ½ inch wide, per yard, . . 5c
697. Same, ¾ inch wide, 55c per piece; per yd., 6c
698. Same, scarlet, ½ inch wide, 45c per piece;
per yard 5c

699. Common Stay Binding, black and white:
700. No. 4, por piece, 2c; per dozen 15c
701. No. 6, " 2c; " 17c
702. No. 8, " 2c; " 18c
703. No. 10, " 2c; " 20c
704. No. 12, " 2c; " 23c
705. No. 14, " 3c; " 26c
706. No. 16, " 3c; " 28c
707. No. 18, " 3c; " 31c
708. No. 20, " 4c; " 33c
709. No. 6, 20 yard pieces,per piece 8c
710. No. 8, 30 " " 10c

English Stay Bindiug.

711. ¼ inch wide, per piece, 2c; per doz . . .21c
712. ½ " " 3c; " . . .33c
713. 1 " " 6c; " . . .65c
714. 12 yard pieces, per piece 12c

Honiton Lace Braid and Cotton Star Braid.

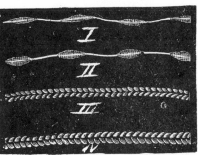

715. I. and II., Honiton Lace Braid.
716. I. Per Yard 5c
717. II. Per Yard. 6c
718. III. and IV., Cotton Star Braid.
719. No. 0. per pce, 2c;per doz.pcs, of 5 yds ea.19c
720. No. 1. " 2c; " " " 21c
721. No. 2. " 2c; " " " 23c
722. No. 4. " 2c; " " " 23c
BEST QUALITY ENGLISH GOODS.
723. No. 1. per pce, 4c;per doz.pcs,of 5 yds, ea.35c
724. No. 2. " 4c; " " " 38c
725. No. 3. " 5c; " " " 45c
726. No. 4. " 5c; " " " 53c

LINEN TAPE.

728.	No. ¼, per piece, 3c; per dozen......29c
729.	No. ½, " 5c; " 48c
730.	No. 1, " 6c; " 65c
731.	No. 2, " 7c; " 75c
732.	No. 3, " 8c; " 88c
733.	No. 4, " 9c; " 95c
734.	No. 5, " 9c; " $1 04
735.	No. 6, " 10c; " 1 12
736.	No. 8, " 12c; " 1 34

DRESS AND CORSET STEELS.

Corset Steels, sizes 11, 11½, 12, 12½, 13, 14, 15 and 16 inches.

737. Sateen covered attachable Corset Steels, with extra piece in center to prevent the steels from breaking, 12 to 15 inches, per pair 8c

738. Corset Steels, double, per pair........8c
739. Corset Steels, kid covered, best, imported, per pair........11c
740. Side Steels, muslin covered, per pair, 5c
741. Corset Steels, spoon shaped, muslin, imported, per pair........21c
742. Corset Steels, spoon shape, kid covered, per pair 25c
743. Celluloid Corset Steels, pr pair, 15, 17, 19c
744. Celluloid Side Steels, per pair.......11c

WIRE DRESS STEELS, ETC.

746. Wire Dress Steels, used in place of whalebone, sateen covered, black or white, 4, 6, 8, 10 and 12 inches long, per dozen.......7c
747. Moschkowitz Clock Spring Dress Steels, with brass tips, very extensively used, from 6 to 12 inches long, per doz., per each...2c
748. Celluloid Dress Steels, 6 to 12 inches. each, 3c ; per dozen......30c
749. Corset Whalebone, per pair.........12c

DRESS REEDS.

750. Dress Reeds, sateen covered, holes in end for sewing on, ½ inch wide, 15, 18 and 21 inches long, per set of 3.............6c
751. Same, ⅝ in. wide, per set of 3 .... 8c

752. Feather-bone entirely new, can be washed and always remain stiff, made of quills and covered with cotton, in black, white and slate, per yard, 12c; per doz. $1 30

DRESS SHIELDS.

GOODYEAR'S RUBBER CLOTH.

		Doz.	Per Pair.
753.	No. 1, small sewed......$0 75		7c
754.	No. 2, medium sewed 1 00		10c
755.	No. 3, large sewed 1 25		12c
756.	No. 1, small gummed.... 1 75		17c
757.	No. 3, large gummed... 2 25		21c
758.	Pure Rubber 2 00		18c
759.	Chamois or oiled silk 29c

760. Goodyear's Rubber-lined Serge Dress Shields, entirely impervious, per dozen, $3 25 ; per pair.........29c
SERGE, WITH PURE RUBBER LINING.

		Doz.	Each.
761.	No. 2, medium $1 00		10c
762.	No. 3, large 1 25		12c
763.	No. 4, extra large......... 1 65		15c

764. Stockinette, made of rubber and cloth, entirely impervious, and very much used (as illustrated), No. 2, medium, per doz., $2 00 ; each.........18c
765. Same, No. 3, large, per doz. $2 25 ; each, 18c

SILK THREAD.

768.	Heminway's 100-yard spools, 9c each ; per doz....95c
769.	Heminway's 24-yard spools, 3c; per doz.........35c
770.	Tsatlee, 100 yards, 5c spool ; per doz 60c
771.	Heminway's Buttonhole Twist, 2c spool; per doz..24c

For Embroidery Silks, see Worsteds.

LINEN THREAD.

772. Marshal's 200-yard, 7c spool ; per doz.... ....80c
773. Skeins, 2 for 5c ; per doz.........29c
774. Linen Floss, 3c skein ; per doz.........30c
775. Carpet Thread, brown, drab, green or scarlet, 3c skein ; per doz.........33c
776. Linen Floss, very fine, for crocheting feath r-edge braid or for lace work, same price as above.
777. Barbour's Linen Thread, 200-yard spools, black, white or unbleached, per spool, 7c ; per doz.........80c
778. Same, 100-yard spools, black only, for sewing on buttons, 5c ; per doz 50c

SPOOL COTTON.

779. Willimantic 3-Cord Cotton, per spool, 4c; per doz. 40c
780. B. B. T. 3-Cord, warranted 200 yards, for hand or machine sewing, per doz.........25c
781. O. N. T. Spool Cotton, per spool, 5c; per doz.....55c
782. Coats' Spool Cotton, per spool, 5c, per doz.....55c
783. Clark's Spool Cotton, per spool, 5c ; per doz.....55c
784. Willimantic 6-Cord Cotton, per spool, 5c; per doz.55c
785. Brooks' Cotton, per spool, 5c; per doz.........50c
786. Hall & Manning's, per spool, 2c; per doz.........33c
787. French Basting Cotton, 500-yard spools, per doz.25c
788. Merrick's ready-wound bobbins for machine, per box 5c
For Knitting and Crocheting Cotton, please refer to Worsteds.

789. Neat Ebony Box, containing 8 spools cotton, thimble and pin cushion...........50c
790. Same in velvet, per box.... ....50c

SHOE AND GLOVE HOOKS.

791. Shoe Button Hooks, black handles, each 1c ; per doz.........10c
792. Shoe Button Hooks, white bone handles, each, 5c ; per doz.........50c
793. Glove Button Hooks, white bone handles, each 5c ; per doz.........50c
794. Cocoa Bola Shoe Button Hooks, rosewood or cocoa bola handles, 6 inches long, each.........6c
795. 8 inches long, each.........7c
796. 10 inches long, each.........8c

WOVEN LETTERS.

797. Letters woven on fine cambric, in red, for marking house linen, etc., any initial, not less than a gross of one initial sold, per gross.........13c

HOOKS AND EYES.

798. Hooks and Eyes, dress, Nos. 3 and 4, white, per box.........10c, 11c
799. Hooks and Eyes, dress, Nos. 3 and 4, black, per box.........12c, 15c
800. Hooks and Eyes, large military, 4c per dozen ; per gross.........39c
801. Nichols' Patent Hooks and Eyes, with catch, black and white, per dozen 7c

SHOE BUTTON FASTENERS.

802. Excelsior Shoe Button Fasteners, simple and strong; box, 6 dozen, full directions, 8c
803. Boss Shoe Fastener, made of a linen cord, same thickness as a shoe lace, with a needle attached, very simple and strong, per dozen, 18c ; each.........2c

CLASPS AND BUCKLES.

804. Garter Buckles, steel or gilt, per pair, 5c
805. Pantaloon Buckles, steel or gilt, each, 1c

WIRE.

806. Bonnet Wire, black or white, per piece, 3c; per dozen.........33c
807. Ribbon Wire, white or black, each, 2c ; per dozen.........19c

TAPE MEASURES.

808. Linen Tape Measure, 60 inches long, each, 3c; per dozen 30c
809. Tape Measures, 60 inches long, printed on both sides, each 6, 8, 10c
810. Linen Tape Measures, printed on both sides, in brass cases, each.........4c
811. Tape Measures, in nickel cases, with stop spring, 60 inches long, each . . . 39c
812. Tape Measures, sewed together, French sateen on one side and American on the other, each.........15c

PIN CUSHIONS.

813. Black enameled tubs, each 5c
814. Tomato Pin Cushions, each . . 12c
815. Strawberry shape, each 5c

DRESS WEIGHTS.

816. Lead Dress Weights, per dozen, 5, 6, 8, 9c

LACES.

817. Laces, linen, shoe, per dozen . . .3 to 4c
818. Laces, flat, silk, each . . . . .7 to 13c
819. Laces, corset, linen, 2½ yards long, round or flat, each, 3c ; per dozen. . .25c
820. Laces, dress, flat, silk, 4 yards long, all colors, each 25c
821. Laces, dress, round, silk, all colors, each 3c ; per dozen 33c
822. Corset Laces, cotton, per doz., 7c ; elastic, each 7c
823. Cotton Corset Lacing, per ball of 100 yards 21c
824. Linen Corset Lacing, per ball of 100 yds, 83c

DRESS BELTINGS.

824a. Silk Serge Belting, black or white, best quality, per yd, 9c; per piece of 12 yds, $1 00

WHALEBONE.

824b. 36 inches long, 9c; subject to fluctuation.

CORD.

825. Picture Cord, all colors, 3c; piece of 18 yards..................................38c
826. Picture Cord, wire, piece of 20 yards, No. 1, ...10c
827. Picture Cord, wire, piece of 25 yards, No. 2, ...12c
828. Window Shade Cord, any color, per dozen yards.................................20c
829. Spring Shade Cord, all colors, per ball..10c
830. Eye Glass Cord, best quality, per yard....5c
831. Silk Watch Guards, fine, each, 8c; medium, 12c; heavy.............................15c

DRESS BRAIDS, ETC.

832. Black Silk Braid, per yard.........4c to 10c
833. Same, all colors, per yard, 7c; per dozen, 80c
834. Tubular bone casing, does not require any sewing as the bone is simply put in the casing which makes it perfect, cotton, per dozen, 35c; per yard.................................3c
835. Silk, per dozen, 50c; per yard............5c

GARTERS.

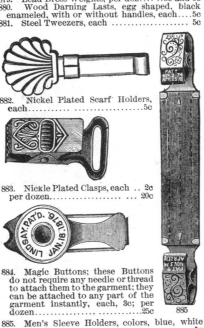

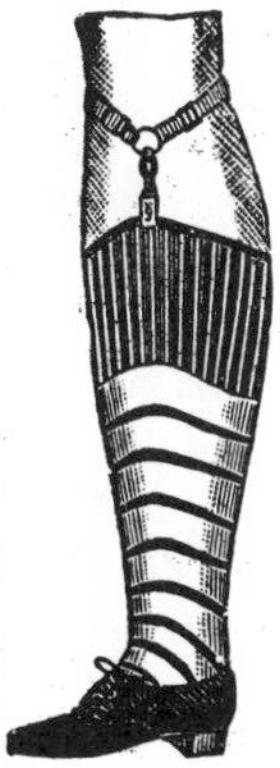

836. Men's Hose supporters, French loom, elastic, each.13c
837. Silk elastic, in white, pink, blue and cardinal, each.....25c
838. Sleeve Elastics, French loom elastic, 4c; silk, colors, pink, white, blue and red..10c
839. Elastic Garters, cotton, ½ inch, per pair.................3c
840. Fancy cotton, with buckles, per pair.................15c
841. Fancy silk, with bows and buckles, per pair........50c 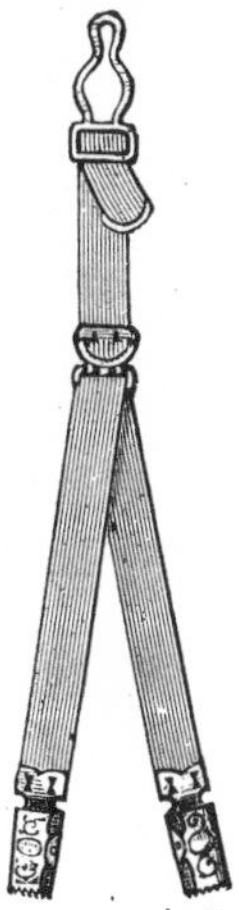
842. Bloomingdale's Improved Stocking Supporter for ladies or children, is much more convenient than the old style stocking supporter, can be adjusted to any size, and fastens on the garment or corset. Ladies who try them once will use no other. White French loom elastic, per pair.......29c
843. Silk, colors, pink, white, blue and cardinal, per pair, 59c
844. Ventilated Garters, silvered' per pair.....................17c
845. Ventilated Armlets, silvered, per pair..............17c
846. Silk, patent clasp, per pair, 10c
847. Stocking Supporters, with patent self-fastening clasps, D. D. or children's.
848. No. 1...........................per pair 5c
849. No. 2, large size .... "　"　8c
850. No. 3, Misses'..................... "　"　12c
851. No. 106, larger size.......... ..... "　"　15c
852. No. 19, Ladies .... "　"　17c
853. No. 6, same style, with band to fasten round waist, all sizes, for ladies or children, size of band from 10 to 30 inches, each......25c

ELASTICS.

854. Black, white and colored garter elastic, ⅞ inch, per yard, 5c; piece...............53c
855. Black and white linen Hat Elastic Braid, per yard..................................3c
856. Silk Garter Elastic, plain, ½ inch, all colors, per yard.................................13c
857. Same, ¾ inch, per yard....................15c
858. Same, ⅞ inch, per yard....................18c
859. Fancy Silk Garter Elastic, 1 inch wide, all colors, per yard.......................25c
860. Silk Elastic Pocket-book Bands, each.....4c
861. Black Silk Hat Elastic Cord, per yard....3c
862. Black Silk Hat Elastic Braid, per yard....5c
863. Same, white, per yard 7c

SUNDRIES.

864. Emery bags, each 6c
865. Beeswax, per cake....... ....3c
866. Eyelets, per gross.................. 14c
867. Wooden Darning Eggs, black enameled, each 5c
868. Wooden Darning Eggs, with handle to hold and needle box at the end, each. 7c
869. Window Shade Tassels, each...........25c
870. Window Shade Tassel Rings, per doz....5c
871. Screw Hooks and Eyes for picture frames, per dozen.................................5c
872. Carpet Tacks, per box, 3c to 4c; postage, per box...6c
873. Tack Hammers, each, 4c to 11c; postage each..................................4c to 12c

874. Picture Nails, with porcelain heads, each 2c; per dozen..................................18c
875. Curtain Rings, for curtains or loop dresses, per dozen...................................3c
876. Button Rings, per box..................12c
877. Key Rings, each....... ....3c and 5c
878. Machine Oil, per bottle...............5c
879. Lead Dress Weights, per doz.....5c and 6c
880. Wood Darning Lasts, egg shaped, black enameled, with or without handles, each....5c
881. Steel Tweezers, each 5c

882. Nickel Plated Scarf Holders, each.........................5c

883. Nickle Plated Clasps, each .. 2c per dozen.................... ... 20c

884. Magic Buttons; these Buttons do not require any needle or thread to attach them to the garment; they can be attached to any part of the garment instantly, each, 3c; per dozen. 15c

885. Men's Sleeve Holders, colors, blue, white and scarlet, cotton..........................5c
886. Same, in silk.... ....10c

NEEDLES.

BLOOD'S

"ALL THE YEAR ROUND"

PLUSH NEEDLE CASE

FULL VALUE IN NEEDLES.

Price, 35 cents.

887. Handsome Silk Plush Case, satin lined, containing 5 papers of needles, bodkins and darning needles.................................35c
888. Leather Needle Case, containing 5 papers of Milward's needles and pocket combined.....39c
889. Fancy Needle Box with 3 papers of needles and thimble....................................21c
890. More Handsome box, 5 papers of needles, thimble and spool of cotton................35c
891. Milward's, per paper....................4c
892. Milliners', very long, per paper...........4c
893. Glove, three-cornered, per paper.........10c
894. Worsted, long eyes, per paper...........5c
895. Darning, per paper....................4c
896. Bodkins or tape, per dozen. ..-. 5c
897. Needles, knitting, per dozen............10c
898. " bone, per dozen........15c
899. " wood, "............12 to 20c
900. " rubber, "............20c
901. Lace Needles, very fine, for making Princess or Honiton lace, each....................7c
902. Needles, Crochet, steel, each, ...3c
903. " " nickel, "......5c, 7c
904. " " rubber, "......7c

905. Needles, Crochet, bone, 5-inch, 3c; 6-inch, 5c; 8-inch, 8c; 10-inch, 10c; 12-inch, 12c.
906. Machine. all makes, each, 2c; per doz....22c
907. Steel, Macrame, each.............. .....2c

HAIR PINS.

908. The Standard Hair Pin Casket contains 100 assorted hair pins, plain, invisible, crimped and waved, each.................................7c
909. Hair Pins, French, per dozen........... ...5c
910. Hair Pins, Kirby's English, paper........ ...4c
911. Hair Pins, Kirby's invisible, per box of 100, 9c
912. Hair Pins, English (100 in a box) per box, 8c
913. Hair Pins, blue steel, per paper..........2c
914. Hair Pins, crimped (don't drop out of the hair) per paper...........................5c
915. Fifty best English Hair Pins, put up in a neat wooden box 5c
916. Rubber, waved or plain, per box of 12....8c

PINS.

917. Pins, American, per paper........ ....2c
918. Pins, ne plus ultra, per paper.............5c
919. Pins, Kirby's best English, per paper 12c, 14c
920. Pins, Neuse's mourning, box of 80 pins.. 3c
921. Pins, American and Howe's mourning, per box.....................................7c
922. Pins, best English mourning, per box....9c
923. Pins, Turney's larger size, white and black, mixed, or white alone, per book....... .....10c

924. Pins, Stewart's Nursery, No. 2, per gross. 42c; per dozen..........................4c
925. Pins, Stewart's Nursery, No. 3, per gross, 55c; per dozen............................5c
926. Pins, Rowley's Nursery, black or white, per box.......................................5c
927. Clinton nickel-plated, with patent catches, best made, No. 2, per dozen, 7c: per gross...75c
928. No. 3, per dozen, 8c: per gross.........85c
929. Stewart's Nickel-plated Safety Pins, No. 1, per dozen, 5c: per gross..................55c
930. No. 3, per dozen, 6c; per gross.........70c
931. Minerva Safety Pins, best and cheapest made, No. 2, per paper, 2c: per dozen, 23c. No. 3, per paper, 3c: per dozen.................30c

HAT AND SHAWL PINS.

932. Pins, like common pins, but very large, for shawl, per paper.........................4c
933. Pins, shawl, with very large jet heads, per dozen.................................4c
934. Hat Pins, with very long jet heads for pinning on bonnets, per dozen 8c
934 A. Same, cut jet heads, each..............2c

TIDY PINS.

935. Plush tidy Spiral pins, colors, cardinal, garnet, olive and peacock blue, best in use, each, 3c: per dozen................................30c

SHOE DRESSING.

936. Brown's per bottle....................8c
937. Saratoga per bottle....................8c
938. Militia, per bottle....................15c
939. Glycerole, an oil preparation, and dressing combined, per bottle...............25c
940. Glycerine Shoe Paste, for kid shoes, box 8c
941. Bixby's Shoe Polish, per box.......3c and 5c
942. Cahii's Shoe Bronze, per bottle.........10c

SHOE DEPARTMENT

Our stock of shoes consists only of reliable and well made goods, and every pair is warranted ; the prices quoted are for strictly first-class goods, and we guarantee them to be low for the class of goods furnished. Shoes returned which are soiled or damaged, or that have been made specially to order, we cannot exchange.   *When taking the measurement be careful to follow the directions below, so as to avoid errors.   Shoes to order, $1 00 extra.*

Directions for Measurement.

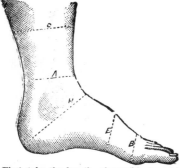

First, take the length of your foot, and to do this remove your shoe, lay a measuring rule upon the floor, with one end against the wall. Set your foot upon the rule, your heel pressed closely to the wall and you can see the exact length of your foot upon the rule. Next, with a tape measure, take the exact size around your foot at all the points designated in the illustration, giving the number of inches. The letter b is where you take the measurement of your foot, e the instep, h the heel, a the ankle and c top of the boot. This will make six measurements in all—length, size of ball, instep, heel, ankle and top. *Boots and shoes made to order we will not exchange, and would request our patrons to exercise great care in giving measurement.*

Information.

The following will explain the letters used for indicating the widths :

A A..............................Extra narrow
A..................................Narrow
B............................Medium Narrow
C...............................Medium Wide
D....................................Wide
E...............................Extra Wide

Definitions of Sizes.

Ladies' sizes are from..............No. 1 to 6
Misses' sizes are from...........No. 11 to 2
Children's sizes are from.........No 6 to 10½
Infants' sizes are from.............No. 1 to 6
Men's sizes are from ....No. 6 to 12
Boys' sizes are from ....No. 1 to 5
Youths' sizes are from...........No. 11 to 2

LADIES' FINE DRESS BOOTS.

Sizes, 2½ to 7.
Widths, A to E.

1. French kid, box toe, French or plain heels.
....$4 00
2. Best French kid, box toe, French or plain heels, hand finished...............$5 00
3. Fine French kid, box toe, French or plain heels, hand-sewed...............$6 00
4. Same, best French kid.................$7 00

We can also furnish any articles not in our Catalogue from other cuts or descriptions furnished us. Our patrons will, however, avoid mistakes by describing explicitly what they wish.

Our next number of this Price List will be issued early in the Fall; we will send a copy free of charge to any one applying for it by postal card or letter.

LADIES' WALKING BOOTS.

Sizes, 2½ to 7.

5. American kid, box toe, all styles heels, widths B to D..................$2 00
6. Fine American kid, B to E.......... 2 50
7. Curacoa kid, A to E............. 3 00
8. Best Curacoa kid, A to E.......... 3 50
9. Best Curacoa kid, hand-sewed, A to E 5 00
10. Pebble goat, B to D............. 2 00
11. Best Pebble goat, B to E..... 2 50
12. Best pebble or straight goat, box toe, all styles heels, A to E. $3 00

LADIES' BOOTS LOUIS XV HEELS.

Sizes, 2 to 6.
Widths, A to E.

13. Fine Curacoa kid, hand sewed......$6 50
14. Fine French kid...... .... 7 50
15. Best French kid.................. 8 00
16. French kid, Wurtemburg heel....... 6 50
To order, extra per pair 1 00

LADIES' WAUKENPHAST.

We desire to call special attention to our Waukenphast shoes, very latest style, and very nobby for ladies wear. The most comfortable shoes manufactured.

Widths, A to E.   Sizes, 2 to 6.

17. Best calf, Curacoa kid, foxed, kid top, hand-sewed...... ....$5 00
18 Best calf, kid top, straight goat, foxed, hand-sewed, tipped or plain, per pair
$5 00

LADIES' COMMON SENSE BOOTS.

Sizes 2½ to 8.

19. Very durable American kid, widths C to E.................................$2 50
20. Best American kid, widths B to E....$3 00
21. Best Curacoa kid, hand finished, A to E...............................$3 50
22. French kid, hand finished, A to E.... 4 00
23. Best French kid, hand finished, A to E 5 00
24. French kid, hand sewed, A to E..... 6 00
25. Best kid, hand sewed, A to E....... 7 00
26. Pebble goat, A to E................. 2 50
27. Pebble and straight goat, A to E.... 3 00
28. Best pebble and straight goat, hand finished, A to E $4 00
29. Best pebble and straight goat, hand sewed, A to E....................$5 50
To order, extra... .... 1 00

OLD LADIES' SHOES.

30. Soft glove kid, front lace, broad soles, low heels.............. ......$1 75, 2 00
31 Morocco, same style as above 1 50

LADIES' NEW STYLE SCALLOP-ED BUTTON BOOTS.

Sizes, 2 to 6.   Widths, B to E.

32. Curacoa Kid....................$3 75
33. French Kid......................... 4 75

LADIES' KID TOP SHOES.

Sizes, 2½ to 7.

34. Foxed American kid, box toe, French heels, B to D....................$2 00
35. Finer Quality, B to E...................2 50
36. Foxed Curacoa kid, box toe, French or plain heels, B to E.....................3 00
37. Best mat kid top, foxed Curacoa kid, box toe, French heels, A. to E.........3 50
38. Mat kid top, foxed French kid, box toe and any style heel, A to E, $4 50. This shoe can be had with cloth top at the same prices.

LADIES' CONGRESS GAITERS.

Sizes, 2½ to 7.

39. Pebble goat, C to D....................$1 75
40. Glove kid, C to E......................1 75
41. Best Glove kid, B to E.................2 50
42. Best American kid......................2 50
43. Best French kid, our own make........4 00
44. Best French kid, hand-sewed..........6 00
45. Peurnella, C to D.............$1 00 and 1 25
46. Peurnella, hand sewed.......1 50 and 2 50

LADIES' OPERA SLIPPERS.

LOUIS XV. HEELS.

Sizes, 1 to 6.

47. American Kid, width B to D.........$2 00
48. Curacoa Kid, width B to D..............2 50
49. French Kid, width A to D..............3 00

LADIES' HOUSE SLIPPERS.

Widths, D, E.   Sizes, 2 to 8.

50. American Kid.......................$1 00
51. Goatskin...............................1 15
52. Glove Kid..............................1 50
53. Serge..................................1 25

LADIES' NEWPORT BUTTON.

Sizes, 2½ to 8.

54. American kid, hand-sewed, C to E.. $1 25
55. Best American kid, hand-sewed, B to E 1 50
56. Curacoa kid, hand-sewed, A to E.... 2 00
57. French kid, hand-sewed, A to E....   2 50
58. Very best French kid, hand-sewed, A to E................................. 3 00
59. Best Curacoa kid, Louis XV. heels, A to E................................. 3 50
60. Best French kid, Louis XV. heels, A to E................................. 4 50

OXFORD TIES

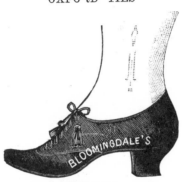

Sizes, 2 to 7.

61. American kid, B to E....   ....$1 50
62. Best American kid, B to E............. 2 00
63. Curacoa kid, B to E.................... 2 50
64. French kid, A to E..................... 3 00
65. Best French kid, A to E. 3 50
66. Best Curacoa kid, Louis XV. heels.... 3 50
67. Best French kid, Louis XV heels 4 50
68. Curacoa Kid, patent leather tips and trimmings............ $2 00 and 2 50
69. French Kid, patent leather tips and trimmings...... ....$3 00 and 3 50
70. French Kid, Louis XV heels ... $3 50, 4 00

PAREPA, or OPERA TOE SLIPPERS

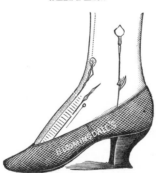

Sizes 1 to 7. Widths A to E.

71. American kid, kid lined............... $1 00
72. Best American kid, kid lined.........   1 25
73. Curacoa kid, kid lined................   1 50
74. Patent leather 1 50
75. French kid............................   2 00
76. Best French kid.......................   2 25
77. Curacoa kid, Louis XV heels $2 00, 2 50
78. Bronze Top French kid, Louis XV heels, 3 00
78a. Bronze kid..... ....   2 00
These slippers can be had in any style of heel desired.

LADIES' DIEPPE TIES.

Sizes 2 to 7.

79. American kid, B to D................ $1 50
80. Curacoa kid, B to E...................   2 50
81. Best Curacoa kid, A to E, Louis XV. heels.................................   3 00
82. French kid, A to E 3 00
84. French kid, Louis XV heels, A to E..   4 00
85. Bronze kid, A to E 2 50

LADIES' BEADED OPERAS.

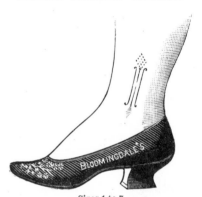

Sizes 1 to 7.

86. American kid, B to D $1 35
87. American kid, hand-sewed, B to E   1 75
88. Best Curacoa kid, hand-sewed, A to E, 2 25
These goods can be had inlaid if desired.

FEDORA SLIPPER.

Sizes 2½ to 7.

89. Fine Curacoa kid, beaded top, with coxcomb bow, B to E...................$2 00
90. Fine Curacoa kid, beaded top, with coxcomb bow, B to E...................$2 50
91. Fine French kid, beaded top and rosette, A to E.................................$3 25
92. Fine Curacoa kid, beaded top, with coxcomb bow, Louis XV heels, A to E.........$3 50
93. Fine French kid, beaded top, with coxcomb bow, Louis XV heels, A to E..........$4 50
94. Bronze kid, beaded top 3 50
The goods can be had inlaid if desired.

LADIES' LACED BUSKINS.

Widths, medium and full.   Sizes 2 to 8.

95. Serge, with elastic in front instead of laced...................................$0 50
96. Same, better quality..................   80
97. Serge, laced, with or without heels,.. 1 30
98. Goatskin, with or without heels 1 25
99. Glove kid, with or without heels...... 1 50

Do not cut or mutilate this book ; by simply referring to the number of the page and article you desire, your order will be understood.
We will send this Catalogue, free of charge, to any one applying for it by letter or postal card.

DANCING PUMPS

100.	Gentlemen's patent leather pumps	$1 75
101.	Gentlemen's patent leather pumps	2 50
102.	Youths' patent leather pumps,	$1 50, 1 75, 2 00
103.	Boys' patent leather pumps,	$1 50, 1 75, 2 00

GENTS' CONGRESS GAITERS.

104.	American caif	$1 50, 2 00, 2 50
105.	French calf	3 00, 3 50, 4 00
106.	Hand-sewed	4 00, 4 50, 5 00
107.	Very best	6 00
108.	Patent Leather, mat kid top	5 00

BOYS', YOUTHS' AND CHILDREN'S CALF BUTTON GAITERS

109.	Boys' "A" calf button, sizes 2½ to 5½,	$2 00, 2 50
110.	French calf	3 00
111.	Youths' American calf, sizes 11 to 2,	$1 25, 1 50
112.	American calf. finer quality,	$1 75. 2 00
113.	French calf, our own make	2 25
114.	Best French calf	2 50
115.	Children's American calf, kid top, sizes 8 to 10½,	1 75
116.	Children's French calf, sizes 8 to 10½,	2 00

GENTS' NEWPORT TIES.

Sizes 6 to 12.

117.	American calf	$1 50, 1 75, 2 00
118.	French calf	$2 50, 3 00, 3 50, 4 00
119.	Hand-sewed	4 50

In ordering goods, please state how you wish them forwarded, by mail, express or freight. If by mail, do not fail to inclose sufficient money to defray the postage. Postal rates to be found on page 2.

GENTS' EMBROIDERED SLIPPERS-

In cloth or velvet.

120.	Assorted patterns	$1 00, 1 25, 1 50
121.	Finer quality	2 00
122.	Our own make	2 50

GENTS' WORKING OR RIDING BOOTS.

Sizes, from 6 to 12.

123.	Calf	$3 50, 4 00, 5 00
124.	Calf, hand-sewed	5 00, 6 00, 7 00
125.	Grain leather	4 00, 5 00
126.	Grain leather riding boots, best quality,	5 50
127.	Patent leather, morocco legs	7 00
128.	Patent leather, morocco legs, hand-sewed,	$10 00

BOYS' BOOTS.

Sizes 1 to 5.

129.	Kip	$1 75, 2 00
130.	Calf	3 00, 4 00
131.	Grain leather	3 00, 3 50
132.	Grain leather, best quality	4 00

YOUTHS' BOOTS.

Sizes, from 11 to 12.

133.	Kip	$1 50, 2 00

CHILD'S BOOTS.

Sizes, from 7 to 10.

134.	Kip boots	$1 25, 1 50

GENTS' WALKING SHOES.

Sizes 6 to 11.

135.	American calf	$1 50, 2 00
136.	French calf	2 50, 3 00
137.	American calf, hand-sewed	4 00
138.	French calf, hand-sewed	$5 50, 6 00

GENTS' GOAT OPERAS.

139.	Morocco goat, plain	$1 25 1 50
140.	Morocco, finer quality	2 00
141.	Boys' goat	$1 00, 1 25
142.	Boys', finer quality	1 50
143.	Children's red and blue goat	1 00, 1 25

GENTS' BUTTON GAITERS.

Sizes 6 to 11.

144.	American calf	$2 50, 3 00
145.	French calf	$3 50, 4 00, 4 50
146.	Cloth top, latest style	3 50
147	French calf, opera toe, hand-sewed	5 50

GENTS' OVER GAITERS.

In ordering the above, it is necessary to state the size of the shoe worn.

148.	Black cloth	$1 00
149.	Black cloth, extra high cut	1 75
150.	Blue or brown cloth	1 25

GENTS' ALLIGATOR OPERAS.

Sizes 5½ to 11.

151.	Colors, garnet, buff and black,	$1 35, 2.00, 2.50 and 3.00
152.	Genuine spotted leopard skin,	$2.25, 2.75 and 3.50

GENTS' OXFORD TIES.

Same quality Low Button at the same prices.

153.	American calf,	$1 50, 1 75, 2 00
154.	French calf	2 50, 3 00
155.	French calf, extra fine	3 50, 4 00
156.	Hand-sewed	4 50
157.	Best patent leather, opera toe	4 00

We can also furnish any articles not in our Catalogue from other cuts or descriptions furnished us. Our patrons, will, however, avoid mistakes by describing explicitly what they wish.

Misses' Button Boots.

Sizes 11 to 2. Widths, A to E.
151. American kid $1.50, 1.75
152. Best American kid 2.00
153. Curacoa kid 2.50
154. Best Curacoa kid 3.00
155. French kid 3.50
156. Pebble goat $1.25, 1 50
157. Better pebble goat 2.00
158. Very best pebble goat 2.59
159. Straight goat 2.50

Canvas Button Shoes.

The uppers of these shoes are made from heavy colored canvas, trimmed with calfskin, and are the most durable and appropriate shoes for seaside or country wear.
160. Child's spring heels 5 to 8 . . . $1.00
161. Childs' Spring heels 8½ to 10½ . . 1.25
162. Childs' heeled 8½ to 10½ 1.00
163. Misses' sizes 11 to 2 . . . $1.25 and 1.50
164. Ladies' sizes 2½ to 7 . . . . . 2.00

Trunks.

190a. Ladies' Zinc Trunks, with hat and parasol boxes and tray,
Sizes,   28,   32,   36 in. long.
Prices, $2.75, 3.50,   4.00
191. Crystallized, $3.50, 4.00,   5.00
192. Packing Trunks, flat top, plain inside, with lock and key,
Sizes,   28,   32,   36 in.
193. Plain . . . . 98c. $1.25, 1.69.
194. Zinc cov'd, 1 tray inside, $1.49, 2.00, 2.69.
195. Duck Dress, flat top and Steamer Trunk, one tray, 28, 32 and 36 inches long, linen lined $5.00, 5.98, 6.39
196. Steamer, one tray, linen lined, 32 and 36 in. long $3.50, 4.00
197. Ladies' Leather Covered Saratoga Trunks, full finished, with hat and parasol boxes and tray, and with iron bottoms,
Sizes,   28,   32,   36 in. long
198. Quality X. Prices, $4.00, 4.50, 5.50.
199.   " XX.   "   5.50, 6.00, 7.00.
200. Same, duck cov'd   5.00, 5.50, 6.50.
201.   " sole leather, 16.00, 17.00, 21.00.
202. Gents' Leather covered Trunks, 28 inches long $7.50
203. Gents' Sole Leather Trunks, 28 inches long, $12.00 ; 30 inches $15.00
204. Gents' Duck Covered Trunks, 28 inches long, $7.00 ; 30 inches $8.00

Infants' Shoes.

WITHOUT HEELS.

165. American kid, B to E, worked button-holes 50c
166. Curacoa kid, A to E, worked button-holes 75c
167. French kid, A to E, worked button-holes $1.00
168. Best French kid. A to E 1.25
169. Infants' shoes, with light counters, for weak ankles, made to order, $1.00 per pair extra.
170. Soft soles, black, blue, white and bronze, and wine color, sizes, 0 to 3 . . . . 30c

Foot Holds.

171. Ladies' 45c
172. Misses' 40c
173. Men's 70c

Ladies' Croquets.

174. Ladies' 45c
175. Misses' 40c
We also have this style in extra light weight gossamer rubbers.
176. Ladies' 65c
177. Misses' 55c

Trunks.

PATENT TRAY TRUNKS.

207. Zinc Saratoga—metal covered, barrel top, wide iron corner bands, iron centre bands, 5 slats on top and 2 around body of trunk, all slats clamped, nickel lock, valance all around, iron bottom, deep body tray, with high hat box in centre. and shirt box on each side, parasol case. Prices 28 in., $6.00; 30 in., 6.50; 32 in., 7.00; 34 in., 7.50; 36 in., 8.00.
208. Saratoga Leather or Duck—barrel top, wide iron corner bands, 2 iron centre bands, 5 slats running lengthwise on top, and 2 around body of trunk, fancy metal clamps on ends of slats, and fancy metal corner protectors, strap hinges, iron bottom, nickel lock, Ristori tray, containing hat box. 2 shirt boxes and parasol case, all covered. Prices, 28 in., $7.35; 30 in., 8.00; 32 in., 8.62; 34 in., 9.35; 36 in., 9.75.
209. Saratoga Fancy Crystal—barrel top, reversed slats on top, upright slats in front of trunk, all slats have fancy metal clamps on the end, nickel lock, fancy metal side bolts, deep body tray, hat box, and shirt box covered, parasol case in front. Prices, 28 in., $6.00; 30 in., 6.70; 32 in., 7.35; 34 in., 8.00; 36 in., 8.62.

Children's Spring Heel.

Sizes 4 to 8.

177a. American kid $1.00
178. American kid, worked buttonholes. 1.25
179. Best American kid 1.60
180. Pebble goat 1.00
181. Pebble goat, worked buttonholes. 1.25
182. Pebble goat, best 1.50
183. Straight goat 1.00
184. Straight goat, worked buttonholes. 1.25
185. Straight goat, worked buttonholes, very best $1.60
185 a. French kid 2.00
Sizes from 8½ to 10½, 25c a pair extra.
Misses' Spring Heel Shoes, sizes from 11 to 2, 75c a pair more than in sizes from 8½ to 10½.

Canvas Laced Shoes.

Same material as the button.
186. Child's spring heels 5 to 8 . . . . . . $1.00
187. Child's spring heel 8½ to 10½ 1.25
188. Child's heeled 8 to 10½ . . . . 1.00 and 1.25
189. Misses' sizes . . . . 1.25 and 1.50
190. Ladies' sizes 1.50

Trunks.

205. Ladies' Plain Saratoga Trunks, with hat and parasol boxes and tray,
Sizes, 28,   32,   36 in. long.
206. Quality X. Prices, $2.50, 2.75, 3.00
   "   XX.   " $3,00, 3.50, 4.00

Have your friends send their address and they will receive our Price List. It enables them to buy New York goods at New York Prices.

All our goods are marked at the lowest prices, which do not include postage. No goods sent by mail, except sufficient money accompanies the order, for postage ; otherwise we will reduce orders, and take out part of goods to the amount of postage required.

Cutlery, Etc.

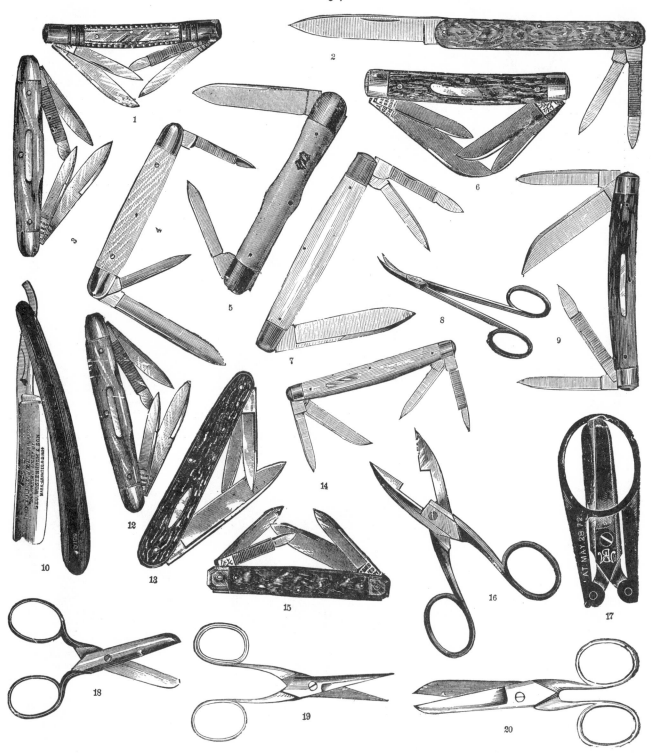

924 TO 928 THIRD AVE., AND 160 TO 164 EAST 56th St., NEW YORK.

77

UPHOLSTERY DEPARTMENT.

In issuing this season's catalogue we have taken pains to present to our patrons the largest and most varied assortment of Upholstery Goods, than ever before had. Our importations have been very large, and we can safely state that a better selection cannot be seen at any other house.

Our stock of Curtains consists of Nottingham, Guipure, Antique, Applique, Madras, Swiss or Tambour, and hundreds of styles not illustrated, equally as handsome and cheap. Our assortment of Lambrequins, Nottingham and Guipure Net by the yard, Bed Sets, Turcoman Portieres, etc., etc., is enormous at remarkably low prices.

It may occur that the exact pattern is sold out when ordered, in such cases we claim the privilege of substituting an equally as handsome design, guaranteeing good value.

CURTAINS, LAMBREQUINS, ETC.

1200. Nottingham Lace Curtain, 50 inches wide, length 3½ yards, per pair.....$2.25

1208. Nottingham Lace Curtains, taped edge, width 57 inches, length 3½ yards, white only, per pair.....$3.50

1201. Nottingham Lace Curtains, width 48 inches, length 3 yards; in a large and handsome assortment of designs; a bargain: per pair.....$1.19

1202. Nottingham Lace Curtains, taped edge, width 58 inches, length 3½ yards, elegant assortment of designs, white or ecru, per pair.....$2.75

1204.   Nottingham Lace Curtains with Madras effect; width, 60 inches; length, 3½ yards; per pair, $4.25.

1205.   Antique Curtains, plain centres; length, 3½ yards; per pair, $5.00.

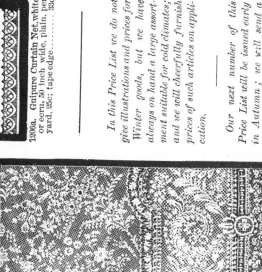

1206a.   Guipure Curtain Net, white or ecru, 50 inch wide, plain, per yard, 25c; tape edge.........33c

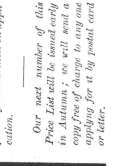

In this Price List we do not give illustrations and prices for Winter goods, but we have always on hand a large assortment suitable for cold climates; and we will cheerfully furnish prices of such articles on application.

Our next number of this Price List will be issued early in Autumn; we will send a copy free of charge to any one applying for it by postal card or letter.

1206.   Nottingham Lace Curtains, taped edge; width, 54 inches; length 3½ yards; in a large and handsome assortment of designs, white, only; per pair, $3.75.

1207.   Imitation Tambour Lace Curtains; width, 60 inches, a large variety of patterns, white or ecru; per pair, $5.00.

No. 1209. French Guipure Lambrequins, width 62 inches, length 48 inches, white, each, $1.00.

No. 1211. Nottingham Lace Lambrequins, width 54 inches, length 42 inches, each 65c.

CURTAIN NETS

1210 a. Nottingham Curtain Net, 36 inches wide, white, per yard, 15c

Have your friends send their address and they will receive our Price List. It enables them to buy New York goods at New York prices.

All our goods are marked at the lowest prices, which do not include postage. No goods sent by mail, except sufficient money accompanies the order, for postage; otherwise we will reduce orders, and take out part of goods to the amount of postage required.

No. 1208. Nottingham Lace Lambrequins width 40 inches, length 87 inches, each 25c.

No. 1219. Nottingham Lace Lambrequins, width 61 inches, length 42 inches, white, each 50c.

CURTAIN NETS.

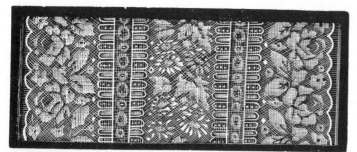

1212.   Guipure Curtain Net, 36 inches wide, per yard..............................12½c

1213.   Nottingham Curtain Net, 40 inches wide, per yard............................18c

1214.   Guipure Curtain Net, white or ecru, 50 inches wide, per yaad... ....25c

1215.   Nottingham Curtain Net, white or ecru, taped edge. 50 inches wide, per yard..40c

1216.   Nottingham Curtain Net, taped edge, 58 inches wide, white or ecru, per yard..48c

Curtains.

NOT ILLUSTRATED.

1217.   A complete line of Nottingham Lace Cuatains, at the following prices, viz.: $1.00, 1.50, 1.75, 2.25, 2.75, 3.25, 4.00, 4.50 and upward.
1218.   Real Antique Curtains, per pair, $5.00, 6.50, 7.50, 9.00 and 10.00
1219.   Swiss or Tambour Curtains, 3½ and 4 yards long, per pair.......... $5.00, 6.75, 7.50, 9.00 and upward.
1220.   Applique Curtains, 3½ yards long, $4.50, 5.00, 6.00 and upward.
1221.   Scrim for Curtains in variety of patterns,44 inches per yard...... ...12½c
1222.   Curtain Net, white or ecru, per yard,   12½c, 16c, 21c, 28c, 35c and 50c
1223.   Curtain Swiss, per yard....12½c, 16c, 21c and 25c
1224.   Colored Madras, per yard... ...12½c, 18c and 25c
1225.   Vestibule Lace, per yard.........15c, 18c and 25c
1226.   Japanese Madras, per yard................12½c
1227.   Mikado Drapery, per yard 25c

Furniture and Slip Coverings.

1228.   Domestic Cretonnes, 32 inches wide, per yard,'   12½c, 15c and 18c
1229.   English Cretonnes, best patterns, per yard, 20c,25c
1230.   Robe Chintz.... ....7c, 8c and 10c
1231.   Raw Silk, 50 inches wide, per yard,   55c, 60c, 75c, 85c and $1.00
1232.   Rich Tapestry, 50 inches wide, per yard, $1.00, 1.25 and 1.50
1233.   Plush, 25 inches wide, for upholstery and fancy work, per yard ....$1.65, 1.89, 2.00 and 2.25

Oilcloths.

1234.   Table Oilcloths, marble and wood patterns, 1¼ yards wide, per yard...............................20c
1235.   Same, 1½ yards wide, per yard.................35c
1236.   Shelf Oilcloth, per yard, 6c; per dozen yards...70c
1237.   Stair Oilcloth, 15 and 18 inches wide, per yard, 8c

Live Geese Feathers.

1238.   Prime Live Geese Feathers, per lb.............75c
1239.   Best Selected Live Geese Feathers,per lb. 85c, $1.00

Canopies.

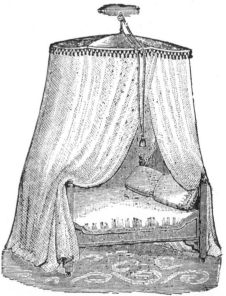

1240   Turn-Over Canopies, gauze netting, 90 inches, 9 yards skirt, white...........................$1.75
1241.   Same, pink............................. 1.85
1242.   Same, 100 inch, white, 10 yards skirt....... 2.15
1243.   Pink.. 2.25
1244.   Same, 108 inches and 11 yards skirt, white.. 2.50
1245.   Pink.. 2.75

Mosquito Netting.

1246.   Mosquito Netting, per piece of 8 yards,white, 38c
1247.   Colors Blue, Buff, Green, per piece of 8 yards, 40c
1248.   Pink, per piece of 8 yards......... 42c

924 TO 928 THIRD AVE., AND 160 TO 164 EAST 56th St., NEW YORK.

81

OPAQUE AND HOLLAND WINDOW SHADES.

  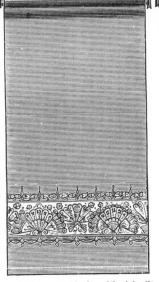 

1249. Opaque Window Shades, with crystalized dado, size 3x6 feet, without fixtures.............45c

1250. Opaque Shades with gilt dado, 3x6 feet, without fixtures......50c

1251. Opaque Shade, with rich gilt dado, 3x6 feet, without fixtures, each... ....58c

1252. Opaque Shade, with rich gilt dado, size 3x6 feet, without fixtures, each.....................67c

The above Shades can be had in the following colors, viz.: olive, brown, slate, buff or ecru, and can be mounted on Hartshorn spring rollers and fixtures, finished with linen fringe or tassels, complete and ready to put up, for 35c per window extra.

Opaque Shades, with any of the dados above illustrated, can be made to order in any size, prices furnished on application, which should be accompanied by the measurements. Our patrons will kindly exercise care in sending the measurements, and state whether they are taken inside or outside of the casings, especially when the shades are to be mounted, as they are cut in exact accordance with the measurements given.

Office and Store Shades of any color or size, including lettering, such as monograms, etc., made to order at short notice; prices furnished on application.

1253. We can furnish Holland Shades, 3x6 feet, in either of the following colors, viz.: white, blue, buff, green, brown, Spanish-olive or slate, mounted on Hartshorn spring rollers with fixtures, and finished with tassels or fringe, complete and ready to put up, for...................39c

1254. Domestic Holland, 36 inches wide, per yard......................12½c

1255. King's Scotch Hollands, all widths, 24 to 54 inches wide, per yard, 15c and upward.

LACE BED SETS.

1256. This ELEGANT NOTTINGHAM LACE BED SET, consisting of two shams and sheet, former price, $8 00, a real bargain....**$3 40**

1257. Other Lace Bed Sets......................................$2 00, $2 50, $2 75, $4 00, $4 50 and $5 00

1258. OUR LEADER. Elegant Nottingham Lace Bed Set, sheet and two shams; a GENUINE BARGAIN.....................**$2 00**

................................$5 00, $6 00, $7 00, $8 00, $9 00, $10 00

1259. Guipure d'Art Bed Sets, each.........

1260. Real Antique Bed Sets, each.......................$9 00, $10 00, $12 00 and upward

PIANO COVERS.

1261. Embroidered Piano Cover, with centre piece, 2
yards square; colors, maroon, garnet, cardinal and
green $2 00
1262. Same size, 2 x 3 yards 2 50

TABLE COVERS.

1265. Silk Embroidered Cloth Table Covers, with
scalloped edges, 1½ yards square; colors, brown,
green, maroon, cardinal and garnet, each, $1 50
1266. Same, 2 yards square, ...2 25
1267. Same, for Pianos, 2x3 yards. 3 25

1271. Tapestry Table Covers, with tinsel, size, 54 inches square;
in various designs $1 95
1272. Other Tapestry Table Covers, 68 inches square. 3 50
1273. Size, 68x84 inches 4 25

1263. Holland Window Shades with
gold dados, size, 3x6 feet, with spring
rollers, fringe and fixtures, ready to
be put up; in brown, spanish olive,
green, blue, white and buff. 50c

1274. Linen Momie, cloth side
board, or table scarf, in white,
pink, blue, red or buff centres
with cream or white borders,
size, 18x72 inches, $1 00
1275. Same, size 18x60,   80c

STAND COVERS.

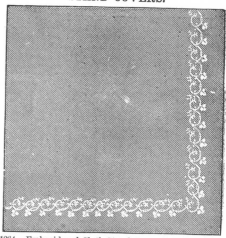

1264. Embroidered Cloth Stand Cover, 1 yard square;
colors, maroon, garnet, brown, cardinal and green,
$1 00

TABLE AND COVERS.

1268. Silk Embroidered Cloth Table Cover with
scalloped edge, 1¾ yards square; colors, brown,
green, maroon, garnet or cardinal, each. $4 00
1269. Same style for piano, size, 2x 3 yards. $5 00
1270. Also a complete line of Piano Covers, better
quality and heavier cloth, each, $7 00, 8 00,9 00 and
10 00

Covers made to order for Grand. Square and Upright Pianos; when sending for prices, please ' send
the name of manufacturer, the number and size.

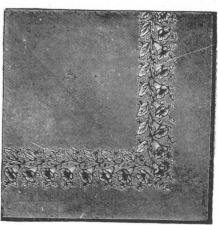

1276. Silk Embroidered Cloth Table Cover, 1½ yds.
square, garnet, brown, cardinal, maroon and green,
$2 50.

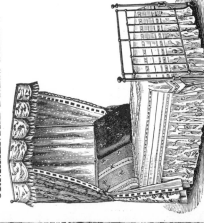

1284. A light symmetrical hollow pillow, by which the sham is kept in a perfectly smooth condition, at the same time concealing the usual sleeping pillow; it can be as easily removed as any pillow while making the bed; it is very light, weighing but a few ounces, but cannot be sent by mail. Thousands are in use, and they are in great demand; colors—pink, blue and red, per pair..$2.00

1282. Turcoman Portieres, raw silk, 3 yards long, 48 inches wide, colors—garnet, blue and gold, with striped dado, per pair............$4.00
1283. Same, 3½ yards long............$4.50

TURCOMAN PORTIERES.

1280. Turcoman Portieres, raw silk in blue, gold and garnet, with rich dado, 48 inches wide, 3½ yards long, per pair............$8.00
1281. Turcoman Portieres, raw silk in gold, blue and garnet, with rich dado, 48 inches wide, 3½ yards long, per pair............$10.50

1278. Heavy Raw Silk "Portieres," in blue, gold and garnet, with rich deep dado, fringed all round, size, 52 inches by 3½ yards, per pair............$6.00
1279. Turcoman Curtains from 3½ to 4 yards long, with a variety of borders, per pair from............$4.50 to $25.00

CARPET DEPARTMENT.

Particular attention is directed to our extensive line of Carpets, Oil Cloths, Rugs, etc., which we are selling at remarkably low prices that cannot be purchased elsewhere at the same figures for the quality of goods furnished. Orders for samples we cannot fill, as it is impossible to see the pattern unless we send at least one yard of the goods. Our patrons may rest assured, however, that if the selection is left to our judgment we will give satisfaction. When ordering, state as near as possible what color and style is wanted.

Carpets.

1356. Tapestry Brussels, fair quality, per yd..50c
1357. Tapestry Brussels, good quality, per yd.55c
1358. Tapestry Brussels, extra good quality, per yard..... ....60, 65, 75c
1359. Tapestry Brussels, double extra quality, per yard ... .80, 90c, $1 00
1360. Body Brussels, extra quality, per yd..$1 00
1361. Body Brussels, double extra quality, per yard...... ....$1 10, 1 20
1362. Velvets, per yard...... $1 15, 1 25, 1 35, 1 45
1363. Wiltons, per yard $1 35, 1 45
1364. Moquettes, per yard $1 25, 1 50

1365. Ingrain Carpets, cotton chain, per yard, 30, 35, 40c
1366. Extra quality, wool filling, per yard, 45, 50, 55, 60c
1367. Kidderminster (equal to the best 3-ply), per yard.................................. ....75c
1368. Extra quality, all wool, Ingrain, per yard, 75c, 85c
1369. 3-ply Ingrain, per yard... ....90c, $1.00

Stair Carpets.

1370. Venetian, per yard..15, 20, 30, 35, 40, 45, 50c

Floor Oil Cloths.

1371. 4-4, 5-4, 6-4, 8-4 per square yard, 25, 30, 35, 40, 50, 60c

Mats and Matting.

1372. Common Cocoa Mats, each 50c
1373. Better quality.................. .... ..89c
1374. Large size.............................$1 25
1375. Wool border Cocoa Mats, good size...$1 65
1376. Same, 36x72.. . .. . $6 19
1377. Same, 48x84. . . . . $9 50
1378. China Matting, plain, per yard . .25, 30, 35c
1379. Checked, per yard . . . 15, 18, 20, 25, 30, 35c
1380. Fancy, per yard 25, 30, 35, 40, 45, 50c

All-Wool Reversible Smyrna Rugs.

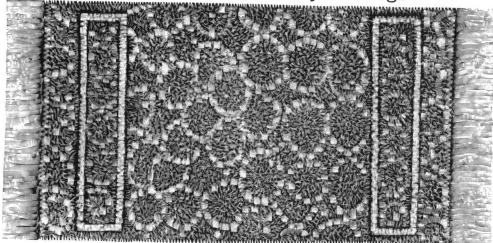

1381.	Single door size, each...79c
1382.	18x36, each..$1.00, $1.10
1383.	21x46, " 2.00, 2.25
1384.	26x54, " 2.88, 3.00
1385.	30x60, " 3.50, 4 00
1386.	30x36, " 2.00, 2.25
1387.	36x72, " 5.25, 5.50
1388.	4x7 feet, each.. 8.50, 9.00
1389.	6x9 " " 17.50

Ingrain Art Squares.

Substitutes for felt crumb cloths. These are ingrain carpets made up and finished with borders.

1390. 2½ yards square, each. $4 75, $5 25
1391. 2½x3 yards, each 5 50, 7 00

1392. 2¼x3 yards, each 5 00, 6 00
1393. 3 yards square, each $6 75, $8 00
1394. 3x3½ yards each 7 75, 9 00
1395. 3x4 " " 9 00, 10 50
1396. 3x4½ " " 10 00, 11 50
1397. 3½x4 " " 10 50, 12 00

1398. 4x4½ yards each 13 50, 15 50
1399. 4x5 " " 15 50, 18 00
1400. STAIR PADS, per dozen $1 00, 1 25
1401. CARPET LINING, yard wide, per yard . .5c
Making ingrain carpets, per yard 5c
Making Brussels and Velvet Carpets, per yd . .6c

HASSOCKS, ETC.

1402. Turkish Ottomans, on rollers, of tapestry carpets; height, 10 inches, width, 13 inches, each.................... .85c
1403. Same, of better quality carpet, each . $1 00

1404. Parlor Hassocks of tapestry Brussels; height, 7 inches, width, 13 inches, each . .49c
1405. Same, of better quality carpet, each . .60c

CARPET SWEEPERS.

1408. The Grand Rapids Carpet Sweeper, with four wheels exposed and entirely self-adjusting; has a rubber band to prevent marring the furniture; is handsomely hand-decorated, and will last for years; it is superior to anything of its kind in the world. Price, $2.98.

1406. Diamond Hassocks, made of Tapestry Brussels; height, 7 inches, width 13 inches, each.................... .75c
1407. Same, of better quality carpet . 85c, $1 00

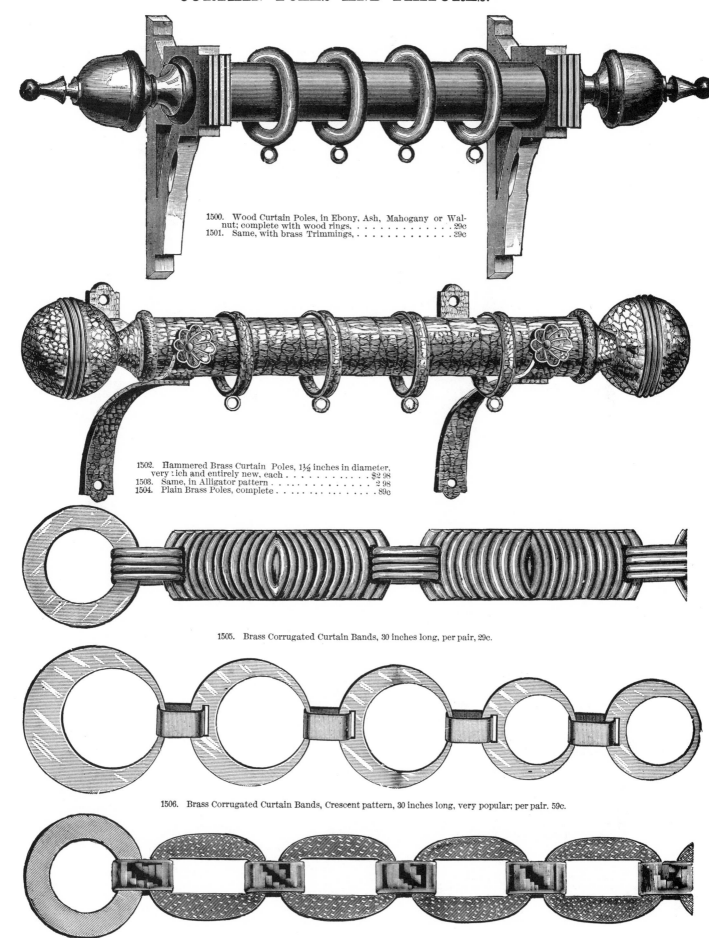

1500. Wood Curtain Poles, in Ebony, Ash, Mahogany or Walnut; complete with wood rings, ... 29c
1501. Same, with brass Trimmings, ... 39c

1502. Hammered Brass Curtain Poles, 1½ inches in diameter, very rich and entirely new, each $2 98
1503. Same, in Alligator pattern 2 98
1504. Plain Brass Poles, complete 89c

1505. Brass Corrugated Curtain Bands, 30 inches long, per pair, 29c.

1506. Brass Corrugated Curtain Bands, Crescent pattern, 30 inches long, very popular; per pair. 59c.

1507. Brass Corrugated Curtain Bands, fancy pattern, 30 inches long; per pair, 49c.

1505. Picture Nails, with screw heads; can be had in amber, crystal, ruby, green and blue, per dozen, 35c.

1506. Handsome Walnut Patent Extension Cornices, (can be adjusted to any window) hand engraved centres and gold inlaid ends, each, 89c.

1509. Handsome Walnut Patent Extension Cornices, with hand engraved centres and ends, inlaid with gold, can be adjusted to any window, each, $2 69.

1507. Picture Hooks, solid brass, bright finished, to fasten on 1¼ inch mouldings. per dozen, 35, 40c.

1508. Gilt Bangles, for fancy work; cut represents full size, per dozen, 5c.

1510. Hammered Rings for decorative purposes, gilt; per dozen, 10c.
1511. Plain brass rings for fancy work, per dozen, according to size, 6, 8 and 10c.

1515. Gilt Crescent, with bangles, cut represents actual size; per dozen, 49c.

1516. Stair Buttons, alligator pattern, in brass or nickel, per dozen, 75c.

1512. Gilt Crescents with star centre, small size, 8c.
1513. Medium size 9c.
1514. Large size, (see cut) 10c.

1517. Patent Drapery Hooks for curtains, lambrequins, etc. per dozen, 5c.

1521. Stair Corners, to prevent dust from collecting in corners of stairs, brass, per dozen, 45c.
1522. Same. nickel. 55c.

1523. Brass Tassel Hooks, bright finish, each, 10c.

1518. Gilt Crescents, small size, per dozen, 5c.
1519. Gilt Crescents, medium size, per dozen, 7c.
1520. Gilt Crescents, large size, (see cut) 8c.

1524. Stair Rods, black walnut, with brass fastenings, 24, 27 and 30 inches long, dozen, 85c.
1525. Same, in brass. ¾ inch diameter, 24 inches long, per dozen, $1 25.
1526. 27 inches long, $1 49.
1527. 30 inches long, $1 75.
1528. One inch diameter, 24 inches long, per dozen, $1 85.
1529. 27 inches long, per dozen, $2 00.
1530. 30 " " " " 2 25.

1531. Brass Headed Upholstery Nails used for all kinds of frame work, per hundred, 15c.

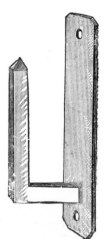

1532. Brass Tassel Hooks, bright finish, each, 10c.

1533. Stair Buttons, brass, nickel or bronze, per dozen, $1 30.

1534. Brass Banner Rods.

Sizes,	8	10	12	15	18	21	24	30 inches long.
Prices,	27	30	42	50	58	67	75	85c each.

1535. With Chain to hang. 15c extra.
1536. Same, plush covered, colors, olive, cardinal and peacock blue.

Sizes,	10	12	14	16 inches long.
Prices,	25	27	29	35c each.

Housekeeping Goods, White Goods, Etc.

In this departmeut we keep all goods appertaining to housekeeping. All the popular brands of sheetings and shirtings in bleached and brown, such as Wamsutta, Utica, Nonpariel, Fruit, Lonsdale, etc., which are always sold at manufacturers' prices.

1542. All Linen bleached Damask Towel, Grecian border and knotted fringe; size, 20x40 inches; each 25c.

1543. Heavy half-bleached Damask Towel, red border; sizes, 24x46 inches; each, 25c; per dozen, $2 75.

1544. Loom Damask Towels; size, 20x40 inches; each, 25c.

1545. Reversible Velour Turkish Towels, Tidy, Chair or Carriage Cover; very handsome, showing red, white and blue colors in each towel; size, 20x48 inches; each, 35c

1546. All Linen Damask Towels, with fancy colored centers; size. 20x40 inches; each, 25c.

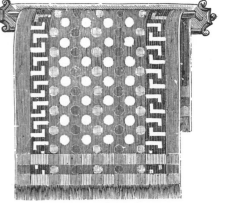

1547. Reversible Velour Turkish Towel.Tidy, Chair or Carriage Cover: very handsome, showing red, white and blue colors in each towel; size, 21x42 inches; each, 25c.

TOWELS.

1548. Half-bleached Damask, per doz., $1 50,1 75 2 00, 2 50, 3 00, 3 50, 4 50 and................6 00
1549. Bleached, with or without knotted fringe; per doz.. $2 00, 2 50, 3 00, 3 50, 4 00, 4 50, 5 00, 6 00, 7 50 and................................9 00
1550. Huck, bleached, per doz., $1 00, 1 20, 1 50, 1 75, 2 00, 2 50 and....................3 00
1551. Fancy Turkish Bath Towels, per doz., $1 50 1 75, 2 00, 2 50, 3 00. 3 50 and............4 00
1552. Same. white, per dozen, $2 00, 2 50, 3 00, 3 50, 4 00, 4 50 and.........................6 00
1553. Turkish Bath Sheets, size, 63x72 inches, each.......................................1 75
1554. Same, 60x90 in., each 2 50
1555. Terry Cloth or Turkish Toweling.[27 irch es wide, per yard, 25, 31, 35. 38, 40 and.........50c
1556. Same, 50 inches wide, for bath sheets, per yard....................................$1 00

TOWELINGS.

1557. Crash, twilled, bleached or unbleached. per yard................................5c
1558. Bleached Scotch Crash, plain or striped, 16 inches wide, per yard, 7c; 18 inches wide, 9c; 20 inches wide.............................10c
1559. Bleached Twilled Crash, 16 inches wide, per yard, 12c; 18 inch, 15c; 20 inch...........18c
1560. Same, unbleached, 16 inches wide, per yd, 10c; 18 inch, 12c; 20 inch....................15c
1561. Russia Crash, per yard, 12½, 15 and....18c
1562. Barnsley Crash, per yard, 15, 18 and....20c
1563. German Toweling, per yard, 12½, 16,22, 25, and.....................................31c
1564. Huck, per yard, 16, 18 and..............20c
1565. Stevens, unbleached, per yard, 10, 12½, 15 and.....................................18c
1566. Stevens' bleached, per yard, 12½, 16 and 18c
1567. Stevens' Twilled, per yard,15, 18 and....20c
1568. Glass Toweling, red or blue checks, per yard, 9, 10, 12½, 15 and....................18c

RUBBER SHEETING.

1569. 27 inches wide, per yard.............39c
1570. 36 " " 49c
1571. 45 " " 59c
1572. 54 " " 79c

LINEN DIAPER.

10 YARD PIECES, BEST QUALITY.

1573. 16 inches wide, per piece, 85c, $1 00.... 1 20
1574. 18 inches wide,per piece,95c,$1 10, 1 25, 1 50 and.....................................1 75
1575. 20 inches wide,per piece,$1 20, 1 35,1 50,1 75, 2 00, 2 25 and.........................2 50
1576. 22 inches wide, per piece, $1 40, 1 50, 1 75, 1 95, 2 10, 2 25 and.....................2 50
1577. 24 inches wide,per piece,$1 75, 2 00,2 25, 2 50, and..2 75
1578. 26 inches wide, per piece, $2 00, 2 25, 2 50, 2 75 and.................................3 00

COTTON DIAPER.

10 YARD PIECES.

1579. 18 inches wide, per piece............50c
1580. 20 " " 55c
1581. 22 " " 64c
1582. 24 " " 69c
1583. 27 " " 72c

LINEN BIBS.

1584. Linen Bibs. with figure of "Jumbo,"woven in each...............................9 and 12c

LINEN DRUGGETTING.

1585. 6-4 yard wide, per yard.. ....50c
1586. 7-4 " " 60c
1587. 8-4 " " 65c
1588. 9-4 " " 70c
1589. 10-4 " " 80c
1590. 12-4 " " 90c
1591. 2½x3 yards, each..................$2 25
1592. 2½x4 " "...................3 00
1593. 3 yards square, each..................2 75
1594. 3x4 yards each.......................3 50
1595. 3x4½ yards each.....................3 80

STAIR CRASH.

1596. 16 inch wide, per yard...... 12½ and 15c
1597. 18 " " 17c
1598. 20 " " 20c

LINEN SHEETING.

1599. 8-4 or 2 yards wide, per yard.....65, 75c
1600. 9-4 or 2¼ " " 75, 85c
1601. 10-4 or 2½ " " 85, 90c
1602. Richardson's 4-4 Family Linen, per yard, 30, 38, 44, 50, 54, 60, 65, 75, 85 and $1 00

PILLOW CASE LINEN.

1603. 42 inches wide, per yard...40, 50, 60 and 75c
1604. 45 " " .45, 60, 75, 85 and 90c
1605. 54 " " .65, 75, 85c and $1 00

RED INLET.

1607. 33 inches wide, per yard 38c

LINEN DRILL.

1608. 40 inches wide, per yard........50 and 60c

TICKINGS.

1609. Fancy Striped, per yard.. ....20c
1610. Ordinary stripes, per yard, 10, 12½, 15, 18 to 30.

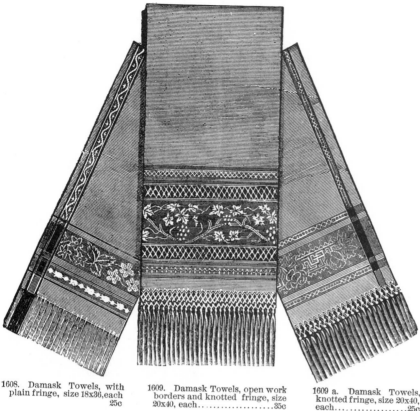

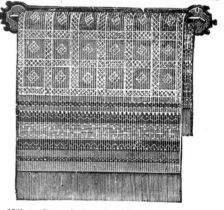

1620. All Linen Huck Towels, knotted fringe, size 18x36, each................................25c

1608. Damask Towels, with plain fringe, size 18x36, each 25c

1609. Damask Towels, open work borders and knotted fringe, size 20x40, each..................35c

1609 a. Damask Towels, knotted fringe, size 20x40, each..................25c

DAMASK.

1610. Unbleached, dice and broken patterns per yard...................... 17c, 20c, 25c and 31c
1611. Loom Damask, unbleached, per yard, 31c, 35c, 40c and 45c
1612. Scotch Damask, unbleached, per yard, 50c, 65c, 75c, 85c and $1 00
1613. Unbleached, with red border, per yard, 35c, 40c. 45c, 65c, 75c, 85c and $1 00
1614. Bleached Scotch Damask, per yard, 40c, 50c and 60c

1615. Bleached German Damask, per yard, 50c, 60c, 75c, $1 00, 1 20, 1 25
1616. "Barnsley" Double Damask, 2 yards wide, per yard..............$1 00, 1 25, 1 50 and 1 75
1617. Turkey Red Damask, warranted fast colors, per yard... 35c, 40c, 45c, 50c, 60c and 75c
1618. Cardinal Damask, 60 to 64 inches wide, per yard...........................80c, 85c and $1 00
1619. Real Vienna Damask, 66 inches wide, per yard ....85c and $1 00

1620 a. Damask Towels with red borders, size 20x40, each........................... .... 18c

All our goods are marked at the lowest prices. which do not include postage. No goods sent by mail except sufficient money accompanies the order for postage, otherwise we will reduce orders and take out part of goods to the amount of postage required.

1621. Bleached Scotch Damask. 64 inches wide, per yard.....50c

1622. Bleached German Damask. 58 inches wide, per yard...........50c

1623. Bleached German Damask, very heavy, 62 inches wide, yer yd, 75c

1624. Bleached Scotch Damask, 62 inches wide per yard....75c

1625. Half Bleached or Loom Damask, with red border, 62 ins. wide. 60c

1626. Bleached Scotch Damask, 68 inches wide per yard..........$1 00

924 TO 928 THIRD AVE., AND 160 TO 164 EAST 56th St., NEW YORK.

89

Table Cloths, D'Oylies, Etc.

1629. All White Linen D'Oylies, or with red or fancy borders, 16 inches square per dozen . .$1 25

1632. Turkey Red D'Oylies, per dozen, 60c, 75c, $1 00, 1 25 and $1 50

1630. All white Linen D'Oylies, or with fancy borders, 11x11 inches, per dozen. . . . 75c

1631. Turkey Red Cloths, 2 yards square, each, $1 45

1633. Plain White Linen D'Oylies, with or without fancy borders, 14 in. square; per dozen $1 00 Oval D'Oylies, per dozen, ... $1 35, 1 50 and 2 00

NAPKINS.

1634. ⅝, per dozen, 50, 65, 75, 85c, $1 00, 1 25, 1 50, 2 00 to $3 50
1635. Same, ¾, per dozen, $1 50, 1 75, 2 00, 2 50, 3 00, 3 50 and $4 00

GERMAN TURKEY RED TABLE CLOTHS.

1636.	1¼	yards square, each	. . . .	. . . .	. . . . 40c
1637.	1½	"	"	"	. . . . 75c
1638.	1¾	"	"	"	. . . . $1 00
1639.	1⅞	"	"	"	. . . . 1 20
1640.	2	"	"	"	. . . . 1 45
1641.	2x2½	"	"	"	. . . . 1 85
1642.	2x3	"	"	"	. . . . 2 00
1643.	2x3½	"	"	"	. . . . 2 60
1644.	2x4	"	"	"	. . . . 3 00

CARDINAL TABLE CLOTHS.

1645.	1¼	yards square, each	. . . . 50c
1646.	1½	"	"	"	. . . . 85c
1647.	1¾	"	"	"	. . . . $1 25
1648.	2	"	"	"	. . . . 1 85
1649.	2x2½	"	"	"	. . . . 2 10
1650.	2x3	"	"	"	. . . . 2 50
1651.	2x3½	"	"	"	. . . . 3 00
1652.	2x4	"	"	"	. . . . 3 60

TABLE SETS.

Particular attention is called to our extensive line of Damask Table Sets, consisting of cover and one dozen ⅝ or ¾ Napkins to match.
1653. 2 yards square, per set. . . . $4 75 to 10 00
1654. 2x2½ " " " . . . . . . .5 50 " 18 00

1655.	2x3	yards square, per set	. . . .$8 00 to 20 00
1656.	2x3½	"	"	"	. . . . .9 50 " 25 00
1657.	2x4	"	"	"	. . . . 10 00 " 30 00

Cloths 2½ yards wide, can be had for $1 00 extra

1658. Cream Lunch Cloths, 2 yards square, with fancy borders, and one dozen D'Oylies to match, per set. $4 75
1659. 2x2½ yards, per set. 5 25
1660. 2x3 " " 5 75
1661. 2x3½ " " 6 50
1662. 2x4 " " 7 00

1663. Damask Cloths, plain white or red borders, and one dozen Napkins to match, 2 yards square, per set, $3 75; 2x2½ yards, $4 25, 2x3 yards, $4 75, 2x3½ yards. $5 50; 2x4 yards, $6 00.

1664, Cardinal Table Covers black or white borders in a variety of patterns; two yards square, each. $1 85

1665. Cream Lunch Cloths, with fancy colored borders, 2x2½ yards and one dozen d'oylies to match. $4 50
1666. Same, in plain cream, or plain white. 4 50

SILK EMBROIDERED FLANNELS.

All Wool.   Yard Wide.

1667.   1½ inch embroidery, per yard 85c

1672.   1 inch embroidery, per yard.............75c

1677.   1 inch embroidery, per yard.............80c

1668.   2¾ inch embroidery, per yard........$1.20

1673.   2½ inch embroidery, per yard........$1.00

1678.   2¾ inch embroidery, per yard.........$1.10
Can also be had in scarlet flannel, embroidered
with either black or white silk twist, at the
same price.

1669.   4 inch embroidery, per yard...........$1.75

1674.   1½ inch embroidery, per yard.........$1.25
Can also be had in scarlet flannel, embroidered
with either black or white silk twist, at the
same price.

1679.   3½ inch embroidery, per yard... ......$1.25

1670.   3¼ inch embroidery, per yard........$1.60
Can also be had in scarlet flannel, embroidered
with either black or white silk twist, at the
same price.

1675.   4 inch embroidery, per yard...........$1.50

1680.   4½ inch embroidery, per yard........$1 55

1671.   3½ inch embroidery, per yard.. ......£1.35
Can also be had in scarlet flannel, embroidered
with either black or white silk twist, at the
same price.

1676.   5½ inch embroidery, per yard.......$2.00

1681.   4½ inch embroidery, per yard.........$1.85

924 TO 928 THIRD AVE., AND 160 TO 164 EAST 56th St., NEW YORK.

91

FLANNEL DEPARTMENT.

1681. White cotton and wool mixed and Domet flannel, ¾ yards wide, per yard,
9, 12½, 15, 18, 25 and 30c

1683. Same, ⅞ yards wide,
10, 12½, 15, 18, 25, 30 and 35c

1684. Same, yard wide, per yard,
35, 40, 45 and 50c

1685. White all-wool [flannel, ¾ yards wide, per yard......25, 31, 38 and 40c

1686. Same, ⅞ yards wide, per yard,
30, 35, 40 and 45c

1687. Same, yard wide, per yard, 45, 50, 55 and 60c

1688. Gilbert's and Ballardvale White Flannel, ¾ yards wide, per yard, 35, 40, 45 and 50c; ⅞ yard wide, per yard, 45, 50, 55 and 60c; yard wide, per yard......50, 55, 60, 65, 70 and 75c

1689. Silk and Wool Flannel, best quality, yard wide, per yard................85, 90c and $1.00

1690. White Shaker Flannel, per yard,
20, 25, 30 and 35c

1691. Same, all-wool, yard wide, per yard,
40, 45, 50, 55, 65, 75, 90c and $1.00

1692. Scarlet Shaker Flannel, all-wool, per yard,
30, 40, 50, 60, 65, 75c and $1.00

1693. Gray Shaker Flannel, all-wool, yard wide, per yard................50, 60 and 75c

1694. Plain Scarlet Flannel, ¾ yards wide, per yard................20, 25, 31, 38, and 40c

1695. Same, ⅞ yards wide, per yard,
30, 35, 40, 45 and 50c

1696. Same, yard wide, per yard......40 and 50c

1697. Scarlet and Navy Blue Twilled Flannel,
25, 31, 38, 40, 45, 50, 60 and 70c

1698. White Twilled Flannel for Bicycle Shirts, Ladies' Suits, etc., 26 inches wide, per yard,
35, 40, 45 and 50c

1699. Gray Twilled Flannel, cotton and wool, per yard................15, 18, 25 and 30c

1700. Same, all-wool, per yard..30, 35, 40 and 50c

1701. Eider Down, in pink, white, blue, cardinal and gray, yard wide, per yard................85c

1702. Jersey Flannels, in entirely new designs, for ladies' sacques, wrappers, etc., 27 inches wide, per yard................55c

1703. Orient Cashmeres, all colors, 27 inches wide, per yard................50c

1704. Striped Homespun all-wool Flannel, white, scarlet and navy blue, 84 inches wide, specially adapted for ladies' skirts, one yard necessary to a skirt, per yard................$1.45

1705. Opera Flannels, all colors, 27 inches wide, per yard................38, 45, and 50c

1706. Striped Flannels, for ladies' and children's dresses, sacques, etc., 27 inches wide, per yd.47c

1707. Colored Canton Flannels, colors, gold, garnet, cardinal, maroon, light, medium and navy blue, dark green, olive and sapphire, for upholstery purposes, 27 inches wide, per yard,
12½, 15 and 18c

1708. Double Faced Plush, 30 in. wide, per yd. 19c

1709. Matelasse or Basket Flannel, 27 inches wide, per yard................45 and 50c

1710. Plaid Flannels, 27 inches wide, per yard,
40, 45 and 50c

1711. Honeycomb Flannel, white only, per yd. 50c

1712. Canton Flannel, bleached or unbleached, per yard............8, 10, 12½, 15, 18, 20 and 25c

1713. Felt, all colors, for upholstery purposes, 2 yards wide, per yard................$1.10

1714. White Table Felt, 64 inches wide, per yd.65c

1715. Same, 60 inches wide, per yard........55c

1716. Same, 68 inches wide, per yard........75c

1718. Green Baize, 54 inches wide, per yd...$1.75

CLOTH FOR MEN'S AND BOYS' WEAR.

1719. Kentucky Jeans and Tricots, per yd. 20, 25c

1720. Tweed and Cassimeres, per yd...40 and 50c

1721. All wool Cassimeres, 50, 60, 75c and $1.00

1722. Waterproof, colors, black, brown, blue, gray and green, per yard. ....75, 85c and $1.00

1723. All wool Ladies' Cloth, 65, 75, 85c and $1.00

CLOAKINGS.

1724. Black Union Beaver Cloths, 54 inches wide, per yard................$1.25

1725. Beaver Cloths, black, per yard......$1.50
A complete line of Cloths. suitable for Wraps, Ulsters, Raglans and Traveling garments, per yard................$1.00, 1.25 and 1.50

FARMERS' SATIN.

1760. 27 inches wide. per yard......50, 65 and 75c

FINE WHITE GOODS.

1726. Berkely Cambric, per yard.......15 and 20c

1727. Lonsdale Cambric, 36 inches wide, per yard................10c

1728. English Nainsook, plain, 27 to 36 inches wide, per yard................18, 20, 25, 31 and 35c

1729. French Nainsook, sheer or heavy, 36 and 48 inches wide, per yard....25, 31, 38, 44, 60 and 75c

1730. Check Nainsook, per yard,
8. 10, 12½, 15 and 18c

1731. Striped, per yard........12½, 15, 18 and 25c

1732. Jones' Cambric, 36 and 45 inches wide, per yard................25, 35, 42 and 50c

1733. Victoria Lawn, per yard,
10, 12½, 15, 18, 25, 31 and 35c

1734. All Over Tucking, per yard,
45, 50, 60, 75 and $1.00

1735. Lace, striped and cluster tucking, per yard
65, 75, 85 and $1.00

1736. Tarlatan, white, per yard,
12½, 15, 16, 18, 25 and 29c

1737. Tarlatan, colored, per yard,
12½, 16, 18, 22 and 28c

1738. Persian Lawn, per yard....20, 25, 30 and 35c

1739. Linon d'Inde, per yard,
12½, 16, 18, 22, 25 and 31c

1740. Plain Swiss Muslin, per yard,
10, 12½, 15, 18, 21 and 25c

1741. Dotted and figured Swiss, per yard,
12½, 16, 18, 22, 25, 31, 36, 40 and 50c

1742. India Mull, cream or white, per yard,
25, 30, 35, 38, 40 and 50c

WADDING, ETC.

1743. Cotton Batting, per pound 15c

1744. Sheet Wadding, white or black, per doz. 24c

1745. White Wadding, per yard................10c

1746. Black   "   " 8c

Send for a Dress Pattern of our own make Black Cashmere, 46 inches wide, 50c per yard.

POSITIVELY A BARGAIN.

See the prices of our Opaque Window Shades, 45, 50, 58 and 67c each,

Holland Window Shades, all complete, 3x6 feet;
....39c

LININGS.

1747. A, Silesia, per yard....................10c

1748. B,   "   " 12½c

1749. C,   "   " 15c

1750. Cable Twills, " 18c

1751. Diamond Twills, per yard................20c

1752. Satin Surah, per yard................25c

1753. Brocades, etc., per yard............31 and 40c

1754. Quilted Satin Linings, all colors, 19 inches wide, per yard................75c

1755. Same, 24 inches wide, per yard........$1.00

THE MOSKOWITCH MODEL WAIST LINING.

EVERY LADY HER OWN DRESSMAKER

Dress Making Simplified.

By using this Model Waist-lining, any person can obtain a perfect fit, as the correct pattern is clearly printed on silesia, with directions where to cut, baste and sew together (thus avoiding the use of paper patterns). Can be had for the mere cost of silesia. In ordering please give bust measure; to obtain the correct size, please take the bust measure one inch tighter than the size intended for the dress. Can be had in white, black, light, medium and dark slate.

(*Refer to advertisement in back part of book.*)

1756. Sizes, 31 to 34, bust, each................39c

1757. Sizes, 35 to 40, bust, each................45c

1758. Sizes, 41 to 44, bust, each. 48c

SHELF OIL CLOTH.

1759. Printed or Perforated Shelf Oil Cloth. A substitute for shelf paper, 12 inches wide, can be had in the following colors, white, pink, light blue, light green, garnet and various wood colors, per yard, 6c; per piece, (12 yards) 63c.

MARSEILLES AND HONEYCOMB QUILTS.

1761. Marcilles crib and cradle spreads, each.
75, 85, 95, $1.00, 1.25, 1.75, 1.90 and 2.00

1762. 9-4, for single beds, each,
$1.65, 1.75, 2.00, 2.50. 3.00 and 3.50

1763. 10x10 for double beds, each,
$1.75, 1.90, 2.25, 2.50, 3.00, 3.75,
4.50, 5.00, 6.00, 7.00, 8.00 and 10.00

1764. 11x11. Extra large size, each,
$3.50, 4.00, 5.00 and upward

1765. Honeycomb and Crochet Quilts, each,
60, 75, 85c and $1.00

1766. Marseilles pattern, each, $1.10, 1.25, 1.35, 1.40

COMFORTABLES, ETC.

1767. Comfortables....65, 75c, $1.00, 1.50 and 2,00

1768. Chintz..............$1.50, 2.00, 2.50 and 3.00

1769. Turkey Red,..............2.00, 2.50 and 3.00

CRIB BLANKETS.

1770. 30x40. Per pair.. ....$1.25

1771. 36x50.   " $1.75

1772. 42x56.   " $2.25

WHITE BLANKETS.

1773. 10-4. Per pair, $1.25, 1.50, 2.00, 2.50 and 3.00

1774. 11-4.   " $3.00, 3.50, 4.00, 5.00 and 6.00

1775. 12-4. Per pair,
$5.00, 6,00. 7.00. 8.00, 9.00 and upward

COLORED BLANKETS.

1776. Brown and Grey, per pair, $1 25, 1.50 and 2.00

1777. Scarlet Blankets, 10-4, per pair, $3 50 and 4.00

1778. 11-4. Per pair............. $5.50 and $6.50

Send for a Dress Pattern of our own make Black Cashmee, 46 inches wide, 50c per yard.

POSITIVELY A BARGAIN.

See the prices of our Opaque Window Shades.
45, 50, 58 and 67c each.

Holland Window Shakes, all complete, 3x6 feet;
. . . . .39c

WHITE INDIA LINEN ROBES.

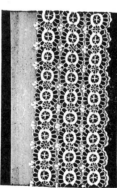

1799. 12 yards India Linen, 33 to 36 inches wide ; 4½ yards wide and 4½ yards narrow embroidery; put up in a neat box and warranted to be sufficient to make up a garment illustrated above; unmade...........$4.00
1800. Same, made up..$7.50
1801. Others not illustrated; unmade......$5.00, 6.00, 7.00, 8.00 and 10.00
Making extra, $3.50, 4.00 and 5.00 each.

EMBROIDERED ROBES.

WHITE EMBROIDERY FOR INDIA LINEN ROBES.

1793. Material for robe, consisting of 12 yards India linen, 4½ yards of embroiderery (as illustrated) and 4½ yards of narrow embroidery, guaranteed to be sufficient to make up robe as garment No. 1799...........$3.50
1794. Same, made up.............................$7.50

1795. Materials for robe consisting of 12 yards India linen, 4½ yards of embroidery as above and 4½ yards of narrow embroidery, guaranteed to be sufficient to make up garment same as No. 1799 ....$4.50
1796. Same, made up..............................$8.50

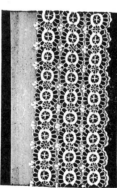

1797. Materials for robe, consisting of 12 yards India Linen, 4½ yards embroidery as illustrated guaranteed sufficient to make up garment illustrated $5.00
1798. Same, made up................................$9.00

WHITE NAINSOOK ROBES.

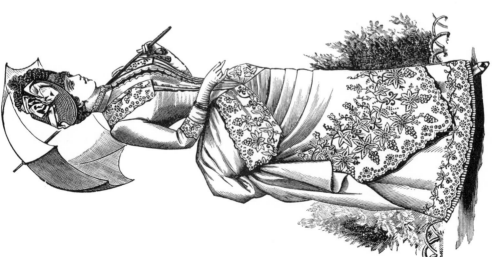

1790. 9 yards plain Nainsook, 40 to 45 inches wide; embroidery 2¼ yards wide, 1¾ yards medium and 5 yards narrow. These materials are put up in a neat box and we warrant them to be sufficient to make up the garment as illustrated above (unmade) $11.98
1791. Same, made up..$16.50
1792. Other styles not illustrated, unmade.......$6.00, 7.00, 8.00 and 9.00
Same, made up. $4.50 extra,

EMBROIDERY FOR CHAMBRAY ROBES.

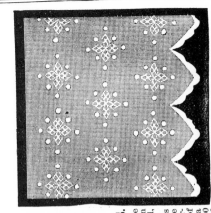

1811. Chambray Robe, consisting of 10½ yards Chambray, 4½ yards of wide embroidery, as illustrated, and 4½ yards narrow, put up in neat box ; price, unmade $8 00
1812. Same, fully made up, price $10 50

1813. Chambray Robe, consisting of 10½ yards Chambray, 4½ yards of wide embroidery, as illustrated, and 4½ yards narrow, put up in neat box ; price, unmade. . . $9 00
1814. Same, fully made up, price. $9 00

EMBROIDERED CHAMBRAY ROBES.

The materials described are guaranteed to be sufficient to make up the above costume, and can be had in the following colors, viz.: gray or mixed, brown, navy, pink and light blue.

1807. Chambray Robe, consisting of 10½ yards plain material, 4½ yards same, edged with wide embroidery (as shown in cut), and 4½ yards narrow embroidery, making a total of 15 yards of material and 9 yards of embroidery ; put up in a neat box ; price, unmade $8 00
1808. Same, fully made up; price $13 00
1809. Chambray Robe, not illustrated, consists of 15 yards of plain, material, 4½ yards of wide and 4½ yards narrow embroidery; put up in box ; price, unmade . . . . $3 25, 4 00, 4 50 and 5 00
1810. Same, made up; price, 6 25, 7 00, 7 50 and 8 00

CHAMBRAY ROBES.

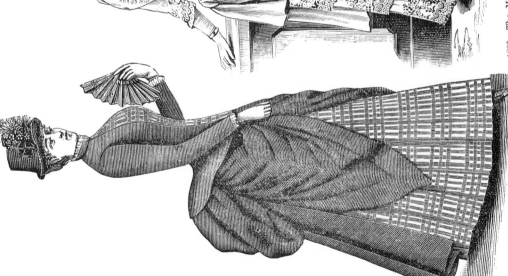

1806. The Moss Stitch Chambray Robe, consisting of 10 yards plain chambray, 4½ yards wide, and 4½ yards narrow, moss embroidery in various designs; colors, gray mixed, navy and light blue, brown or pink, put up in a neat box ; unmade. . . . . $4 00 and 4 50 For making, $4 00 extra. The same material can be had, if desired, for 12½c per yard.

TOILE du NORD ROBE.

1804. The material is fine quality Seersucker and can be had as above illustrated or entirely plaid or striped. The entire garment consists of 13 yards, very neatly put up, with the above plate enclosed ; price unmade. $1 75
1805. Same, made up. $3 50

Silks, Satins and Velvets.

Particular attention is called to our extensive line of staple dress silks in black and colored, consisting of the most reliable brands of European and American manufacturers, such as "Guinet," "Bonnet," or "Bellon," (European) and "Givernaud Bros.," (American); these brands are guaranteed to equal any silk manufactured.

We recommend the "BLOOMINGDALE BROS. RELIABLE BRAND," and warrant it to give satisfaction in every respect, our written guarantee to that effect if desired, will accompany every dress pattern delivered.

Notwithstanding the advance of from 35 to 40 per cent. on the price of raw silks since last season, we are still selling them at the same price as heretofore, being enabled to do so by having placed large orders prior to the advance, giving our patrons the benefit thereof.

When ordering samples of Silks, Dress Goods, etc., do not fail to state colors, styles and prices desired, and whether same is intended for dress or trimming purposes.

Black Gros-Grain Silks.
Bloomingdale Bros' Reliable Brands.

No.	Quality.	Width.	Price per yard.
2000.	A,	20-in	$1 00
2001.	B,	21-in	1 20
2002.	C,	22-in	1 50
2003.	D,	22-in	1 65
2004.	E.	22-in	1 75

N. B.—To parties sending us club orders for 50 yards of either of the above qualities we will allow a discount of 5 per cent.

"Bellon's Cashmere Finish."

No.	Quality	Width	Price per yard.
2005.	O,	20-in	$0 90
2006.	A,	20-in	1 00
2007.	B,	20-in	1 25
2008.	C,	22-in	1 75
2009.	D,	22-in	2 00
2010.	E,	22-in	2 25
2011.	F,	24-in	2 50
2012.	G,	24-in	2 75
2013.	H,	24-in	3 00

C. J. Bonnet & Cie's Lyons Silks.
MOST RELIABLE SILK MADE.

No.	Quality.	Width.	Price per yard.
2014.	0,	20-in	1 00
2015.	1,	20-in	1 20
2016.	2,	22-in	1 49
2017.	3,	22-in	1 69
2018.	4,	22-in	1 89
2019.	5,	24-in	2 09
2020.	6,	24-in	2 59
2021.	7,	24-in	3 09
2022.	8,	24-in	3 59
2023.	9,	24-in	3 89

Tapissier Freres' Grease-Proof Silks

No.	Quality.	Width.	Price per yard.
2024.	100,	20-in	$0 90
2025.	200,	20-in	1 10
2026.	300,	20-in	1 20
2027.	400,	22-in	1 50
2028.	500,	22-in	1 70
2029.	600,	22-in	1 90
2030.	700,	22-in	2 10
2031.	800,	22-in	2 30

Antoine Guinet's Silks.
"OUR MOST POPULAR BRAND."
Every yard warranted to wear.

No.	Quality.	Width.	Price per yard.
2032.	30,	19-in	$0 60
2033.	40,	19-in	0 69
2034.	50,	20-in	0 80
2035.	60,	20-in	0 85
2036.	70,	20-in	0 98
2037.	80,	20-in	1 08
2038.	90,	20-in	1 28
2039.	100,	21-in	1 48
2040.	110,	21-in	1 68
2041.	120,	22-in	1 88
2042.	130,	22-in	2 08
2043.	140,	23-in	2 28
2044.	150,	23-in	2 48

"Givernaud Bros. Renown American Black Gros-Grain Silks."
Every yard warranted to wear.

No.	Quality.	Width.	Price per yard.
2045.	A,	23-in	$1 00
2046.	B,	23-in	1 15
2047.	C,	23-in	1 25
2048.	D,	21-in	1 25
2049.	E,	21-in	1 39
2050.	F,	22-in	1 50
2051.	G,	23-in	1 75

Black Ottoman Silk.
For dresses or wraps.

No.	Quality.	Width.	Price per yard.
2052.	A,	30-in	$1 00
2053.	B,	20-in	1 35
2054.	C,	30-in	1 50
2055.	D,	30-in	1 75
2056.	E,	30-in	2 00

Colored Gros-Grain Silk.
Full assortment of colors.

No.	Quality.	Price per yard.
2057.	100	$0 75
2058.	200	0 85
2059.	300	1 00
2060.	400	1 20
2061.	500	1 50

2061A. Full line of white and evening shades, 18 inches wide; per yard, 95c.
2061B. Same, 20 inches wide; per yard, $1 25, 1 50.

Black Tricotine.

2062. 19 inches wide; per yard ..... $1 00 and 1 25
2063. 20 "   " 1 50

Summer Silks.
CHECKED AND STRIPED.

2064. 18 inches wide. per yard, 35c, 40c. 45c, 55c, 60c and 75c

Lining Silks.

2065. Marceline; black, white and colored, per yard ..... 40 and 50c
2066. China Silk, black, white, per yd. 35 and 45c
2067. Black and white serge ..... 50 and 75c
2068. Lustrine silk, black only, per yard, 60, 75c and $1 00

Surah Silks.
BLACK AND COLORED.

2069. 20 inches wide, per yard, 65, 75, 85c and $1 00

China Pongee Silks.

2070. Per piece of 19 to 20 yards, $4 50, 5 00, 5 50, 6 00, 6 50, 7 00, 8 00 and 9 00

India Silks and Foulards.

2071. 22 inches wide, per yard, 75c, $1 00, 1 25 and 1 50

Crépe de'Chene.

2072. 24 inches wide, per yard ..... $1 20 and 1 40

Black Satin.

No.	Quality.	Width.	Price per yard.
2073.	A,	19-in	$0 50
2074.	B,	19-in	0 65
2075.	C,	19-in	0 75
2076.	D,	19-in	1 00
2077.	E,	22-in	1 25
2078.	F,	22-in	1 50

Colored Satins.

No.	Quality.	Width.	Price per yard.
2079.	A,	19-in	32c
2080.	B,	19-in	40c
2081.	C,	19-in	50c
2082.	D,	19-in	65c
2083.	E,	19-in	75c

Black Brocade Satin.

2084. 19 to 20 inches wide, per yard, 65, 75, 85 and 98c
2085. 23 inches wide. per yard; $1 10, 1 25 and 1 50

Colored Brocade Satin.

2086. 19 to 20 inches wide, per yard, 75c, $1 00 and 1 10
2087. Two-toned, per yard, 75c, $1 00, 1 25, 1 50

Black and Colored Satin Rhadames and Merveilleux.

No.	Quality.	Width.	Price per yard.
2088.	A,	20-in	$0 95
2089.	B,	20-in	1 10
2090.	C,	20-in	1 25
2091.	D,	22-in	1 50
2092.	E,	22-in	1 85

Black and Colored Satin Radzimir and Satin Duchesse.

No.	Quality.	Width.	Price per yard.
2093.	A,	20-in	$1 00
2094	B,	20-in	1 10
2095.	C,	20-in	1 25
2096.	D,	20-in	1 50
2097.	E,	22-in	1 75
2098.	F,	22-in	2 10

Black Silk Velvets.

No.	Quality.	Width.	Price per yard.
2099.	A,	19-in	$1 00
2100.	B,	19-in	1 20
2101.	C,	20-in	1 50
2102.	D,	20-in	1 75
2103.	E,	20-in	2 00

Colored Silk Velvets.
40 DIFFERENT SHADES.

No.	Quality.	Width.	Price per yard.
2104.	A,	19-in	$1 00
2105.	B,	19-in	1 25
2106.	C,	19-in	1 50
2107.	D,	20-in	1 75
2108.	E,	20-in	2 00

Black and Colored Brocade Velvets.
IN PLAIN AND FRIÉSÉ EFFECTS.

2109. 19 to 22 inches wide, per yard, $1 65, 1 75, 2 00, 2 50 and 3 00

Black and Colored Embossed Velvets.

2110. Rich designs, 19 inches wide, per yard, $1 25 and 1 50
2111. Two-toned Brocade Velvet, 19 inches wide, per yard ..... $2 00, 2 50, 3 00 and 3 50

Dress Velvets.

2112. 24 to 26 inches wide, per yard, $2 00, 2 50, 3 00, 3 50, 4 00, 4 50 and $5 00

Velveteens.
THE RENOWN BOULEVARD BRANDS.

No.	Quality.	Width.	Price per yard.
2113.	A,	22-in	$0 50
2114.	B,	22-in	0 65
2115.	C,	22-in	0 75
2116.	D,	22-in	1 00

2117. Elberon Black and Colored Twill Velveteen, 22 inches wide, per yard $1 10

Plush.

2118. 19 inches wide, all colors, per yard . . $1 25
2119. 24 "   "   "   "   "
$1 69, 1 89, 2 00 and 2 25

Corduroys.

2120. 28 inches wide, all colors, per yard, 69 and 75c

Dress Goods Department.

CASHMERES.

2121. All-wool, in all the most fashionable colors, 40 inches wide, per yard, 42, 50, 69 and 75c

COLORED DRESS GOODS.

2122. Shoodah Cloth, 40 inches wide, per yard, 45, 55, 62 and 75c
2123. Worsted Diagonals, 36 to 42 inches wide, per yard . . . . .45, 52, 62 and 75c
2124. Worsted Serges, 42 inches wide, per yard, 50, 59, 69, 75 and 85c
2125. Satin Berber, 42 inches wide, per yard, 75, 85 and $1 00
2126. Tricots, 36 inches wide, per yard, 50 and 60c
2127.   "   45   "   60, 75 and 85c
2128. Tricots, 54 inches wide, per yard, 75, 90c and $1 00
2129. Camel's Hair, 42 inches wide, per yard, 69, 75, 85c
2130. Boucle, 42 inches wide, per yard, 35, 40 and 45c
2131. Boucle, 40 inches wide, per yard, 60, 75c and $1 00
2132. Boucle, 50 inches wide, per yard, 69, 85c, $1 00, 1 25 and 1 50
2133. Homespun, 36 to 40 inches wide, per yard, 40 and 50c
2134. Homespun, 50 inches wide, per yard, 75, 85c and $1 00
2135. Cheviot and silk mixtures, 40 inches wide, per yard 55c
2136. Melrose Suiting, 42 inches wide, per yard, 60, 69 and 75c
2137. Valencia, 22 inches wide, per yard, 30, 35 and 45c
2138. Drap d'Alsac. 42 inches wide, per yard, 40, 50, 60 and 75c
2139. Gro-Tunis Cloth, 22 inches wide, per yard, 25, 30 and 35c
2140. Alpine Lustre Cloth, 22 to 27 inches wide, per yard . . . . 30, 35 and 40c
2141. Alpine Lustre Cloth, 40 inches wide, per yard . . . . 60, 75 and 85c
2142. Crape La Favor Cloth, per yard, 50, 60 and 75c
2143. Crape de Tunis Cloth, 22 inches wide, per yard . . . . 25, 33, 38 and 45c
2144. Algerian, 40 inches wide, per yard, 40, 49, 59 and 69c

LACE, NUN'S VEILING AND ALBA-TROSS CLOTH.

2145. Lace Bunting, all colors, 26 inches wide per yard 15c
2146. Same, all wool, 40 inches wide, 50, 60, 69, 75, and 85c
2147. Plain and Figured Nun's Veiling, 22 inches wide, per yard . . . . 15, 18 and 25c
2148. 40 inches wide, per yard, 45, 50, 60, 69, 75c
2149. Albatross Cloth, 42 inches wide, all wool, per yard . . . . . 45, 50, 55, 60, 69, and 75c

DOMESTIC DRESS GOODS.

2150. Cashmeres, single width. per yard, 10, 12½ and 15c
2151. Double width, per yard, 12½, 18, 20, 25, 31c
2152. Brocades, per yard . . . .12½, 15 and 18c
2153. De Beiges, per yard . 12½, 15, 18, 25 and 35c
2154. Same, all wool, 40 inches wide, per yard, 50, 60, and 70c
2155. Satin Berber, per yard, 20, 25, 30, 39 and 45c
2156. Heather Suitings, per yard . . 8, 10 and 12c
2157. Satin Foule, per yard . . . . 15, 18 and 25c
2158. Plaids, single width . . . .25. 33, 38 and 45c
2159. Same, double width, per yard, 40, 50, 60, 75 and $1 00
2160. A complete line of Cashmere, Nun's Veiling and Albatross Cloth, in all the evening shades, per yard . . 55, 65, 75, 90c and $1 00

MOURNING GOODS DEPARTMENT.

2161. Superior Crape ....per yard, 50, 60 and 75c
2162. Courtauld's Crape, 4-4, measures 28 inches wide, per yard, 75c, $1 00, 1 50 and 2 00
2163. Courtauld's Crape, 5-4, measures 35 inches wide, per yard, $1 50, 2 00, 2 50, 3 00, 3 50 to 5 00
2164. Courtauld's Crape, 6-4 for veiling purposes, 42 inches wide, per yard, $2 00, 3 00, 3 50, 4 00, 5 00, 6 00 and upward
2165. All-wool Nun's Veiling for mourning veils, 26 to 48 inches wide, per yard, 65, 75c, $1 00, 1 25, 1 50, 2 00

BLACK CASHMERE, ETC.

CAN BE HAD IN BLUE AND JET BLACK.

2166. Wool Face, equal to all wool, 36 inches wide, per yard . . . . 40, 45 and 50c
2167. Wool Face, 45 inches wide, per yard, 50c, a great bargain.
2168. Black Cashmere, all wool, 40 inches wide. per yard, 42, 50, 55, 60, 69, 75, 85, 98c, $1 10 and 1 25
2169. Silk Warp, Henriettas, 36 to 40 inches wide, per yard, 75, 90c, $1 00, 1 15, 1 25, 1 40, 1 60, 1 85 and 2 00
2170. Drap 'd Ete, 46 inches wide, desirable for wraps, per yard, $1 25, 1 50, 1 85, 2 25, 2 50
2171. Crape Cloth, 36 to 40 inches wide, per yard, 50, 60, 69, 75, 85c and 50c
2172. Satin Berber, 36 to 40 inches wide per yard, 33, 38, 45 and 50c
2173. Same, 42 inches wide, per yard, 75, 85c and $1 00
2174. Shoodah Cloth, 40 inches wide, per yard, 50, 65, 75, 85c and $1 00
2175. Camel's Hair, 40 inches wide per yard, 62, 75, 89, 95c, $1 10 and 1 25
2176. Prunelle Cloth, per yard, 60, 69, 75 and 89c
2177. Tamise Cloth, per yard, 50, 59, 69, 79 and 89c
2178. Satin Face Brocades, 42 inches wide, per yard. . . . . .75, 85 and 95c

2179. Satin Soliel, 42 inches wide, per yard, 85, 95c and $1 00
2180. Ottomans, 42 inches wide, per yard, 85c, $1 00 and 1 25
2181. Tricot, 36 inches wide, per yard 50c
2182.   "   45   " 65, 85. 90c
2183. Worsted Diagonals, 36 to 42 inches wide, per yard. . . . . .45, 55 and 65c
2184. Flannel Suitings, 36 inches wide, per yard, 39, 45, 49c
2185. 54 inches wide, per yard, 49, 65, 75, 85 and 98c
2186. Drap d' Alma. 22 inches wide, per yard, 25 and 30c
2186a. Boucle, per yard. . . . . .75, 85 and 98c
2187. Armures, 22 inches wide, per yard 25c
2188. Nun's Veiling, 36 to 40 inches wide, per yard. . . . . .50, 60, 69, 75, 85c and $1 00
2189. Albatross Cloth, 40 inches wide, per yard, 50, 60, 69 and 75c
2190. Alpaca and Brilliantine, per yard, 20, 25, 29, 33. 36, 45, and 50c
2191. Lace Buntings, 22 inches wide, per yard, 12½ and 15c
2192. Same, double width, per yard, 18, 25, 45, 50, 60 and 75c

COTTON DRESS GOODS.

We desire to mention the extensive line of these goods which we constantly have on hand. During the past few years these goods have taken the lead for the city trade, and are very fashionable at watering places.

2193. Sateens, French, plain colors, per yard, 30c
2194.   "   "   figured, per yard, 25, 30 and 33c
2195. Domestic Sateens, in plain colors, and figured, per yard. . . . .12½, 15, 18. 20 and 25c
2196. Batiste, 30 inches wide, per yard, 10 and 12½c
2197.   "   40   "   18, 20 and 25c
2198. Lawns, plain and figured, per yard, 8, 10 and 12½c
2199. Lattice, or open work, per yard. . . .12½c
2200. Chambrays, plain colors, per yard, 10, 12½ and 15c
2201. Imported Chambrays, per yard, 20 and 25c
2202. American Ginghams, per yard. 8, 10, 12½c
2203. Scotch Ginghams, per yard, 15, 18, 20 25c
2204. Embroidered Ginghams, per yard, 12½, 15 and 18c
2205. Seersucker, per yard. . . . . .10, 12 and 15c
2206. Crinkled Seersucker, per yard, 11½, 15. 18c
2207. Linen Lawn, per yard. . . . . .12½, 15 and 18c
2208. Percales, per yard . . . . .10, 12, 16 and 18c
2209. Indigo Blue Percale, per yard. . . .16 and 18c
2210.   "   "   Foulard   "   8 and 10c
2211. Foulard, per yard. . . . . .8, 10 and 12½c
2212. Prints, new styles, per yard. . . . .6, 7 and 8c
2213. Furniture Prints, per yard. . . . . . . .8 and 9c
2214. Cretonnes, per yard. . . . .10, 12½, 18 and 20c
2215. Turkey Red. . . . . . . .8, 10, 12½, 18 and 20c

HAMMOCKS.

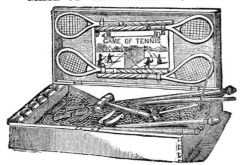

2216. Cotton Hammocks, ten feet long. $0 98
2217. Better quality. 1 49
2218. Mexican, white or colored. 1 25
2219. Spreader. . . . . .25c each
2220. Pillows. . . . . .25c "

GAME OF LAWN TENNIS, ETC.

2221. Lawn Tennis, complete. $5 00
2222. Archery per set. . . . .$2 00, 3 50, 5 00 to 15 00

GARDEN TOOLS.

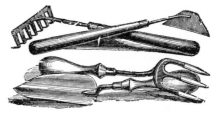

2223. Garden Tools, per set. 25, 50, 75c

CROQUET.

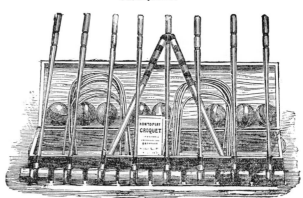

2224. Croquet, per set, complete. . . . .$1 00, 1 50, 2 00, 3 00 and 4 00

CARMEN.

2210. Lace Bonnet, full crown of tan colored lisse, faced with brown velvet, roses on the edge, finished with jabot of lace, bead aigrette and velvet ribbon bow to match, strings of the same; can be made in all colors, $5.00, 6.25 and 8.00.

LILLY.

2211. Black Lace Poke, crown of chantilly net, 3 rows of lace on rim. finished with a full jabot of the same and picot edge ribbon of any color; can also be made of jet lace, $6 00, 8.00 and 10.00.

QUEEN.

2212. Queen Coronet Bonnet, fine Milan straw with fancy bugle edge, trimmed with French lace, and flower with aigrette attached, ribbon strings, $4.50 and 6.00.

CAPPELLO.

2213. Fine Milan Straw, faced with velvet and bead edge, trimmed with cardinal velvet ribbon and hyacinth flowers, $4.00, 5.50 and 7.00.

WOODLAND.

2214. Leghorn Shade Hat, faced with oriental lace, and trimmed with heavy jabot of the same, finished with ribbon bows. $3.75 and 5.50.

2215. Same style, trimmed with mull, $2.50 and 3.50.

AVENUE.

2216. Fine Milan Straw, faced with velvet and jet gimp, trimmed with colored crape and finished with velvet ribbon bows and jet ornaments, $5.00 and 7.00.

DAUVRAY.

2217. Mourning Bonnet, crown of soft folds of crape and full shirred rim, trimmed with crape loops, and strings of the same; ribbon strings if preferred; $2.75, 3.50 and 5.00.

JULIA.

2218. Black Lace Hat, made of chantilly net, soft crown and shirred rim, finished with beads on one side, ornaments round the crown and tips, towards the back; can also be made of white lace, $8.00, 9.50 and 10.50.

HUSSAR.

2219. Mourning Hat of crape, heavy folds on rim, plain band round the crown, finished with fan trimming of the same in front, $2.75, 3.75 and $5.00.

924 TO 928 THIRD AVE., AND 160 TO 164 EAST 56th St., NEW YORK.

97

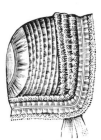

2220. Bonnet of Oriental lace trimmed with satin ribbon, suitable for a child from 2 to 8 years of age, $1.55.

2221. Fine Swiss Cap, corded in space or clusters with triple row of lace ruching, 69, 83c and $1.33

2222. Infants' Oriental lace cap, with full lace and ribbon ruche; *very pretty*, sizes, 1 mo. to 2 yrs. 93c

2223. Other Lace Caps, 50, 75c, 1.25, 1.50, 1.75 and upward.

2224. The "Greenaway" Cap, of fine hamburg embroidery and full lace ruche, sizes, 1½ to 5 yrs., 58c

2225. Other Caps, same style, 75c, 1.25 and $1.50

2226. Child's Normandy swiss embroidered and tucked with full ruche sizes, 2 to 7 years, 63c.

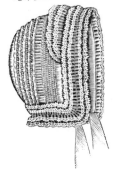

2227. Swiss Cap, shirred and corded with very full fluted ruche, wide swiss ties, sizes, 6 mos. to 6 years, 62c.
2228. Other Corded Caps, all sizes, 88c, 1.00, 1.15 and $1.48.

2229. The "Greenaway;" Cap of hamburg embroidery, full lace ruche, *very handsome*; sizes, 2 to 7 years, $1.29.
2230. Other Caps, same style of Oriental lace, 2.50 and 3.25

2231 The "Gretchen," Cap of hamburg embroidery, trimmed with Italian lace, sizes, 1 to 5 years, 79c.

2232. Very fine nine cord swiss cap with full double ruche, sizes, 1 to 6 years, 30c.

2233. The "Mayflower," Cap of open work embroidery with triple row of lace ruching, sizes, 6 mos. to 6 yrs., 73c

JOCKEY.

2234 Fine Milan straw hat, trimmed with white satin, ribbon and buckle, faced with navy blue velvet and full lace ruche, suitable for little boy; sizes, 6 to 6¾. Price. $4.25.

2235. Boys' Jockey Cap, of straw, sizes, 6⅛ to 6¾, 98c and $1.25.
2236. Same style in cloth, $1.15.

2237. Child's sun hat, of cambric, will wash equal to new, sizes, 6 mos. to 4 years, 42c.

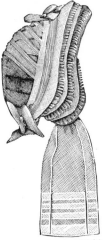

2238 Hat of Oriental lace and shirred mull brim, trimmed with mull to match; suitable for a girl or miss $1.65

2239. Ladies' Dress Caps, made of black Brussels net, and black French lace, handsomely trimmed with satin ribbon; all black, or black and purple, or white, 1.65, $1.88.

2240. Widow's White Cap, made of tarlatan, with fine folds across crown, and three rows of crepe ruching inside, 1.10, $1.35.

2241. Ladies' Dress Cap, made of black Brussels net, and black French lace handsomely trimmed with satin ribbon; all black, or black and purple or white, 1.10, 1 25 and $1.35.

2242. Hand made Swiss Caps, sizes, 1 mo. to 1 year, 30, 42 and 60c.
2243. Child's shade hat of fine cambric, hand made, will wash equal to new, 1.25 and $1.75.

UNTRIMMED HATS.

2246. Parisian.   2247. Hussar.   2248. Adrienne.   2249. Seadrift.

2250. Baronet.   2251. Patti.   2252. Bon Ton.   2253. Melrose.

2554. Jaunty.   2255. Fashion.   2256. Katie.   2257. Jewel.

2258. Oxford.   2259. Modjeska.   2260. Queen.   2261. Saxon.

The above Hats can be had in Union Milan, black and colored, 49c. In fine straw, 88c and $1.15.
In English Milan, 1.49, 1.65 and $1.75.

2262. Amazon; in Union Milan, black and
    colored, 49c.
2263. Fine straw, 88c and $1.15.
2264. English Milan, 1.49, 1.65 and $1.75.

2265. Dolly; hat for a child, in pearl, loop or Milan straw,
    white or colored; sizes, 6¼ to 6¾, 65, 88c and $1.50.

2266. Glen; plain or mixed straw, 25c.

CHILDREN'S TRIMMED HATS.

TAM O'SHANTER.

2267. Child's "Tam O'Shanter," of plain or mixed straw; sizes, 6¼ to 6¾, $1.35.

2268. Mixed Straw Sailor Hat; sizes, 6½ to 6¾...........50 and 75c

KATE.

2269. Fancy straw, trimmed in all colors..............95c

POLO.

2270. Boys' polo cap, in plain or mixed cloth, 6¼ to 7; 25c, 39c and 75c.

RESCUE.

2271. Plain or fancy straw, trimmed with satin ribbon and buckle, all colors......$1.10

EVELYN,

2272. Fancy straw, trimmed with satin ribbon and ornaments, $1.00 and 1.35.

DOT.

2273. Sizes, 6 to 6¾; mixed straw, 75c; white English Milan, $1 00 and 1 25

GARRICK.

2274. Very stylish hat, fine English Milan straw, trimmed with heavy silk cord, satin picot edge ribbon and hussar pompon, entirely new, white or colors.............$3.25

CANOTIER.

2275. Plain or fancy straw, trimmed with satin ribbon and fancy cord, all colors,......88c

DILEMNA.

2276. Fine straw, with fancy edge, trimmed with satin ribbon, all colors..........$1.15

ZEPHYR.

2277. Plain or fancy straw trimmed with satin ribbon and cord in all colors,...............$1.15

MEN'S AND BOYS' HATS.

Men's Sizes 6¾ to 7¼.   Boys' Sizes 6¼ to 7.

2278. Boys' hats, plain or mixed straw, ...50c, 75c and $1.25
2279. Manilla 50c
2280. White Mackinaw..............$1.00

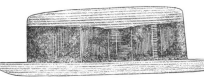

2281. Men's hats, plain or mixed straw, $1.00, 1.50 and 1.75.
2282. Manilla . ...75c.
2283. White Mackinaw...............$1.50

2284. Boys' hats, plain or mixed straw 50c, 75c and $1.25
2285. Manilla 50c
2286. White Mackinaw...... ....$1.00

2287. Men's soft hats, fine wool felt, black, brown or gray $2.00
2288. Extra Fine Felt.....................$2.50
2289. Beaver Felt... ....$3.00 and 3.50

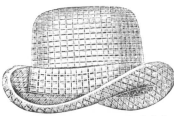

2290. Men's hats of plain or mixed cloths, to match suits......$1.50, 2.00 and $2.50

2291. Men's plain or mixed straw Derby hats, $1.00 and 1.50.

2292. Men's Derbys, black, brown or gray, wool felt..................$1.00
2293. Extra fine felt....... ..$2.00 and 2.50

2294. Men's soft hats, fine wool felt, black, brown or gray....................$2.00
2295. Extra fine felt....................$2.50
2296. Beaver felt....... ....$3.00 and 3.50

2297. Men's derby, black, brown or gray wool felt................$1.00
2298. Extra fine felt.... ..$2.00 and 2.50

Flowers, Tips and Millinery Trimmings.

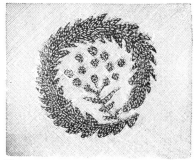

2300. All Silk Chenille Pompons with leaves, aigrettes and wood beads, very handsome, 49c

2301. Plumes and Feathers, black; each, $1.00, 1.50, 1.65, 2.00, 2.75, 3.00, 3.50, 4.00, 4.50, 5.00, 5.50, 6.00 and 7.00.
2302. Plumes, white and colored, $1.25, 1.75, 2.00, 2.25, 2.50, 3.00, 3.42, 4.00, 5.00, 5.50 and 6.00.

2303. Jet Crowns. assorted patterns, each, 50, 65, 87, 98c, $1.25 and 1.98.

2304. Ostich Tips, black and colored, very rich, per bunch, $3.49

2305. Ostrich Pompons, with aigrettes, each, $1.00.

2306. Jet Pompons, per bunch, 49c.

2307. Colored Ostrich Tips, per bunch of 3, 69c, $1.29 to 3.49.
2308. Single, all colors. each, 50c, 75c, $1 10 to 1.50.

2309. Ostrich Tips, black, per bunch of 3. .47, 75c. $1.00, 1.55, 2.25 and 2.75.
2310. Single, each, 50, 65, 75c, $1,00, 1.25 and 1.50.

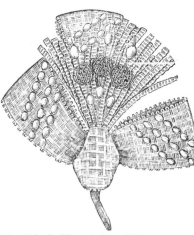

2311. All Silk Military Pompon, in cream, white, beige, yellow, pink, light blue, cardinal and black, entirely new 21c

2312. Fine Spray of satin blossoms, leaves and piquets, assorted colors, each, 63c.

2313. Striped Silk and Straw Ribbon Sprays of crimped silk braid, ornamented with satin and metal beads; colors, straw, beige, brown, yellow, black and cream, 59c.

2314. Very fine spray made of cluster of tiny rosebuds, large open and half blown buds, leaves and piquets, 98c.

2315. Silk Plush Hussar Pompon, in white, cream, beige, yellow, pink, light blue, cardinal and black, 29c.

2316. Fine Spray, made of satin fancy flowers, satin leaves and grasses, assorted colors, 83c.

2317. Very fine Monture of flowers, with fine French piquets and leaves all colors, 95c.

2318. All Silk Chenille Bird Pompon, entirely new, in white, cream, beige, yellow, pink, light blue, cardinal and black, 15c.

2319. Handsome Spray of satin leaves and French piquets, with small velvet blossoms, all the new shades, 98c.

2320. Spray of velvet tulips, fine grasses and leaves, assorted colors, 47c

2321. Bunch containing two clusters of lilies of the valley and lily leaves, white only 65c

2322. Bunch of two sprays made of fine fancy fruit, covered with chenille, leaves and grasses, assorted colors, 85c

2323. Bunch of two sprays, made of half closed dasies, small flowers, leaves and grasses $1 00

2324. Handsome cluster of drooping satin blossoms mixed with fine piquets, wheat and satin leaves, assorted colors, $1 00

2326. Very fine monture of dandelions mixed with plush and satin leaves, yellow only, 93c

2327. Bridal Wreath, including ear drops, breastpin and bouquet, price, $1 00, 1 35, 1 50, 1 75, 2 00, 2 50, 3 50 to 5 00

2328. Handsome spray of satin rose, half blown rose buds, fine French piquets and leaves, assorted colors $1 19

2325. Handsome cluster of satin lilacs, sweet pea blossoms, fine piquets, natural leaves, assorted colors. . 93c

2329. Elegant fruit monture mixed with velvet leaves and fine drooping piquets, assorted colors 85c

2330. Bunch of fine roses and buds in all shades.25c

2331, Cluster of fine blossoms, grasses and natural leaves, assorted colors . .63c

2332. Very fine spray of velvet and satin primroses, satin begonia leaves and French piquets, assorted colors, 98c

2333. Bunch of two sprays made of fine flowers, drooping blossoms, leaves and piquets, assorted colors $1 15

3334. Fine French Buds, in all shades, per dozen . 25c

ARTIFICIAL FLOWERS.

(Not Illustrated.)

2335. Roses, all colors, each, 4c; per dozen, . .47c
2336. " " " 10c; " $1 00
2337. " " " " . . . 15, 20 and 25c
2338. Rosebuds, large, all colors, per doz., 25, 40, 50, 60c
2339. Violets, double, yellow white and violet, 3 dozen for 45c
2340. Violets, single, 3 dozen for 45c
2341. Buttercups, soft stems, all colors, per doz. 10c
2342. Daisies, small, all colors, per dozen. . .15c
2343. Poppies, each, 4c; per dozen. 45c
2344. Moss, per package 15c
2345. Snow Balls, per bunch 25c

MOURNING FLOWERS.

2346. Mourning Flowers, per spray.
50, 75c, $1 00, 1 39 to 3 50
2347. Mourning Spray of black leaves, silk roses and buds . . . . . . $1 50, 1 75, 2 00, 2 50 and 3 50

2348. Mourning Spray of black silk wheat, with drooping jet . . . . $2 00, 2 25, 2 50 to 3 50
2349. Mourning Spray, consisting of jetted leaf, with jetted pique . . . $1 00, 1 25, 1 50, 1 75 to 2 50

MILLIMERY TRIMMINGS.

(Not Illustrated.)

We have a complete line of hat crownings, all the latest novelties, in straw, beige, yellow, black, cream and brown, on hand, very handsome and rich.

2350. Straw Crowning, 12 inches wide, per yard, $1 69
2351. Ribbed Gauze Cloth, silk crowning, 12 inches wide, very handsome, per yard . . $1 69
2352. Plaid Straw Crowning, 9 inches wide, per yard 98c
2353. Porcupine Straw Cloth Crowning, 12 inches wide, all colors, per yard $1 69

2354. All Silk Ring Gauze Crowning, 9 inches wide, all colors, per yard $1

RIBBONS TO MATCH CROWNING, FOR BOWS, SAME COLORS.

2355. Silk Gauze, with raised cord effect, 2 inches wide, per yard 49c
2356. Porcupine Ribbon, 2 inches wide, all colors, per yard 49c
2357. Plaited Straw Ribbon, 2 inches wide, all colors, per yard 39c
2358. Ribbed Gauze Ribbon, all colors, per yard, 69c
2359. Striped Straw Ribbon, all colors, per yard, 29c
2360. Silk Ring Gauze Ribbon, 2 inches wide, per yard .39c
2361. A full line of hat cords, solid gold or silver or mixed tinsel with colors, per yard, 10, 15, 25c
2362. A complete line of gilt, silver and steel hat braids, per yard . . . . . . 15, 25 and 50c

NOTICE.—In order to forward fragile articles, such as Trimmed Hats, etc., by mail without getting crushed or damaged in the least we will pack them in tin boxes, which do not weigh any more than paper boxes, and will charge our patrons the ACTUAL COST PRICE for the same, from 15 to 25 cents, according to size. These tin boxes will also be found very useful in the household.

FANS.

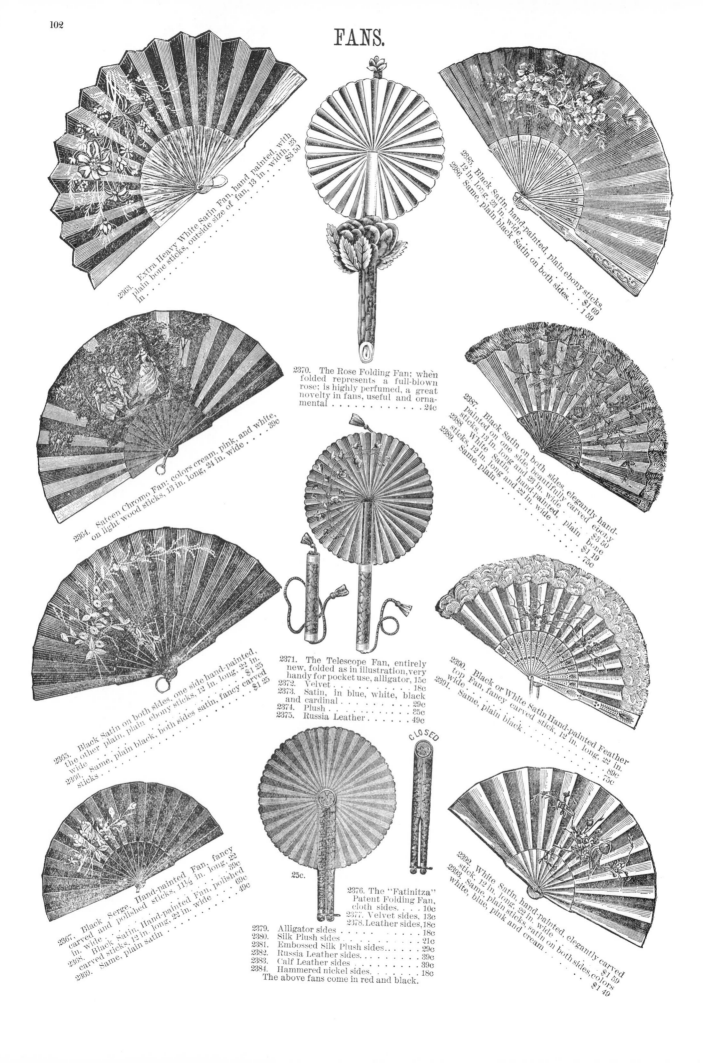

2363. Extra Heavy White Satin Fan, hand painted, with plain bone sticks, outside size of fan, 13 in. width, 23 in. $3.50

2364. Sateen Chromo Fan: colors cream, pink, and white, on light wood sticks, 13 in. long, 24 in. wide 39c

2365. Black Satin on both sides, one side hand-painted, the other plain, plain ebony sticks, 12 in. long, 22 in. wide $1.25
2366. Same, plain black, both sides satin, fancy carved sticks $1.25

2367. Black Serge, Hand-painted Fan, fancy carved and polished sticks, 11½ in. long, 22 in. wide 39c
2368. Black Satin, Hand-painted Fan, polished carved sticks, 12 in. long, 22 in. wide 69c
2369. Same, plain satin 49c

2370. The Rose Folding Fan; when folded represents a full-blown rose; is highly perfumed, a great novelty in fans, useful and ornamental 24c

2371. The Telescope Fan, entirely new, folded as in illustration, very handy for pocket use, alligator, 15c
2372. Velvet 18c
2373. Satin, in blue, white, black and cardinal 29c
2374. Plush 25c
2375. Russia Leather 49c

2376. The "Fatinitza" Patent Folding Fan, cloth sides 10c
2377. Velvet sides, 13c
2378. Leather sides, 18c
2379. Alligator sides 18c
2380. Silk Plush sides 21c
2381. Embossed Silk Plush sides 29c
2382. Russia Leather sides 39c
2383. Calf Leather sides 39c
2384. Hammered nickel sides 18c
The above fans come in red and black.

CLOSED

25c.

2385. Black Satin, hand painted, plain ebony sticks, 13 in. long, 23 in. wide $1.69
2386. Same, plain black Satin on both sides . . . 1 59

2387. Black Satin on both sides, elegantly hand-painted on one side, beautifully carved ebony sticks, 13 in. long and 22 in. wide . . . plain $3.50
2388. White Satin, hand-painted, plain bone sticks, 12 in. long and 22 in. wide $1 19
2389. Same, plain 75c

2390. Black or White Satin Hand-painted Feather top Fan, fancy carved stick, 12 in. long, 22 in. wide 89c
2391. Same, plain black 75c

2392. White Satin, hand-painted, elegantly carved stick, 12 in. long, 22 in. wide $1 59
2393. Same, plain satin sticks, satin on both sides, colors white, blue, pink and cream $1 49

Men's, Youths' and Boys' Clothing.

Regular sizes for men are from 34 to 44 breast measures; for youths 33 to 37 breast, and boys 4 to 13 years of age. Extra sizes will cost a proportionate advance.

Rules for Self-Measurement.
Take measure with great care, and give the correct height and weight.

FOR A PAIR OF PANTS.

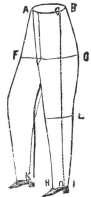

Inches

1. From A to B round the waist...........
2. From C to D top to bottom ....
3. From center of fork, close up, down to K for length of leg inside, keeping the leg straight down........... ....
4. F to G round the seat....................
5. L round the knee.. ....
6. From H to I round the bottom..... ....

FOR A COAT.

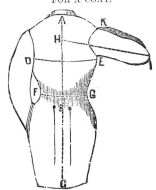

Take these measures outside the Coat.

Inches

7. From A to B................. ....
8. Continuing on to C for length... .... ..
9. From H to I for elbow joint........ ...
10. Continuing on to K for length of sleeves, Take these measures under the Coat.
11. From D to E round the breast.........
12. From F to G round the waist...........

FOR A VEST.

13. Height.........................inches
14. Weight.... ....lbs.

Take these measures over the Vest.

Inches

15. From 1 at center of back of neck round the inside edge of the collar to height required for top button................
16. From top button to 2,for length in front.
17. From 3 to 4 round the breast..... ...
18. From 5 to 6 round waist...............

Fig. 1. 2400 to 2402. Fig. 2. 2403 to 2407. Fig. 3. 2408 to 2411. Fig. 4. 2412 to 2413. Fig. 5. 2415 to 2417.

Fig. 1. 2400. Boys' Jersey Suit, laced with silk cord in Navy Blue.

| Size | 4 | 6 | 8 | 10 | 12 years. |
Price $3.00 3.50 4.00 4.50 5.00 each.

2401. Jersey Suit with sailor collar, trimmed with blue Hercules braid, one of the most stylish suits of the season.

Size 4 6 8 10 12 years.
Price $3.25 3.80 4.45 5.05 5.70 each.

2402. Boys' Jersey Suits, made of the finest imported jersey cloth, buttoned down front.
Size 4 6 8 10 12 years.
Price $5.00 5.60 6.20 6.80 7.60 each.

Fig. 2. 2403. "The Webster," plaited back and front, with belt, well-made and very nobby, satinet in dark mixtures...................$2.25
2404. Fancy Union Cassimere, gray and brown, mixed............ ....$3.00

2405. Imported Twilled Cassimeres, all wool, gray and brown.............. ....$4.75
2406. Blue Cheviots, all wool...............$5.50
2407. Corduroy, colors, blue, brown and drab; will be very stylish this season......... ...$6.50

Notice.

A pocket dictionary, handsomely bound in cloth will be presented to every purchaser of the Webster Suit.

Fig. 3 2408. "The O K" suit, knife plaited, front and back; very stylish and elegantly made; suitable for boys from 4 to 13 years of age, brown and gray mixed cottonade. ...$2.25
2409. Union Cassimeres, brown and gray plaids $3.00.
2410. Fine all-wool cassimeres, in gray, brown and garnet, plaid checks, also Oxford mixtures, $4.00
2411. Gray and brown, Scotch tweeds $5.00

Fig. 4. 2412. "The Webster Norfolk" suit, a nobby suit for school wear, suitable for boys from 4 to 13 years of age; made of the best materials, and the very best workmanship. Fancy Union Cassimeres, all dark mixtures, $3.00
2413. All-wool Domestics, Cassimeres, grays, browns, and an immense assortment of patterns.......................................$4.00
2414. Imported all-wool Cheviot, color blue $5.00

Notice.
A Webster pocket dictionary given to every purchaser of the above suit.

Fig. 5. 2415. The "Rough and Ready" a school suit, single breasted, round or square bottom and buttoned high.; so well made that the most careless boy will find it difficult to wear out the suit. Union Cassimere brown and gray plaids and mixtures... ....$3.25
2416. All-wool Cheviots and tweeds........$4.00
2417. All-wool and silk mixtures $6.00
2418. Indigo blue pontusic flannel..........$6.00
2419. Slater's blue tricots...................$7.00

Fig. 6. 2420 to 2423.   Fig. 7. 2424 to 2427.   Fig. 8. 2428 to 2430.   Fig. 9. 2431 to 2434.   Fig, 10. 2435 to 2440.

Fig. 6. 2420. "New Brunswick," a beautifully made suit with corded plaits back and front, new this season; age, 4 to 13 years; union cassimeres in a large variety of plaids and mixtures.....................................$3 50
2421. All wool and silk mixed.. .. .. .. 5 00
2422. Worsted Diagonals for dress, blue, black and brown...............................$7 50
2423. Silk and wool pin checks, very fine $9 00
Fig. 7. 2424. Norfolk Suit with belt, a beautiful suit for dress, made in the most stylish manner and of the best materials, suitable for a boy 4 to 13 years of age; fine imported worsteds, blue gray and brown..................$8 50
2425. Corkscrews, all wool, blue, black and brown, fast colors..................$7 00
2426. Imported Corduroys, gray, blue and brown.............................$10 00
2427. Velveteen, bound with silk braid, blue, black and brown $10 00

Fig. 8. 2428. The "Newport," a neat suit made of all wool, dressy mixtures; age, 4 to 13 years; union cassimeres, in brown plaids, $3 25
2429. Fine all wool twilled cassimeres, brown, gray and light gray..... ....$4 00
2430. All wool Cheviots, blue and brown.... 6 00

Fig. 9. 2431. Imported Worsteds, fine diagonals, back, blue and brown...... ....$9 00
2432. The "O. K. Norfolk" a very pretty suit, slightly different than the Webster, fancy union cassimeres............. ....$3 25
2433. All-wool Cassimeres, brown and gray, 30 different patterns................ ... .$4 50
2434. Blue, all-wool Tricot.................$6 00

Fig. 10. 2435. Sailor Suit, blue, brown and gray, cottonade.. ... .$1 50

2436. Union Cassimeres. brown and gray. $2 00
2437. Blue Flannel, fast colors, embroidered collar...........................$2 50 and 3 00
2438. Fancy Plaid Cassimeres, embroidered collars................................$3 50
2439. Gray and Brown Tricot, embroidered collar.....................................$4 50
2440. Middlesex Flannel, embroidered collar, $4 75

The above prices are for plain suits only; same, with box plaited blouse, 25c extra, or knife plaited, 50c extra.

Notice.

A patch piece for mending is sent with every one of our boys' and children's suits.

When ordering clothing for children from 3 to 11 years of age, it is only necessary to state the age, and whether large or small according to age

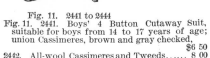

Fig. 11. 2441 to 2444

Fig. 11. 2441. Boys' 4 Button Cutaway Suit, suitable for boys from 14 to 17 years of age; union Cassimeres, brown and gray checked, $6 50
2442. All-wool Cassimeres and Tweeds...... 8 00
2443. Blue Flannel, all wool ..$6 50, 8 00 and 9 00
2444. Fine Worsted Diagonals, blue, black and brown .... $10 00 and 12 00
Youths' sizes, 33 to 37 breast, $2 00 extra.
Fig. 12. 2445. Boys' School Suit, with Norfolk jacket; age, 14 to 17 years; satinette......$6 00

Fig. 12. 2445 to 2450.   Fig. 13. 2451 to 2456.
2446. Union Cassimeres............... ......$7 50
2447. All-wool Cassimeres............. ...... 9 00
2448. Fine Tweeds and Cheviots...........$11 00
2449. Norfolk Jacket, separate......$4 00 to 6 50
Youths' sizes, 33 to 37 breast, $1 50 extra.

Fig. 13. 2451. Boys' Single Breasted Sack Suits, round or square corners; age, 14 to 17 years; union Cassimeres, plaids and pin checks...$4 50
2452. All-wool Cassimeres, brown and gray mixtures.................................$7 00
2453. Silk and Wool mixtures, gray and brown, $9 00
2454. Blue, brown and black corkscrews, $12 00 and 14 00

Fig. 14. 2457 to 2461.
2555. Blue Flannel·······......$6 50, 8 50 and $10 00
Youths' sizes 33 to 37 breast measure, $2 00 extra
Fig. 14. 2457. Boys' Fly Front Overcoat; age, 13 to 18 years; union cassimeres.............$4 50
2458. All-wool Cassimeres...............$6 00
2459. Home-spun................. .... 8 00
2460. Kerseys, brown and gray $10 00
2461. Diagonals, black. brown and gray.....12 00
2462. Youths' sizes, 33 to 37 breast, $10 00 extra

924 TO 928 THIRD AVE., AND 160 TO 164 EAST 56th St., NEW YORK.

105

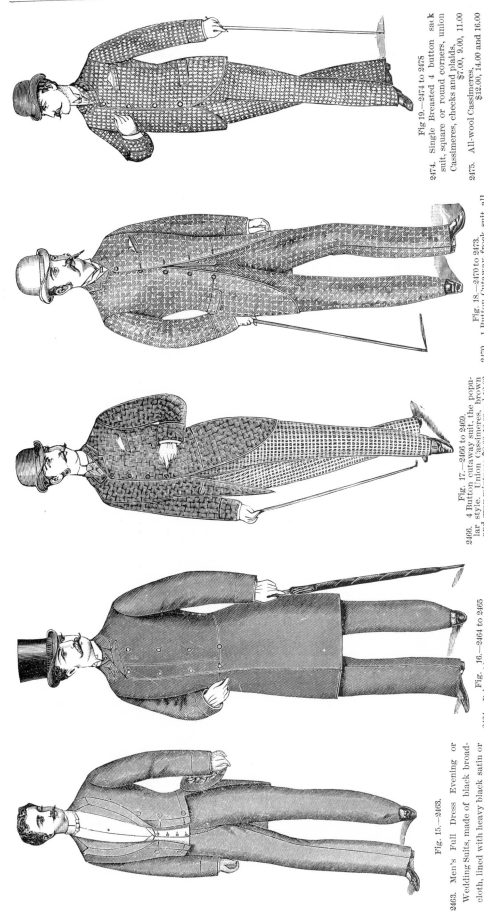

Fig. 15.—2463.

2463. Men's Full Dress Evening or Wedding Suits, made of black broadcloth, lined with heavy black satin or serge $28.00, 30.00, 35.00, 40.00

N. B.—In ordering the above, please exercise great care in giving measurements, so as to avoid errors.

SUITS. Not Illustrated.

2479. Skeleton Sack Suits, coat made with lapseams, without lining. Blue Flannel Pontonsuc Mills, ... $10.00
24·0. Blue Flannel Slater Mills. $12.00
2481. Blue Flannel Middlesex Mills. $13.00
2482. Blue Serges, ... $12.00
2483. Uniform Suits, Grand Army, double breasted, fly and eyelets, ... $12.00 and 14.00
2484. Conductors, single breasted, fly and eyelets . . . . . $12.00 and 14.00
2485. Fat Men's Suits, 40 to 50 breast measure all wool cassimeres and cheviots, brown and gray mixtures . . . . . $11.00 to 24.00

Fig. 16.—2464 to 2465

2464. Prince Albert suits in black, blue and brown diagonals and corkscrews, ... $15.00, 17.50, 20.00 and 25.00
2465. Wide Wale diagonals, *new*, black and blue, ... $17.00 and $30.00 Silk faced extra. . . . . . $2.00 The coat and vest can be furnished without the pants *less ¼* the price of suit.

Fig. 17.—2466 to 2469.

2466. 4 Button cutaway suit, the popular style. Union Cassimeres, brown and gray mixtures $8.00, 10.00 and 12.00
2466a. All-wool Cassimeres, ... $13.00, 14.00, 15.00 and 17.00
2466b. Imported Cassimeres in plaids and checks . . . . . $18.00, 20.00 and 22.00
2467. All-wool Corkscrews, ... $12.50, 15.00, 18.00 and 20.00
2468. Imported worsted, Diagonals and Corkscrews, $20.00, 23.00 and 25.00
2469. Blue Flannel, ... $10.00, 12.00, 14.00 and 16.00

COATS. Not Illustrated.

2486. Blue Flannel . . . . . $14.00 to 18.00 A liberal discount on large orders for conductors and uniform suits.
2487. Clergymen's Coat, best black cloth. . . . . . $16.00 and 18.00
2488. Knight Templar's Coats. . . . . . $15.00, 17.00 and 19.00 A liberal discount allowed on large orders.

Fig. 18.—2470 to 2473.

2470. 1 Button Cuttaway frock suit, all wool cassimere $9.00, 11.00 and 13.00
24f1. Corkscrew, blue, brown and black $11.00, 15.00 and 18.00
24f2. Wide Wale Diagonals. . . . . . $20.00 and 23.00
2473. English Mohair. $23.00

ALPACA COATS.

2489. Black Alpaca. . . . . . $1.35 and 1.50
2490.   "   "   silk finish. . . . . . $2.00 and 3.00
2491.   "   "   warp. . . . . . $3.50 and 4.50
2492. Striped and checked mohair. $2.50
2493. Linen Coats, ... $1.00, 1.25 and 2.00

Fig 19.—2474 to 2478

2474. Single Breasted 4 button sack suit, square or round corners, union Cassimeres, checks and plaids. $7.00, 9.00, 11.00
2475. All-wool Cassimeres $12.00, 14.00 and 16.00
2476. Corkscrews, blue, brown, gray and black, ... $12.00, 15.00, 17.00
2477. Blue Flannel, ... $8.00, 10.00, 12.00
2478. Fine Imported Worsteds, $18.00, 20.00 and 24.00

ALPACA AND LINEN DUSTERS.

2494. Linen Dusters. . . . . . $1.25, 1.75 and 2.25
2495. Gray Mohair Dusters. . . . . . $2.50 and 3.00
2496. Drab   "   Ulsters. . . . . . $3.00 and 3.50

SEERSUCKER SUITS.

2497. 50 different patterns of shrunk seersucker checks and plaids. . . . . . $3.25 and 2.75
2498. Coat and vest, ... $2.00 and 2.75
2499. Boys' Seersucker coats, large variety of patterns. $1.35

LINEN SUITS.

2500. All Linen . . . . . $3.75, 4.50 and 5.00
2501. Blue and brown Marseilles. $4.50

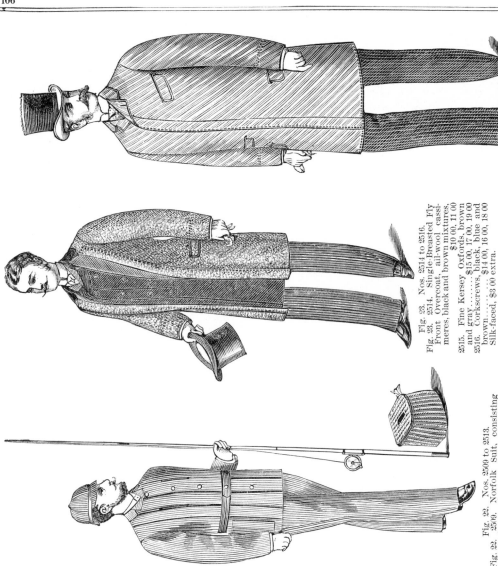

Fig. 24. Nos. 2517 to 2521.

Fig. 24. 2517. Men's Single-Breasted Long Roll Spring Overcoats of wool diagonals and cassimeres. $5 50

2518. Union Cassimeres, brown and gray..........$8 00

2519. Corkscrews, brown and gray..........$10 00

2520. All-Wool Kerseys, silk-faced, gray and brown..........$14 00

2521. All-Wool Diagonal, silk faced, blue and black..........$16 00

Fig. 23. Nos. 2514 to 2516.

Fig. 23. 2514. Single-Breasted Fly Front Overcoat, all-wool cassimeres, black and brown mixtures. $10 00, 11 00

2515. Fine Kersey Oxfords, brown and gray..........$15 00, 17 00, 19 00

2516. Corkscrews, black, blue and brown..........$14 00, 16 00, 18 00

Silk-faced, $3 00 extra.

PANTALOONS.

2522. Union Cassimeres, in stripes, hairlines, etc..........$2 00, 2 50

2523. All-Wool Cassimeres, stripes, check and plaids, $3 00, 3 50, 4 00, 4 50

2524. Fancy Worsteds, stripes and plaids..........$5 00, 5 50, 6 00

2525. Chevoits, black and blue,..........$3 50, 4 25

2526. Diagonals and Corkscrews, blue, brown and black,..........$5 00, 5 50, 6 00

2527. Black Doeskin, for full dress,..........$5 00, 5 50

2528. Blue Flannel, $4 50, 5 00, 5 50

2529. Fat Men's Pantaloons, 40 to 48 waist, 30 to 34 inseam, $2 75 to 6 00

Fig. 22. Nos. 2509 to 2513.

Fig. 22. 2509. Norfolk Suit, consisting of jacket and pants, all-wool cassimeres, brown and gray..........$6 00

2510. Chevoits, blue, brown and gray. ..$7 00

2511. Middlesex, blue flannel..........$9 00

2512. Scotch Tweeds..........$10 00

2513. English Mohair, blue, brown and gray..........$10 00

PANTALOONS.

2530. Separate Long Pants for boys and youths, of mixed and striped cassimeres, ages 2 to 17 years. ..$2 00, 2 50, 3 00, 3 50

2531. Boys' Short Pants, ages 4 to 13 years, dark mixed cottonades..........65c

2532. Union Cassimeres..........$1 00, 1 50

2533. All-Wool Cassimeres..........$2 00, 2 50

2534. Corduroy, blue, brown, gray, $2 00

2535. Corkscrew, blue, brown, black, $2 25

Fig. 21. Nos. 2506 to 2508.

Fig. 21. 2506. Long Roll Cutaway Suits, very stylish, fine wool and silk mixtures... $16 00, 20 00, 24 00

2507. Wide Wale Diagonals, blue and black......$17 00, 21 00, 26 00

2508. Imported Worsted Diagonals, blue.. ......$18 00, 20 00, 24 00

NORFOLK JACKETS.

Fig. 20. Nos. 2503 to 2505.

This suit comes only in the best quality of goods.

Fig. 20. 2503. Long Roll Sack Suit of all-wool cassimeres, fancy plaids and mixtures,
..........$15 00, 20 00, 25 00

2504. Fine Diagonals, blue, brown and gray, $16 00, 18 00, 21 00, 23 00

2505. Imported Tricots, black and blue.. ....$20 00, 24 00, 28 00

NORFOLK JACKETS.

2536. Shrunk Seersuckers, checked..........$2 50

2537. Silk Mohair, checks and plaids..........$2 75, 3 50

2538. Blue and Brown Serge.. ....$4 50, 6 00

2539. Fancy Cassimeres.. . ...$4 50, 5 50

924 TO 928 THIRD AVE., AND 160 TO 164 EAST 56th St., NEW YORK.

107

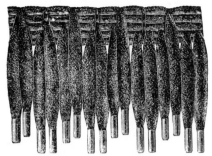

2644. 4 row leech pattern, all silk chenille fringe, 5 inches deep, with chenille heading and jet bugle ends; black, per yard 69c
2645. Black, with natural wood bead ends, per yard, 79c
2646. Same, all colors, without bugle ends, per yard, 69c

2647. Silk tape mourning Fringe, 4½ inches wide, per yard 65c

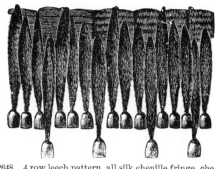

2648. 4 row leech pattern, all silk chenille fringe, chenille heading and bell shape jet ends. 5½ inches deep, black only, very handsome and heavy, per yard $1.29

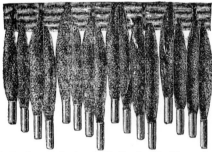

2649. 4 row extra heavy all silk chenille fringe, chenille heading and jet bugle ends 6 inches deep, black only, per yard 89c
2650. Same, with natural wood rosary bead ends, black, per yard $1.19

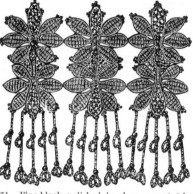

2651. Fine black polished bead ornament trimming, with satin cord and jet drops, 6½ inches deep, per yard $1.39

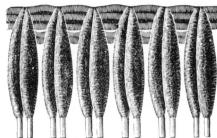

2652. 2 row leech pattern, all silk chenille fringe, with chenille heading and jet bugle ends, 4½ inches deep, black only, per yard 49c

2653. Black satin cord bead passementerie 3 inches wide, per yard. 39c

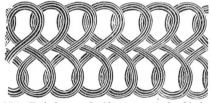

2654. Entirely new braid passementerie, black, seal brown, navy blue and bottle green, 3 inches wide, per yard 69c

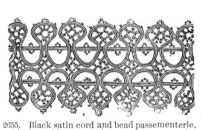

2655. Black satin cord and bead passementerie, 3 inches wide, per yard 25c

2656. Plain black satin cord passementerie, 2 inches wide, per yard 35c

2657. Wood bead and silk galoon, seal brown, with natural wood beads entirely new and very fashionable, 1¾ inches wide, per yard $1.19
2658. Same, 2½ inches wide, per yard $1.49

2659. Plain black satin cord passementerie, 2¼ inches wide, per yard 49c

2660. Plain black satin cord passementerie, 2½ inches wide, per yard 59c

2663. Silk bead galoon trimming, entirely new, with cut jet drops, 2 inches wide, in black $1.29
2664. Same, with plain drops, per yard $1.29
2665. Same, brown, bronze and green beads, per yard . . . $3.49

2662. Black satin cord passementerie, heavily beaded with large and small beads, very stylish, 2½ inches, per yard 89c

2661. Black satin cord and all bead passementerie, with cut beads in centre, very heavy and rich, 2½ inches wide, per yard $1.19

2666. Black satin cord and bead passementerie, studded with cut jet nail heads, very rich, 2¾ inches wide, per yard $1.69

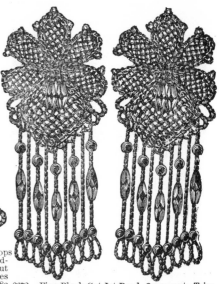

2667. Fine Black Cut Jet Bead Ornament Trimming, made entirely of beads, very rich, 7 in. deep, per yard................ ....$2 69

2668. Cut Bead Drops with 5 fine hollow cut beads, 3 inches long, each......14c
2669. Per doz..$1 49

2670. Cut Bead Tassel Drops with fine cut bead ball heading and 4 fine hollow cut beads at bottom, 2¾ inches long, each 8c
2671. Per dozen ... .75c

2672. Fine Black Cut Jet Bead Ornament Trimming, made entirely of beads, very rich, 6½ inches deep, per yard.... ... .$2 98

2677. Black Beaded Ball ,Drops, very fashionable, per dozen..... ...25c
2678. Same, of plain black silk, round or oblong, per gross, $1 00; per dozen........10c
2679. Same, colored silk, per gross, $1 50; per doz.15c
2680. Colors to order, per gross, $2 00; per doz.20c

2675. Black Silk twisted cord and chenille ornaments, with beaded ends, 6 inches long, each....35c
2676. All colors, each.........39c

2681.Black twisted silk cord and chenille ornaments, with beaded ends, 5 inches long, each........25c
2682. All colors, each.......35c

2683. Very Rich and Fancy Fourageur made of silk and satin cords 10 inches wide, black...............$1 40
2684. Same, in colors...............$1 50

2673. All-Silk Hussar Ornament,worn military style, very fashionable, black 89c
2674. Same, in seal brown, navy blue, bottle green, garnet and slate....... ....$1 29

2687. Black Twisted Silk Cord and Chenille Fourageur, with bead ends.... ....59c
2688. All colors, each........... ....65c

2688a. Black Silk Twisted Cord and Chenille Fourageur, with jet bead ends, very rich, each 75c
2688b. All colors............... ....85c

2685. Plain Silk Cord Loops 8 inches long, black, each...19c

2686. Beaded Satin Cord Loops, 7 inches long each..15c

PARASOL COVERS.

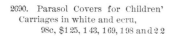

2690. Parasol Covers for Children' Carriages in white and ecru, 98c, $1 25, 1 43, 1 69, 1 98 and 2 2

2691 Oriental Lace Covers in white and ecru,........$2 75, 3 25 and 4 75

2692. Ladies all Spanish Parasol Covers in black, white and ecru, $2 25, $2 98 and 3 25

2693. Ecsurial Lace Covers, black, white and ecru....$2 59, 3 15 and 4 25

2694. All Silk Spanish Lace Covers white.................$3 75, 4 95, 5 75

2689. Beaded Satin Cord Loops, 8 inches long, each.............. .18c

PARASOLS.

Our assortment of Parasols and Sun Umbrellas is larger than that previously had, including the latest styles, shapes and shades.
The coaching and canopy top parasols as described below are the most fashionable this season. The coaching is a plain parasol with a heavy stick and can be had lined or unlined. The canopy top is entirely new, is a flat top with a dome shape inside, is very pretty and unique. There is no doubt, however, that the plain black parasol, trimmed with black Spanish lace, will be used extensively, also in fancy colors to match costumes with or without lace, and lace-covered parasols in black, cream or colored.
When ordering, please give us an idea of what you require, we will use our best judgment in the selection, which as a rule, gives great satisfaction.

COACHING PARASOLS

LYON'S PICADILLY PARASOLS.

2697. Lyon's celebrated Picadilly, 10 rib paragon frame, canopy top, dome shape inside, fine natural stick, plaited border of same material, cord and bone ring, changeable silk lining, which produces a very pretty effect, fine twilled silk, black only ...$6 50

2697a. Heavy Satin, in black, garnet, cardinal, bronze, blue, myrtle green, brown, cream and ecru.......................$7 50

2698. Same, in pongee.............. ...$7 50
2699. Heavy Black Gros Grain Silk, for mourning....... ....$8 50

MOURNING PARASOLS.

2700. Gros Grain Silk, coaching shape, 8 ribs, paragon frame, black ebony handles, ...$2 50

2701. Same, 10 ribs....... ....$3 50

2702. Gros Grain Silk, 10 ribs, paragon frame, silk lined, straight edge stitched, ebony handles...............................$3 75

2703. Same, trimmed with 3½ inch silk tape fringe....... .. ..$6 50

LYONS MIGNON PARASOLS.

2704. Lyon's Mignon, plain satin, dome shape inside, trimmed with 4 inch all silk Spanish guipure lace, silk lined, 10 ribs, paragon frame, black, cardinal, bronze, blue, plum, myrtle green, brown, cream and ecru.................................$5 99

2705. Same shape, very heavy black satin, trimmed with 4½ inch Spanish guipure lace, heavy silk lining. $6 89

2706. Same shape, extra heavy, best black satin, trimmed with 6 inch all silk Spanish guipure lace heavy silk lining...........................$10 00

2707. Plain Satin, 22 inches long, 8 ribs, gilt frame, natural wood handles, in black, navy blue, garnet, cardinal, brown, beige, green and myrtle...........97c
2708. Same, much better quality, same colors$1 39
2709. Same, changeable satin, plain satin borders, 10 ribs, colors as above.............$1 25
2710. Extra heavy plain satin, 10 rib paragon frame, colors as above $1 7
2711. Changeable Satin, same colors......$1 75
2712. Black Surah, with light or black wood handles, silk cord and tassels............$2 00
2713. Same XX heavy satin, canopy top, silk cord and tassels, colors as above..........$2 00
2714. Same XXX heavy satin, canopy top, colors as above. $2 50
2715. Same in pongee, 10 rib paragon frame, silk cord and tassels $2 00
2716. Better quality, pongee, lined, 10 rib paragon frame, bamboo stick, silk cord and tassel............$3 00
2717. Black Surah, for mourning. canopy top, 10 rib paragon frame, ebony handles, silk cord and tassel....$2 25
2718. Brocade Satin, navy blue, cardinal and black, 10 rib paragon frame, silk cord and tassel. $2 25
2719. Much better quality brocade satin, same colors.... ....$2 75
2720. Same, cardinal with Roman stripes, 10 rib paragon frame, very rich and stylish $2 75
2721. Same, in extra heavy brocade satin, navy blue and black grounds with cardinal squares, 10 rib paragon frame, one piece English stick, silk cord and tassel, entirely new this season.......$4 00
2722. Changeable Silk, colors cardinal, navy blue and garnet, with covers to match, 10 rib paragon frame, fancy English carved handles. $3 75

LYON'S LOUIS XV. PARASOLS.

2722a. Celebrated make of Lyon's fashionable parasols, entirely new, plain satin, coaching shape, 8 rib paragon frame, extra long handles, very light in weight, black, garnet, cardinal, bronze, blue, myrtle green, brown, cream and ecru, very popular style.....................$2 98
2723. Brocade Satins, black, garnet, cardinal, bronze, blue, myrtle green, brown, cream and ecru......................................$3 50
2724. Bayadore stripes, running from the tip of the rib to the stick, colors as above.........$5 98

SUN UMBRELLAS.

QUALITY X.

2725. Silk serge sun umbrellas .steel frames, natural sticks, 24 in. long, black only, quality X, assorted wood handles.$1 50
2726. Light horn handles.... 1 75
2727. Celluloid " .. 2 00
2728. Nickle plated " 2 00
2729. Ivory " 2 50
2730. Sterling Silver" 2 39
2731. Ebony, for mourning, 2 00

QUALITY XX.
PARAGON FRAMES.

2732. Assorted wood handles 2 00
2733. Light horn " 2 25
2734. Celluloid " 2 50
2735. Nickle plated " 2 50
2736. Ivory " 3 25
2737. Sterling Silver " 2 75
2738. Ebony, for mourning..2 50

QUALITY XXX.

Paragon Frame.
In colors brown, blue, black and green, extra heavy.

2739. Bamboo handles.....$2 50
2740. Light horn " 2 75
2741. Celluloid " 3 00
2742. Nickle plated" 3 00
2743. Ivory " 4 00
2744. Sterling Silver handles3 50
2745. Ebony, for mourning, 3 00

QUALITY XXXX.

2747. English Silk serge, in brown, blue, black and green, paragon frame, one piece English stick..................$3 50
2748. Light horn handles.... 4 00
2749. Celluloid " ... 4 50
2750. Sterling Silver" ... 5 00
2751. Double-faced silk serge sun umbrellas, paragon frame, black outside and red and blue inside, one piece English stick, 24 inch $2 75
2752. 26 inch............. $3 50
2752a. Same with sterling silver handles, 24 in. $3 95; 23 in. $4 50

Serge, Alapaca and Laventine Sun Umbrellas.

2753. Black Serge, 24 inch long, assorted wood handles.............59c
2754. Same, with bone handles...69c
2755. Black Alapaca, with one inch satin border, 24 inches long, assorted natural wood handles......$1 00
2756. Black Mohair, 24 inches long, with one inch satin border, assorted natural wood handles......$1 25
2757. Black worsted Zenilia with one inch satin border, 24 inches long, assorted natural wood handles...$1 25
2758. Black Union Silk Laventine, very strong and durable, 24 inches long, natural wood handles....$1 69
2759. Same, with black handles, for mourning...................$1 79
2760. Same, with pearl inlaid buffalo horn handles.................$1 89
2761. Special Sun Umbrella, black satin serge, very handsome and durable, entirely new this season and for sale by us only: 24 inches long, natural wood handles...$1 75
2762. Light horn handles........ 2 00
2763. Celluloid handles........ 2 25
2764. Ebony handles for mourning, ...$2 25

BLACK BROCADE SILK PARSOLS.

2765. Black brocade silk parasol, lined, black or cardinal silk cord and tassel, *without lace*, 10 rib gilt paragon frame, fancy carved wood handles.................................... $3.50

2766. Same, with 5-inch all silk Spanish guipure lace... .... $4.75

2767. Black brocade silk, 10 rib paragon frame, fancy carved wood handles, lined with cardinal, garnet or blue all silk changeable linings, or plain black or white trimmed 4½ inch silk escurial lace silk cord and tassel...... ....$6.50

COLORED SATIN PARASOLS.

2768. Heavy satin; 10 rib paragon frame, ecru, cream beige, cardinal and navy blue, trimmed with 5-inch cream color all silk spanish guipure lace, changeable silk linings, canopy top, silk cord and tassels, fancy carved wood handles..... ... ...$5.00

MISSES' COACHING PARASOLS.

2769. Plain satin colors, garnet, cardinal, light and navy blue, 15-inches long, fancy carved wood sticks................................$1.00

2770. Same, with blue or red checked satin $1 25

2771. Same, with fancy metal ring top......$1.39

2772. Plain heavy satin, colors, garnet, cardinal, light and navy blue, 10 rib, fancy carved handles, 15 inches long........................$1.39

2773. Extra heavy satin, same colors, 10 rib paragon frame, 17 inches long.................$1.69

2774. Same, in checked satin, colors, blue or cardinal.............................$1.85

BLACK SATIN PARASOLS, LACE TRIMMED.

2775. Black satin, with either black or cardinal lining, trimmed with 4½ inch silk Spanish lace, silk cord and tassels, assorted fancy wood handles.......... ....$2.25

2776. Same, heavier satin....................$2.50

2777. Good satin, trimmed with 4½ inch all silk spanish lace, 10 rib gilt frame, black or cardinal, lined with silk cord and tassel..... ....$2.69

2778. Black satin surah, black or cardinal lined, trimmed with 4½ inch all silk Spanish guipure lace, 10 rib paragon gilt frame, fancy carved wood handles, silk cord and tassels.......$3.50

2779. Heavy black satin, lined in black, cardinal or white, trimmed with 4½ inch all silk Spanish guipure lace, 10 rib gilt frame, fancy carved wood handles, silk cord and tassels......$3.50

2780. Black silk surah, lined in cardinal, black or white, trimmed with 4½ inch all silk spanish guipure lace, canopy top, 10 rib gilt frame, fancy carved wood handles, silk cord and tassel.......................................$4.00

2781. Heavy black satin, with cardinal, garnet or blue changeable silk linings, or plain black or white, trimmed with 4½ inch all silk Spanish guipure lace, 10 rib gilt paragon frame, fancy carved wood handles, silk cord and tassel $4.25

2782. Same, extra heavy black satin.......$5.00

2783. XX heavy black satin, lined with colors as above, trimmed with 5 inch heavy all silk Spanish guipure lace, canopy top, 10 rib paragon frame, fancy carved wood handles, silk cord and tassel.... ....$6.00

2784. XXX extra heavy black satin, lined as above, trimmed with 4½ inch all silk escurial lace, 10 rib paragon frame, imported fancy carved wood handles, silk cord and tassel; this parasol is very rich and stylish and is as good as any sold last season for $12.00; each.......$9.00

N. B.—Any of the above can be had with black handles for mourning.

PLAIN BLACK SATIN PARASOLS.

2785. Plain black satin parasols, with pinked edge, unlined, 20 inches long, assorted natural wood handles. $1.00

2786. Same, lined.....................$1.50

2787. Black satin, pinked edge, black or cardinal lined, 20 inches long, gilt rib, assorted fancy wood handles, silk cord and ring.........$1.75

2788. Heavy black satin, pinked edge, black or cardinal lined 10 rib paragon frame with gilt or black ribs, assorted fancy wood handles, silk cord and tassel............................$2.50

2789. Same, in extra heavy satin...........$3.50

2790. Black surah satin, black or cardinal lining, pinked edge, 20 inches long, gilt frame, assorted carved wood handles, silk cord and tassel $2.50

2791. Same, 10 rib paragon frame..........$3.25

N. B.—Any of the above can be had with black handles for mourning.

SATIN PARASOLS WITH SILK LACE COVERS.

2792. Heavy black satin, with all silk Spanish lace covers, with cardinal, garnet or blue, changeable silk linings, or plain or black or white; 10 rib paragon frame, fancy carved wood handles, silk cord and tassel.............$6.50

2793. Extra heavy black satin, with all silk escurial lace covers, linings as above, 10 rib paragon frame, fancy carved wood handles, silk cord and tassel..................¿9.50

N. B.—The above two styles can be had in cream at same prices.

MISSES' AND CHILDREN'S PARASOLS.

2794. Misses' figured sateen parasols, colors, blue and cardinal, assorted wood handles, 9 inches.....................................25c

2795. Same, 11 inches........................33c

2796. Same, 14 inches 39c

2797. Misses' plain satin parasols, colors, blue, pink and cardinal, white handles, 9 inch....65c

2798. Same, 11 inches.........................85c

2799. " 14 " $1.19

2800. Figured satin, colors as above, 14 inches long.......................................85c

2801. Same, with china silk lining, 14 inches long, $1.65

PONGEE SILK PARASOLS.

2802. Pongee silk parasols, trimmed with 5 inch silk Spanish guipure lace, lined to match, 10 rib gilt frame, silk cord and tassels, bamboo handles.... ....·......... $3.00

2803. Better quality, canopy top............$4.00

2804. Same with fine imorted fancy carved handles. $5 00

2805. Same, brocaded pongee, entirely new, trimmed with 5 inch Spanish Guipure lace, changeable silk lining all colors, 10 rib paragon frame, fine carved wood stick, silk cord and tassel, very handsome and stylish........$6.00

LACE PARASOL COVERS.

N. B.—For illustrations and prices of parasol covers, refer to page **108**.

UMBRELLAS.

School Umbrellas.

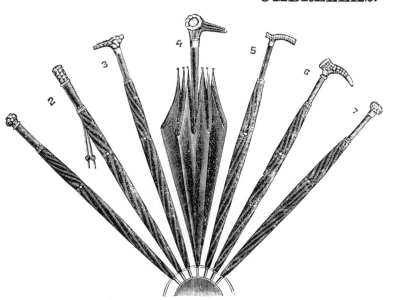

2806. **No. 1.** 26 inch, all Silk Serge, Paragon Fame, genuine Sterling Silver Knob......$2 29
2807. No. 2. 26 inch, heavy Silk Serge, Paragon Frame, genuine Sterling Silver Knob....$2 89
2808. No. 3. 26 inch, all Silk Serge, Paragon Frame, with Buck Horn Shape, genuine
Sterling Silver Handle, with Gold band 4 98
2809. No. 4. 26 inch, all Silk Serge, Paragon Frame, genuine Buck Horn handle.......... 3 98
2810. No. 5. 26 inch, all Silk Serge, Paragon Frame, genuine Sterling Silver handle...... 4 69
2811. No. 6. 26 inch, extra heavy English Twilled Silk, Paragon Frame, Buck Horn
shaped handle of genuine Sterling Silver.. 7 69
2812. No. 7. 26 inch, all Silk Serge, Paragon Frame, genuine Sterling Silver knob........ 2 49
N. B. Any of the above can be had in 28 inch, $1.00 extra.

2813.	Gingham, 24-inch...................................45c
2814.	Zenella, 24-inch.................... ....59c
2815.	Alpaca, 24-inch $1 00
2816.	Satina, 24 inch....................................1 25
2817.	Silk, 26-inch......................$2 25, 2 50 and 3 50

(UMBRELLAS NOT ILLUSTRATED.)

2818. Gingham, natural wood handle, 26-inch, 50c; 28-
inch...69c
2819. Zenella, natural wood handle, 26-inch 69c; 28inch..79c
2820. Waterproof, natural wood handle, 26-inch, 69c; 28-
inch...79c
2821. Satina, natural wood handle, 26-inch, $1 50 and 2 00
28-inch...................................$1 75 and 2 25
2822. Alapaca, natural wood handle, 26-inch, $1 25, 1 50 and
2 00; 28-inch.............. ....$1 50, 1 75 and 2 25
2823. Mohair, natural handle, 26-inch, $3 00; 28-inch....$3 50
2824. Silk, English stick, 26-inch, $1 98, 2 25, 2 50, 3 00, 4 00
and 5 00: 28-inch...................$3 50, 5 00 and 6 00
2825. Silk, celluloid handle, 26-inch.... ....$4 69

Intials engraved on handles, 25c.. per letter.

CANES.

For prices refer to previous catalogue. Prices and description cheerfully furnished.

BABY CARRIAGES.

. Very handsome reed body, upholstered in sateen, with ribbon
rawn through, nickle plated rod, satin parasol, with lace edge, the
unning gear of selected ash, shaved spoke wheels, best steel
springs...$15 00

Other Baby Carriages.

7. Reed bodies, upholstered in Rama selesia, parasol.....$6 19
8. Fine Rattan Carriage, lined in silk plush, extra quality, satin
parasol with lace edge, ribbon drawn through, (refer to cut on
page 151). This is one of the finest rattan bodies that can be
had... ....$25 00

2829. Baby Carriages, upholstered throughout in fancy figured goods fluted and
rolled back, panel and beaded body, continuous nickel plated rail, highly
ornameted and finished..$11 50

A full line of Carriages constantly on hand. Illustrations and Prices cheerfully furnished on application.

Upholstery Fringes.

Upholstery Fringes can only be had in the following combination of Colors: viz., shaded reds, olive and cardinal, olive and peacock, peacock and red, old gold and cardinal, olive and cardinal, gold and cardinal and all upholstery colors; we cannot furnish the fringes in solid colors but they can be made to order at an additional cost of 50 per cent. above schedule prices.

2900. Heavy Worsted Bullion Fringe, 4 inches wide, per yard.............. ....12c

2903. Worsted Upholstery Fringe, with all-silk tassels, mixed with gold tinsel; colors, all cardinal, cardinal and olive mixed, and cardinal and peacock blue mixed, 5 inches deep, entirely new and very rich, per yard... ....59c

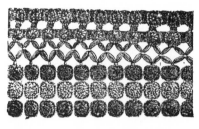

2906. Silk and Worsted Mixed Ball Fringe, mixed with gold tinsel, 4½ inches wide, per yard.....................................41c

2901. Worsted Ball and Silk Spike Fringe, 3½ inches deep, per yard.,... ....39c

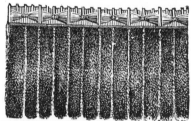

2904. Worsted Chenille Fringe, 3 inches wide, per yard, 10c; 4 inches.......... ....15c

2907. Worsted Fringe, mixed with gold tinsel 3 inches wide, per yard............... ..... 21c

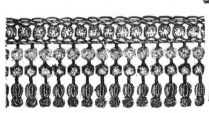

2902. Silk and Worsted Ball Fringe, mixed with gold tinsel and silk-covered ball ends, 4 inches wide, per yard.... ....39c

2905. All-Silk Upholstery Fringe, colors, peacock blue, old gold and cardinal mixed, olive, cardinal and peacock blue mixed, entirely new and very rich, per lyard................. .... 98c

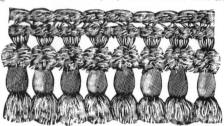

2908. Worsted Upholstery Fringe, with silk molds and mixed with tinsel colors, cardinal and old gold mixed, cardinal and peacock blue mixed, cardinal and olive mixed, 3½ inches deep, per yard........29c

Ornaments, Etc.

2909. Cotton Curtain Bands, all colors, each, 15c
2910. Silk   "   "   "   "   29c
2911. Silk Furniture Gimp, black and colored, piece of 36 yards, 75c; per dozen.............30c

2912. Plush Gimp, per piece of 36 yards, $2 25; per dozen..................................75c
Cord Tassels and Gimps, made for furniture, in any color,

2914. Heavy Silk Twisted Cord, for cushions, very soft, per yard..........................10c

Worsteds, Zephyrs, Etc.

2915. Shetland Floss, 12 oz. to the lb.; Black and white, per lb., 85c; per 2 oz. hank, 12c; all colors, per lb., 95c; per hank...............14c

ANGORA WOOL, ETC.

2916. Angora Wool, very soft and glossy for knitting hoods, shawls, etc., white and gray, per ball.....................................16c
2917. Crimped Wool or Fairy Zephyr,12 oz. to lb., black and white, per lb., $1 00; per hank of 2 oz......................................14c
2918. Colored, per lb., $1 15; per hank of 2 oz.,16c
2919. Pompadour Wool, all colors, per ball...13c
2920. Arrasene, in worsted; per dozen, 15c; 2 skeins for...................................3c
2921. Arrasene in silk, per dozen, 21c; per skein, 2c
2922. Germantown Wool, best quality, 16 oz. to the lb.; black and white, per lb., 75c; 2 oz. hank, 11c
2923. All colors, per lb., 85c; 2 oz hank........13c
2924. Ombre, per lb., 95c; 2 oz. hank...........14c
2925. Worsted, best quality Berlin Zephyr, in 2, 4, or 8 folds; or as some call, splits, single or double; weight, 8 oz., without paper, or 16 oz. full at double the price. Black and white, 75c per lb., or 5c per oz.; all colors. 90c per lb., per oz....................................6c
2926. Saxony Wool, 12 oz. in box; black and white per lb., 90c; per hank of 2 oz., 13c; all colors, per lb., $1 00; per hank...........14c
2927. German Knitting Wool, extra superfine quality, 16 oz. to the lb. Black and white, per lb., 95c; per 1-4 lb.....................25c
2928. Mixed, per lb., $1 00; per 1-4 lb..........25c
2929. All colors, per lb., $1 05; per 1-4 lb 27c

2930. Balmoral, per lb., $1 15; per 1-4 lb 30c
2931. Shetland Wool, 12 oz. to the lb. Black and white, per lb., 95c; per hank of 2 oz...... 13c
2932. All colors, per lb., $1 00; per hank of 2 oz...................................14c
2933. Cashmere Wool. 16 oz. to the lb. Black and white, per lb., $140; per hank of 2 oz....18c
2934. Colors, per lb., $1 50; 2 oz. hank........20c
2935. Black and white, per hank.............18c
2936. Colors..................................19c
2937. Crewel Wool, all colors, per skein, 3c; per dozen....................................30c
2938. Ice Wool, all colors, per box of 8 balls, 39c; per ball....................................5c

CHENILLE, ETC.

2939. For Embroidery, 3c skein, 33c per dozen; heavy, 18 yard pieces, all colors... '........23c
2940. Trimming, heavy, all colors, 10-yard piece, 45c; 5c per yard ; extra heavy 10-yard piece, 65c; per yard...............................7c
2941. Chenille Cord, per yard, 7c; per piece...63c
2942. Silk and Chenille Mixed Cord, all colors, per yard...................................10c

DEXTER KNITTING COTTON, 8 BALLS TO THE LB.

2943. Nos. 6, 8, 10, 12, per lb., 44c. ball.........6c
2944. Nos. 14 and 16, per lb., 48c; ball.........8c
2945. Nos. 18 to 30, per lb., 55c; ball...........8c
2946. All colors, per ball......................7c

MADONNA COTTON.

For Crocheting and Marking.
2947. Madonna Crochet Cotton, white and all colors, per ball............................5c

2949. Madonna Marking Cotton, all colors, per skein.....................................2c

EMBROIDERY SILK.

2950. Embroidery Silk, plain. white, black and colored, per dozen, 7c; per bunch of 25 skeins, 12c
2951. Shaded Embroidery Silk, 2 skeins for 3c; per dozen..................................17c
2952. Filling Silk, black, white and all colors, per skein, 3c; per dozen...................33c
2953. Black and White Embroidery Silk, oz. spools, 58c; half-oz. spools, 38c; 1-8 oz. spools,9c
2954. Purse Silk, spools. black, white, and all colors....................................9c
2955. Heminway's best quality knitting, per ball......................................35c
2956. Saddler's Silk, black and white, bunch of 25 skeins, 25c; 2 skeins for....................3c

CROCHET COTTON.

2957. Clarke's white crochet cotton, per spool, 5c; pink, per spool..........................6c
2958. Marshland's white crochet cotton, all numbers, from Nos. 2 to 20 per ball.........9c
2959. Macrame flax, Barbour's linen, for making fringe or lace, per lb........................58c
2960. Same, white cotton, per lb...............25c
2961. Colored cotton, per ball of 4 oz..........10c
2962. Books, with full instructions for macrame work, each.................................25c
2864. D. M. C. crochet cotton, white and colors, per ball...................................14c
2965. Houschild's crochet cotton, white, per ball........... ....18c

TETZER'S GERMAN KNITTING COTTON.

8 SKEINS TO THE LB.

2066. White, Nos. 4, 65c per lb; hank 9c
2067. " " 6, 66c " " 9c
2968. " " 8, 67c " " 9c
2969. " " 10, 68c " " 9c
2970. " " 12, 69c " " 9c
2971. " " 14, 70c " " 9c
2972. " " 16, 72c " " 10c
2973. " " 18, 74c " " 10c
2974. " " 20, 76c " " 10c
2975. " " 22, 79c " " 10c
2976. " " 24, 82c " " 11c
2977. " " 26, 55c " " 11c
2978. Colored Turkey Red, Nos. 6, 8, 10 and 12; per lb., $1 89; hank. 12c
2979. Navy blue and seal brown, brown and white, blue and white, and black, mixed, per lb., 59c; hank 8c
2980. Mixed red and white, red and blue, red and black, per lb., 69c; hank. 11c
2981. Marking Cotton, all colors, per dozen, 17c; per skein 2c
2982. Mending Cotton, on cards, per dozen, 8c; per skein 1c
2983. Angora Mending Wool, per dozen, 30c; per skein .3c
2984. Balbriggan Mending Cotton, per dozen,20c; per skein 2c

NEW MATERIAL FOR EMBROIDERY PURPOSES.

2985. Tinsel, Gold and Silver, per ball 10c
2986. " Threads, Gold and Silver, 1 oz. spool, all colors 18c
2987. Etching Silk, for outlining embroidery, per spool, all colors 5c
2988. Pearl Chenille, entirely new, all colors; per piece of 6 yards 9c
2989. Pearsall's Wash Silk, all colors, per dozen, 45c; per skein 4c
2990. Heminway's Wash Silk, per dozen, 44c; per skein 4c
2991. Braidine, entirely new, per dozen, 23c; per skein .2c

IRON EMBROIDERY HOOPS.

2992. With straps for lap or table use, each $1 25

WOOD EMBROIDERY HOOPS.

2992 a. Wood embroidery hoops, 5, 6, 8, 10 and 12 inches, per pair 8c

CANVAS, ETC.

2993. Java, white. 18 in., 9c: 27 in., 15c; 36 in., 26c
2994. Java, buff, drab, brown and black,18 in...15c
2995. Java, pink and blue, 18 in 25c
2996. Java, scarlet, 18 in 25c
2997. Honeycomb, white, 18 in., 15c; 27 in., 30c; 36 in 38c
2998. Honeycomb, black, brown, slate and buff, 18 in 21c
2999. Honeycomb, pink, 18 in 25
3000. Honeycomb, scarlet, 18 in 38c
3001. Penelope or working, 27 in 17c
3002. Railroad, black and white, 18 in . . .15c
3003. Worsted Canvas, buff, black, scarlet, drab, green, pink; 18 in 43c
3004. Linen Aida, natural colors, 18 in., 21c; 27 in., 35c; 36 in 45c
3005. Worsted Aida Canvas, in all colors, 18 in. wide, per yard 59c
3006. Crash, 18 in 19c
3007. Turkish Toweling, 18 in 40c
3008. Linen Momie, natural colors, 18 in . . .29c
3009. Linen Congress, 18 in., 25c; 27 in., 40c; 36 in 59c
3010. Burlaps, plain . . . . .15 to 30c
3011. Linen Java, natural color, 18 inches wide, per yard 27c
3012. Same, white, 18 inches, per yard 29c
3013. Cotton Congress, 18 inches wide, per yard, 19c
3014. All silk bolting cloth, new, 24 inches wide, per yard 89c
3015. Pongee, all colors, 19 inches wide, per yard 69c
3016. Crape de Chene, 24 inches wide, all colors, per yard $1 39
3017. Roman satin, 50 inches wide, all colors, per yard $2 25

STAMPED LINEN FOR OUTLINING.

3018. Small Tidies, 10 inches square . . 15 and 25c
3019. Large Tidies, 15 inches square, 35c and 49c
3020. Splashers, 24 inches long and 12 inches wide . . . . 25, 39, 69 and 98c
3021. Scarfs, 18 inches wide and 72 inches long, 97c, 1.29 and $1.49 each.

WOOD EMBROIDERY FRAMES.

3023. Wood embroidery frames, 10, 15, 20, 25, 30 and 36 inches square; per set 29c

ART EMBROIDERIES.

BEADS.

3025. Colored Embroidery Beads, all colors, per bunch 15c
3026. Black Pressed Beads, per bunch, 2c; ten bunches 15c
3027. Black Cut Beads, per bunch, 8c; ten bunches 70c
3028. Silver-lined Beads, per bunch 4c
3029. Gold-lined Beads, per bunch 4c
3030. Large Glass Beads, per bunch 3c
3031. Wax Beads, all sizes, per string 5c
3032. Cut Steel Beads, per bunch . . . 10 and 12c
3033. Gold Cut Beads, per bunch . . . 12 and 15c
3034. Bugles, black box, per lb 50c
3035. Crystal Beads, mass of ten bunches; 100 strings 11, 14c
3036. Necklace Beads, gold, per string 6c
3037. Silver Trimming Beads, per string 6c
3038. Gold Trimming Beads, per string 6c
3039. Satin Beads, white and colored, per string, 6c
3040. Smoked Roman Pearl Necklace Beads, per string 12c

Besides the Beads described above, we have a full line of wood, rosary and all styles of black and colored fancy beads too numerous to mention; samples sent on application.

PERFORATED BOARDS.

3041. White, per sheet, 4c; per dozen 40c
3042. Black and colored. per sheet, 5c; per dozen, all colors 45c
3043. Cardinal, per sheet, 6c; per dozen . . .65c
3044. Silver and Gold, linen-lined, imported, per sheet 29c
3045. Domestic, silver and gold, linen-lined, per sheet 12c
3046. Unlined, per sheet 6c
3047. Collar, Cuff, Handkerchief and Glove Box, plain 12c
3048. Tin foil to put under mottoes of fancy work; size 8½x21 inches, per sheet, 2c; per dozen 20c

FELT BABY CARRIAGE ROBES.

3049. Felt baby carriage robe, handsomely lined with selicia, each, 1.50, 2.50 and $3,50,

Our stock of art embroideries this season, consists of every description of worsted and materials for fancy work. Artistic embroidery done to order and mounted. Instructions given in all branches of ornamental works, or books furnished. A feature for the decoration of chairs, brackets, sofa cushions, etc., etc., is the Japanese Tidy made of pongee in natural colors, such as old gold, terra cotta and olive: it is outlined with silk and trimmed with brass ornaments. We also have embossed plush tidies, which can be worked in different ways according to taste, or can be left plain; some are outlined with embroidery silk and trimmed with chenille or brass ornaments. All of the above are constantly in stock, and can be made to order.

3049 a. Satin Chair Tidies.fringed and stamped,to be outlined; size, 17x33 . . . .$1.33

FELT AND PLUSH GOODS.

(NOT ILLUSTRATED.)

3050. 6-4 Felt Table Covers, handsomely embroidered . . . . 2.50, 3.50 and $5.50
3051. 8-4 . . . . 3.50, 4.50, 6.50 and $7.50
3052. Plush Lambrequins, handsomely embroidered . . 6.50, 8.00, 10.00, 15.00, 20.00 and $25.00
3053. Plush Table Covers, handsomely embroidered, 4-4 . . . 8.50, 10.00, 15.00, 20.00 and $25.00
3054. Same, 5-4 . . . . . . 16.50, 18.00 and $25.00

3055. Same, 6-4 . . , . . . 21.50, 25.00 and $35.00
3056. Plush Piano Cover, handsomely embroidered . . . . 39.00, 50.00 and $65.00
3057. Plush Table Scarfs, handsomely embroidered . . . . . .6.00, 8.00, 10.00 and $15.00
3058. Plush Piano Scarfs, handsomely embroidered . . . . . 8.00, 10.00, 12.00, 16.00 and $18.00

3059. Arrasene Worsted, 2 skeins for 3c; per dozen 15c
3060. Same, silk, per skein, 2c; per dozen 21c

3061. Soft silk plush balls, all colors, per dozen, 20c; each . .2c
3062. Crewel Tassels, per dozen 15c

3063. Plush crescents, per dozen, 40c; each, 3½c
3067. Silk apples, per dozen, 23c; each, .2c

3064. Silk and chenille tinsel drop, with tinsel ball end,per dozen 75c; each 7c
3065. Large silk plush balls, per dozen, 30c; each, 3c
3066. Silk chenille crescent ornament. with brass cornucopia, per dozen, 65c; each.. 6c
3067. All silk mold ornaments, chenille ends, per dozen, 55c; each 5c
3068. Triple plush balls, per dozen $1.10 each 10c
3069. All silk chenille ornament, with filigree ball, entirely new,per dozen, 65c; each 6c

Green's Popular Silk Plush Chenille Appliques.

THE COMBINATIONS ARE ARTISTICALLY ARRANGED, AND PRESENT A VERY NATURAL AND RICH APPEARANCE.

3072. No. 1. Spray of flowers, 12 inches long and 10 inches wide; very nice for screens, etc.; combination, cardinal, olive and old gold with gold and silver tinsel; very handsome $1.69

3073. No 2. Spray of daisies and leaves. 11 inches long and 7 inches wide, combination, white flowers, yellow centres and olive leaves and stem 98c

3074. No 3. Spray of pansies and leaves, 10 inches long and 7 inches wide; purple flower, olive and old gold leaves and stem $1.29

3075. No. 4. Spray of daisies, leaves and buds 10½ inches long and 7 inches wide; cardinal flowers, olive stem and leaves 59c

3076. No. 5. Spray of cardinal roses, with olive leaves and stem, 9 inches high and 6 inches wide 39c

3077. No. 6. Buttercup spray; yellow flowers olive, stem and leaves, very rich, 6 inches long and 5 inches wide . . 39c

3078. No. 7. Pansy spray; purple pansy and olive stem, and leaves, very neat; 7 inches wide 18c

3079. No. 8. Spray of roses and leaves; pink roses and buds olive stem and leaves, 7 inches long and 4 inches wide . 29c

3080. No 9. Flowers, shape of leaves; olive leaves and cardinal stem, 5½ inches long 15c

3081. No. 10. Sunflower spray; cardinal flower, yellow centre and olive leaves 49c

3082. No.11. Pink roses; olive leaves and garnet stem, 7 inches long 18c

3083. No. 12. Pansy shape; purple flower and olive stem, 4 inches long 5c

3084. No. 13. Clover; olive leaves and garnet stem, 3 inches long 4c

3084. Felt Mantle Lambrequins, handsomely embroidered, 2½ yards long, 2 inch velvet band trimmed with silk ornaments; colors, cardinal, garnet, olive and peacock blue, $1.69.

3085. Heavy Silk, Plush Tidy embroidered in 4 corners, with silk tinsel and plush combination flowers centre; colors, cardinal, garnet, olive and peacock blue, bordered with cardinal and trimmed with crewel tassels, 14 inches square, $2.29.

3086. Felt Table Scarfs, corners handsomely embroidered with velvet and plush flowers, 52 inches long, and 17 inches wide, colors, cardinal, garnet, olive and peacock blue, $1.19.

3087. Plush Tidy, handsomely embroidered with silk flowers, outlined with tinsel, 14½ inches square, bordered with crewel tassels; colors, cardinal, garnet, olive and peacock blue, $1.49.

3088. Felt Table Scarfs, handsomely embroidered with plush flowers, 6 inch silk plush band and silk and worsted mixed ornaments lined with silesia, 52 inches long and 17 inches wide; colors, cardinal, garnet, olive and peacock blue, $3.49.

3089. Felt Table Cover, handsomely embroidered with felt flowers; 36 inches square, colors. cardinal, garnet, olive and peacock blue; Price, $2.59.

3090. Felt Table Scarf, handsomely embroidered with felt and plush flowers and square of silk plush trimmed with crewel tassels, 52 inches long and 17 inches wide; colors, garnet, cardinal, olive and peacock blue, $2.75.

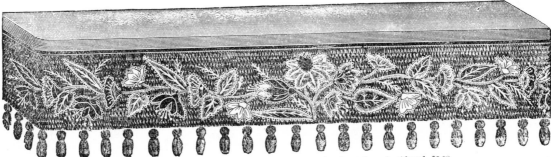

2031. Mantel Lambrequins of plush, 2½ yards long, handsomely embroidered, $9.98.

3092.   Mantle Lambrequins, 2½ yards long, trimmed with silk ornaments, 1½ inch plush band; colors, cardinal, garnet, olive and peacock blue... .....$1 19

3093.   Felt Tidy, handsomely embroidered with plush and silk flowers; colors, cardinal, garnet, olive and peacock blue, 17 inches square
89c

3094. Silk Plush Scarfs with silk applique flowers, hand embroidered, trimmed with silk tassel, 18x25 inches...$3 00

3095.   Felt Tidy, handsomely embroidered with plush flowers and outlined with tinsel, 17 inches square; colors, cardinal, garnet, olive and peacock blue.................$1 19

3096.   Silk and Worsted Spikes; per dozen, 45c; each..... . 04c.

3097.   Silk Plush Table Scarfs, handsomely embroidered, 18 inches wide and 55 inches long $8 49
3098.   Piano Scarfs, same pattern, 18 inches wide, 92 inches long...$13 29

3099.   Silk Chenille Tassels, in all colors with tinsel ends and tinsel tops, 3¼ inches long; per dozen, 75c; each........07c

Willow Ware.

Of Willow Ware we have everything in connection with the line. Office Baskets, plain and trimmed from $1 00 to $5 00 Hair Pin Baskets, from 15c to 50c; Key Baskets, from 15c to 75c; Knitting Baskets, for holding ball of knitting cotton, 25c to $1 00.

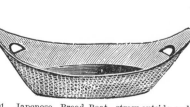

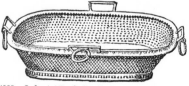

4000.   Infants' Stands, $1 00, 1 50, 4001.
2 00, 2 50 and 3 00.

4001.   Japenese, Bread Boat, straw outside and red inside.........................25c

4002.   Infants' Baskets, 49, 59, 79c, $1 00, 1 25 1 50 and 1 75, according to size and quality. For fancy trimmed Infants' baskets, refer to illustration in Infants' Wear Department.

4003.   Work Basket, round, white or colored, 9 to 11 in. diameter, 20, 25, 35, 40c

3125. Japanese Leather Pocket Book, with card case and purse attachment, calf lined and imported novelty lock. Price $1.39

3126. Men's Pocket and Bill Book combined, with strap or clasp; French calf, all leather................$1.00

3127. Buckhorn Leather Card Case and purse attachment, all leather lined, Price 59c

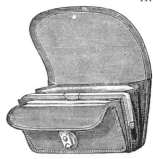

3128. Ladies' fine French calf Pocket Books, black or red............49c

3129. Japanese Leather Pocket Book, with card case and purse attachment, all leather lined, fine imported lock. Price........................ ..$1.25

3130. Ladies' French calf Pocket Books, with writing tablets and pencil attachment..................................59c

3131. Men's Pocket Books, real alligator........ ....$1.19

3132. Ladies' real Alligator Pocket Books, five inside and one outside compartment; nickel trimming, bellows shape $1.75

3133. Men's calf Wallets or Card Cases, leather lined..........$1.00

3134. Latest Novelty purse and fan combination; alligator purse, leather lined, with fan folding in purse, very handy. Price......59c

3135. Ladies' real Alligator Pocket Book $1.00

3136. Real Alligator Card Case, leather lined... .... $1.00

3137. French calf Cigar Case, engraved nickel frame, hand embroidered, satin lined.......$1.39

3138. Men's Calf Leather Companions, containing mirror, comb, glove hook and ear cleaner......23c

3129. French Calf Cigarette Case, in black, red or brown, sliding cover, ...39c

3140. French Calf Cigar Case, in black and red, nickel frame, satin lined...................63c

3141. Calf Pocket Case, containing comb and French plate mirror......16

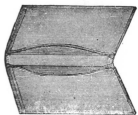

3142. Buckhorn leather chatelain purse, Price..........97c

3146. Genuine Alligator Purse, leather lined. 25c

3147. Change Purses of soft French kid, with steel clasps and inside partition, very strong, ...15c

3143. Ladies' fine French calf Pocket Books, with writing tablet and pencil attachments..................49c

3144. Ladies' or Misses' fine French calf Pocket Book, with writing tablet and pencil attachment..............49c

3145. Fine Calf pocket Toilet Case, containing scissors, comb, plate mirror, nail cleaner and court plaster, very neat and handy. ...75c

3148. American Russia Card Case leather lined, 4¾ in. long....25c

3147. New style Opera Bag, of black and tan alligator, 9 inches long, nickel frame . . . 49c
3148. Same, grained leather, back only, 9 inches long 98c

3149. Japanese leather hand bag, all leather lined, 9 inches long, blocked bottom, stitched all around, with inside and outside pockets, black or tan $1.69

3151. Real Alligator Club Bag, with lock and key, 10 inches, $4.19; 12 inches... . . . . $5.19

3151. Alligator Hand Bag, with inside and two outside pockets, flap and lock, blocked bottom, stitched all round, 9 inches long, black or tan. 89c

3152. Alligator Bag, with two outside pockets, flap and lock. pocket inside, calf lined, nickel and leather handles. heavy nickel frame, blocked bottom, stitched all round, 9 inches long $1 59

3153. Alligator Bag. fancy calf leather front trimmings, inside and outside pocket, blocked bottom, stitched all around, 8½ inches long.. $1 1½

2154. Alligator Hand Bag, with fancy work of real leather in front, inside and extra outside pocket. blocked bottom, stitched all round, 7 inches long, tan or black 49c

3155. Alligator Hand Bag. inside and extra outside pocket, fancy calf leather front, blocked bottom, stitched all round, 8 inches long, tan or black 69c

3156. Alligator Hand Bag, inside and extra outside pocket, 7 inches long, tan or black 39c

3157. Alligator Leather Club Bag, linen lined, nickel lock, tan or black, very neat and strong; cheapest bag ever made.
Sizes, 9 10 11 12 13 14 15 inches.
Price $1.19 1.29 1.39 1.49 1.69 1.79 1.89 each.

3158. Alligator Leather Satchel. linen lined, nickel lock, very neat, durable, tan and black
Sizes, 9 10 11 12 13 inches.
Price, 89c 93c 97c $1.29 1.39 each,

3159. Alligator Leather Satchel, linen lined, outside pocket, nickle yale lock, tan and black.
Sizes. 9 10 11 12 13 inches.
Price. $1.19 1.29 1.39 1.49 1.59 each.

3160. Alligator Leather Gladstone Valise, linen lined, fine nickel lock and sewed grain handle, tan and black.

Sizes,	14,	16,	18,	20
Price,	$2.97,	3.49,	3.89,	4.19.

3163. Telescope Duck Traveling Cases. Sizes, 14, 16, 18, 20, 22, 24 in. long Prices, $1.19, 1.39, 1.69. 1.89, 2.19, 2.50

3164. Ladies' Grain Leather Satchel, nickel plate trimmings, leather lined, inside and outside pockets, colors, red, black or brown.
Sizes, 6, 7, 8, 9, 10 in.
Prices, $1.00, 1.25, 1.50, 1.75, 2.00
3165. Without outside pockets.
Sizes, 8, 9, 10 inches.
Prices, 75c, $1.00, 1.25

3171. Men's Valises, Duck,

	14,	16,	18,	20 inches
Sizes				
Prices	$1.75,	2.25,	2.75	3.00

3172. Grain Leather,

		16,	18,	20 inches
Sizes				
Prices		$3.50,	4.25,	4.75

3173. Split Leather,

	14,	16,	18,	20 inches
Sizes				
Prices	$1.50,	2.00,	2.50	2.75

3174. Rubber Cloth,

	14,	16,	18,	20 inches
Sizes				
Prices	69c,	89c,	$1.00,	1.25

Above bags are all linen lined and have outside pockets, with the exception of the rubber cloth.

3161. Men's Grain Leather Gladstone Bag, two straps and buckles outside, linen lined, very strong and neat. Sizes, 14, 16, 18 inches. Prices, $2.75, 3.00, 3.25.

BELTS.

3166. Alligator Belt, with 2 and 3 straps and buckles, leather lined, black or tan, 2 inches wide, 21c; 2½ inches...35c
3167. Real Alligator, 2 straps and buckles, black or tan, 2 inches wide....................69c

3175. Ladies' Traveling Satchels, Rubber Cloth,

Sizes,	9,	10,	11,	12,	13 inches.
Prices,	50,	60,	70,	80,	90c

3176. Split Leather,

Sizes,	9,	10,	11,	12,	13 inches.
Prices,	69,	79,	89,	98,	$1.25

3177. Grain Leather,

Sizes,	9,	10,	11,	12,	13 inches.
Prices,	$1.75,	2.25,	2.50,	2.75,	3.25

Above satchels are all linen lined, have outside and inside pockets and lock and key. Grain leather can be had in either red, brown or black; the other in black only.
3178. Morocco,

Sizes,	9,	10,	11,	12,	13 inches.
Prices,	$3.00,	3.50,	4.00,	4.50,	5.00

These are leather lined, have nickel or leather covered frames and lock and key. They are imported, and are of the very best workmanship.

3162. Grain Leather Club Bag, heavy nickel frame, with lock and key, leather lined, tan, brown or black. Sizes, 12, 14, 16 inches long. Prices $2.49, 2.98, 3.49

3168. Neat Antique Leather belt in tan or black, closes with adjustable buckles of all leather; can also be had of alligator or canvas, 2 inches, 39c same, 2½ inches 49c

SKATE BAGS.

SKATE BAGS.

3169. Canvas Belts, in cotton, with 2 and 3 straps, colors, black, navy blue, white and cardinal, 2½ inches wide, 10c; 3 inches wide,................17c
3170. Same, in worsted, 2½ in. wide, 21c; 3 in. 39c
Canvas Belts for boys, one strap and buckle, colors, white, black, navy blue, cardinal and red, white and blue mixed, 2 in. wide, each.......12c

3182. Box shape, stitched all round, two straps and buckles, leather handle and two rings for shoulder straps, inside leather pocket for oil can, very strong; 12 inches long, and made of heavy alligator leather, each.............................$1.49

Shoulder Straps for Skate Bags.

3183. Leather, 46 inches long....................21c
3184. Better quality, with patent clasps, 43 in. long................................25c

3179. Bellows shape, bottom stitched round, leather handle with two straps and buckles; bound with leather, two rings for shoulder straps and lined with duck; inside leather pocket for oil can; very neat and strong, 12 inches long, heavy duck, each 59c
3180. Grained Rubber Cloth, each..............95c
3181. Alligator Leather....................89c

Do not cut or mutilate this book; by simply referring to the number of the page and article you desire, your order will be understood. We will send this Catalogue, free of charge, to any one applying for it by letter or postal card.

HAIR GOODS.

Our Hair Goods counters are in charge of the most practical hair dressers, who understand hair work in all its branches. Every article necessary for the dressing of the hair in the fashionable style furnished to match all shades of hair at the most reasonable rates. Hair Goods, made to order, we cannot exchange. **WHEN ORDERING GOODS, DO NOT FAIL TO INCLOSE SAMPLE OF HAIR.**

3200. Ventilated Pompadour, with back hair, $3.75.

3204. Fluffy Langtry Ventilated, with back hair, $2.50.

3208. Roman Knot, 3.00, 4.00 and $5.00

3201. Chatelain Twist or Braid 3.50.

3205. Tuck-up Switch, 3.00, 4.00 and $5.00.

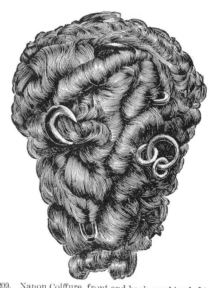

3209. Nanon Coiffure, front and back combined, $4.00

3202. Langtry Montague, $1.00.

3206. Ventilated Empress, $2.50.

3210. Superior, 75c.

3203. Perfection Pin; per pair, 33c.

3207. Fedora, 89c.

3211. Back Coiffure, $3.00

924 TO 928 THIRD AVE., AND 160 TO 164 EAST 56th St., NEW YORK.

121

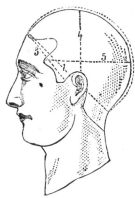

**Method of Measuring
the Head.**

No. 1. Around the Head.
" 2. From forehead to nape.
" 3. From ear to ear across the crown.
" 4. From ear to ear across the forehead.
" 5. From temple to temple.
" 6. Across the neck.

3212. Langtry Bang, 40c.

SMITH'S PATENT FIFTH AVENUE HAIR CRIMPERS, Etc.

3213. Crimps the hair in less than an hour without use of heat or other injury, per pair. . . 3c
3214. Common Sense Hair Crimpers, all colors, per dozen 3c
3215. Kid Hair Curlers, per dozen 9c

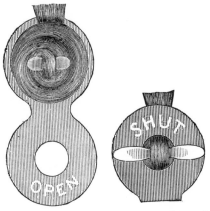

3216. Montague Curl Clasps, made in three colors, black, brown and blonde. Bend the arms of the clasp upright, wind a small lock of hair around them; afterwards place the ends of the hair between the arms and close the other half of clasp over, allowing the arms to pass through the hole, then bend them down to place tightly; after removing the clasp, disturb the locks slightly with comb or brush. Hair differs greatly in its nature; while that of some people curls readily, that of others is more obstinate. If the Montague does not work satisfactorily with your hair dry, try it moist; if you still do not succeed in obtaining the required result, use a little bandoline . . . . . . .8c per dozen

All our goods are marked at the lowest prices, which do not include postage. No goods sent by mail except sufficient money accompanies the order for postage, otherwise we will reduce orders and take out part of goods to the amount of postage required.

SPECIAL.
Real Hair Switches.

In ordering Hair Goods, do not fail to inclose a sample of your hair.

In ordering Hair Goods, do not fail to inclose a sample of your hair.

3217. Try one of our $1 00 Switches, made of 23-inch superfine hair, very short stem; weight, 3½ oz., in all shades. Real value $3 50.

Real Hair Switches.

Our Hair Switches are all hand-woven, and made of the very best quality of human hair.

X QUALITY.

3218. 3   3 oz., 16 inches long 40c
3219. 3½ " 24   "   " 75c
3220. 4   " 28   "   " $1 00
3221. 4½ " 30   "   " 1 50

XX QUALITY.

3222. 3   oz., 28 inches long $2 00
3223. 3½ " 30   "   " 3 00
3224. 4   " 30   "   " 3 50

XXX QUALITY.

3225. 3½ oz., 28 inches long $4 00
3226. 4   " 30   "   " 5 00

XXXX QUALITY.

3227. 3½ oz., 30 inches long $6 00
3228. 4   " 30   "   " 9 00

Hair Goods.

3229. Puffs . . . . .19c to $1 25
3230. Curls, for sets of two 1 00
3231. Chatelaine Braid . . . . . . .1 49 to 6 00
3332. Frizzles on pins, 15c; per yard 50c
3233. Perfections on pins, each 15c
3234. Finger Puff Rolls, per set 10c
3235. Pompadour Rolls . . . . .7 and 8c
3236. Nets, invisible, for front hair, real hair, single, 4c; double, 5c; per dozen, single, 40c; double, 55c.
3237. Back Nets, silk, each . . . .3, 7, 10 and 15c
3238. All kinds of front pieces, redressed, each, 15c
3239. Marchard's Blonde Hair Bleach, Bloomingdale Bros., agents. Four applications will turn the hair a golden blonde; not injurious. Full directions on each bottle. Per bottle. 79c

When ordering hair goods, do not fail to inclose sample of hair.

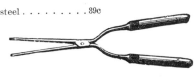

3240. Hair Pinchers, all steel 39c

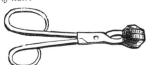

3241. Hair Curlers, steel handles, each 25c
3242. Same, wood handles 39c

3243. Ladies' Wigs, 6 00, 8 00, 10 00, 12 00, $15 00 and upward.

3244. Reversible Small 50

3245. Nanon Ventilated $1 25

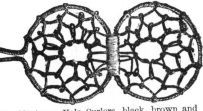

3246. Montague Hair Curlers, black, brown and blonde, per dozen 15c

3247. Fluffy Fedora Hair Curlers, make a large and perfectly round curl, which gives the hair an elegant light and fluffy appearance; per dozen 15c

3247. Triple-plated Pickle Stand, fine pressed glass, fork attached . . $1.87

3249a. Brass or nickle-plated Cuspidores. . . . . . . : . . . . 53c each

3248. Triple-plated 5 bottle Castor, engraved bottles, new design $2.97
3249. Other styles . . . . $1.25 and upwards

3250. The Unique Pickle Bowl, colored glass, heavily plated stand $1.93

3251. Triple-plated Tilting Pitcher. double wall, handsomely chased and hand engraved $10.50

3252. Triple-plated Butter Dish, handsomely chased, new design $2.00

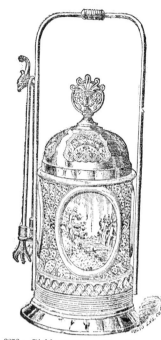

3253. Pickle Stand, with with tongs. heavily plated, handsome pressed glass bottle 93c

3254. Very Unique Card Stand, triple-plated, handsomely chased $3.13
3255. Other designs . . . . $1.00 and upward.

3256. Cake Stand, new design, triple-plate . . . $3.25

3257. Very elegant berry dish, canary or blue colored glass, triple plated stand, one of the most popular dishes this season.... . . ..$4 13

3258. Napkin Rings, triple plated, neatly chased 9c

3259. Square berry dish, canary or blue colored glass, heavily plated stand,... ....$2 75

3260. 3 piece set, triple plated, neatly chased, very popular design, $8.25.

SILVER PLATED CUTLERY.

ROGERS BRO'S A 1 GOODS.

3261. Tea spoons, tipped pattern, per dozen $2 58
3262. Table spoons and forks to match,... $4 75
3263. Tea spoons, fancy patterns, per doz $2 78
3264. Table spoons and forks to match, per dozen....................................$5 50
3265. Rogers Bro's No. 12 Table Knives, per dozen....................$3 75
3266. Same, dessert size....................$3 50
3267. Child's Set on fancy card, knife, fork and spoon, Rogers & Bro.'s make, tipped......85c
3268. Satin lined, imitation morocco case, School Set, containing knife, fork and spoon, Rogers & Bro.'s silverware ....—$2 39

MUSICAL INSTRUMENTS.

3282. Harmonicas. Tin, zinc plates 6 or 8 holes...5c
3283. Tin, zinc plates, ebonized mouthpiece, double row holes, 10 holes, 20 reeds, 10c; 12 holes, 24 reeds, 15c; 16 holes, 32 reeds, 20c; 20 double holes, 40 reeds 45c
3284. Richter Harmonicas, with bells, German Silver covers, brass plates, extension ebonized handles, 10 holes, single, 1 bell, 20 reeds, 35c; 20 holes, 2 bells, 20 reeds................................45c

3274. Accordions Six keys, 4-fold bellows, 2 box basses, single reeds, plain imitation rosewood, paper bound bellows, with white kid corners........83c
3275. Same, 8 keys, 5 folds.................$1 00
3276. Ten keys, 6 folds.................$1 25
3277. Ne plus ultra patent, 8 gilt keys, nickel keyboard cover, imitation rosewood top, 2 basses.$1 70
3278. Same, with 10 keys.................$1 98
3279. Ten keys, 6-fold bellows, kid corners, imitation rosewood; fine toned accordion........$2 25
3280. Ten keys, 6-fold bellows, kid corners and edges bound with black glazed oil cloth imitation rosewood, ebonized moulding and fancy gilt border..$2 75
3270. German Violins; full size, good quality.........89c
3271. Violins, "Paganini"..$1 50
3272. Violins, "Ole Bull"...$1 89
3273. Others, $2 50 and upward.

3281. Ten keys, imitation rosewood, ebonized mouldings; 1 stop, 2 sets keys, 2 basses and 2 rows trumpets; a handsome accordion.. . ...$3 75
Any of the above can be had with bell, if desired, 50c extra.

3285. Tin Music Box, with crank, round, plain, playing one air, assorted tunes..... ....89c
3286. White Wood, 4¼x3 inches, glass cover inside, picture of Harvest Home in colors on cover; 2 airs; "Chorus of Pages." from "La Petit Duc," Lecoq, and National Hymn. $5 50
3287. Handsome Music Boxes, japanned tin, size 4¼x2¼ inches, spring movement, picture of Falls on the Rhine at Scharffhausen on cover; 3 airs, "Daughter of Madam Angot." Lecoq; waltz, "Aus dem Reicher der Tane," Faust, and "Nebelhorn Polka," Starke.................................$6 50
3288. Black Horn Case, 4¼x2¾ inches, with raised picture Chateau of Chillon on cover; 3 airs; "On the Beautiful Rhine." waltz, Kelar Bela; "Sorry Her Lot." Pinafore and "Beautiful Blue Danube." waltz, Strauss.......... ... .$8 00

3289. Banjo, size, 10 inches, sheep skin tack head, maple rim, imitation black walnut neck...................$1 25
90. Same, 11 inches...$1 50
91. Size, 11 inches, 4 brass brackets, handsome maple rim, imitation black walnut neck, sheepskin head..$2 00
3990. Banjo, size, 11 inches, with 8 brass brackets, imitation rosewood rim, black walnut neck, brass hoops, calfskin head and inlaid fronts.................$3 89
Other styles, $7,50 upward.

All kinds of Musical Instruments constantly on hand.

Novelties in Brass Ornaments.

3292. Brass Smoker's set, canoe shape, very pretty $1 25

3293. Solid Brass Easel; height, 5 inches; width, 3½ inches, each 15c

3294. Brass Match Safe and Ash Tray; height, 5½ inches; width, 5 inches 69c

3295. Brass Thermometer and Match Safe, 6 ins. high, 98c

3296. Solid Brass Easel; height, 7½ inches; width, 4½ inches 49c

3297. Brass Match Safe; height, 4½ inches, width 3 inches 69c

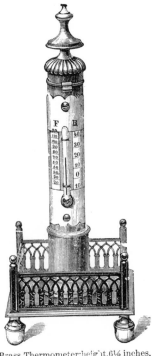

3298. Brass Thermometer; height 6½ inches, $1 49

3299. Brass Call Bell; height, 5½ inches; width, 2¾ inches 98c

ALBUM EASELS.

3301. Solid Brass; height, 14 inches; width, 7 inches 75c

3302. Same, 18 inches high and 8 inches wide $1 00

3303. 20 inches high, 9 inches wide $1 39
Same, nickle plated, 25c extra.

Whenever you send us money with an order for goods, and fail to hear from us within ten days after sending the order, please inform us of the fact by letter or postal card, as lost money can be more readily traced when looked after at once. Customers in California or on the Pacific Coast should write within fifteen days after sending.

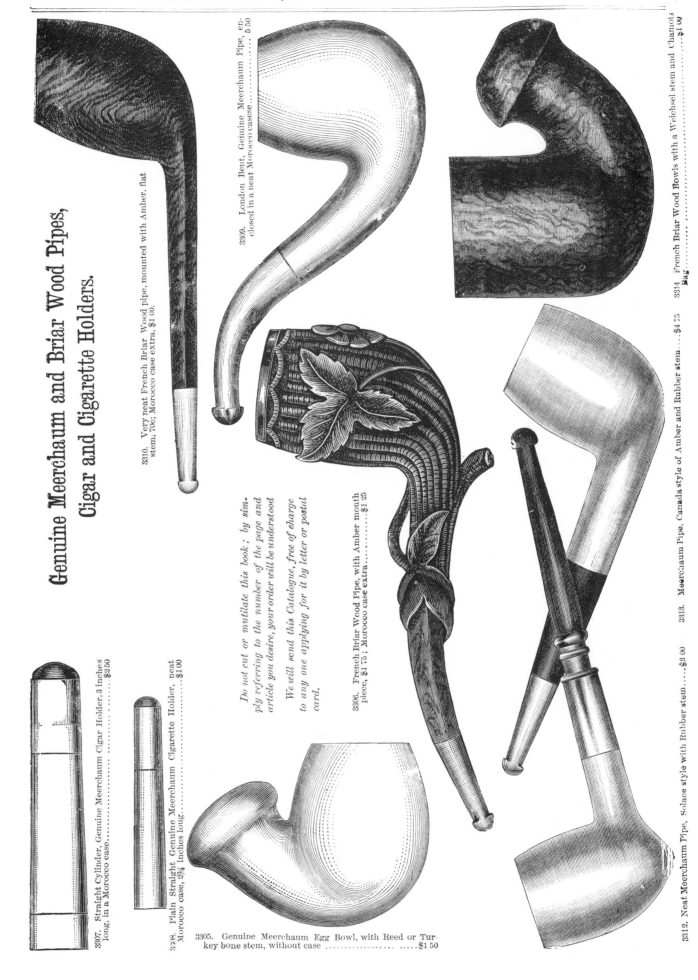

Genuine Meerchaum and Briar Wood Pipes, Cigar and Cigarette Holders.

3310. Very neat French Briar Wood pipe, mounted with Amber, flat stem; 70c; Morocco case extra, $1 00.

3309. London Bent, Genuine Meerchaum Pipe, enclosed in a neat Morocco casee....5 50

3314   French Briar Wood Bowls with a Weichsel stem and Chamois Bag.......$1 00

3313. Meerchaum Pipe, Canada style of Amber and Rubber stem....$4 75

Do not cut or mutilate this book; by simply referring to the number of the page and article you desire, your order will be understood

We will send this Catalogue, free of charge to any one applying for it by letter or postal card.

3306. French Briar Wood Pipe, with Amber mouth piece, $1 75; Morocco case extra............$1 25

3307. Straight Cylinder, Genuine Meerchaum Cigar Holder, 3 inches long, in a Morocco case..............$2 50

3308. Plain Straight. Genuine Meerchaum Cigarette Holder, neat Morocco case, 2¾ inches long........$1 00

3305. Genuine Meerchaum Egg Bowl, with Reed or Turkey bone stem, without case $1 50

3312. Neat Meerchaum Pipe, Solace style with Rubber stem....$3 00

Combs and Hair Ornaments.

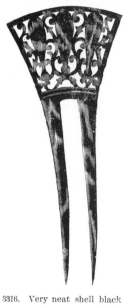

3314. Very neat shell black or amber horn dagger, 6 inches long.................................58c
3315. Very neat shell black or amber horn dagger 6 inches long.................................44c

3316. Very neat shell black or amber hair pin, 3½ inches long................35c
3317. Same, 5 inches long, ...58c

3318. Shell, black or amber hair pin, 4 inches long......30c
3319. Same, 5½ inches long.........42c

3320. Neat Shell, black or amber hair pin,
Size,   3,   3½,   4,   5 inches.
Price, 5c,   6c,   9c, 11c each
3321. Neat shell black or amber hair pin,
Size. 2½, 3, 3½, 4½, 5, 5½, 6, 7 in
Price, 4, 5, 6, 8, 9, 10, 11, 15c ea.

3322. Ladies' shell black or amber horn comb.............58c

3325. Shell black or amber hair pin, 3½ inches long........20c
3326. 4¼ inches long.........22c
3327. 5¼ inches long. 29c

3329. Rubber Comb, dull or polished 65c

3323. Ladies' shell black or amber horn comb....65c

3330. Neat Rubber comb, dull only... ,...........88c

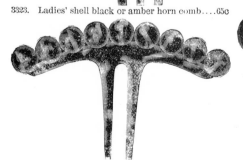

3324. Ladies' shell black or amber horn comb, very neat.. ....33c

3228. Shell black or amber horn comb.29c

3331. Very neat dull finished comb.............65c

3332. Very neat Rubber Lace Pin, dull finished, 58c

3333. Handsome Rubber Lace Pin, dull only 65c

3334. Very neat Rubber Lace Pin, dull finished, 66c
3335. Earrings to match, per pair 66c

3336. Handsome Rubber Lace Pin, dull or polished 59c
3337. Earrings to match, per pair 66c

3339. Neat Rubber Lace Pin, dull or polished, 65c
3340. Earrings to match, per pair 65c

3341. Pretty style of Lace Pin, dull or polished 66c
3342. Earrings to match, per pair 59c

3343. Neat Rubber Lace Pin, dull or polished 66c

3344. Elegant Rubber Lace Pin, dull or polished.

3345. Imitation Ivory Pin, entirely new and very pretty $1.39
3346. Same, in Real Ivory $4.75

3347. Very neat Rubber Earrings, with 18 kt. rolled gold wires, dull finished only, per pair 66c

3348. Handsome Rubber Earrings, with 18 kt. rolled gold wires, per pair 69c
3349. Pin to match, dull finished only 69c

3350. Very neat Rubber Drops, with 18 kt. rolled gold wires, dull finished only, per pair, 66c
3351. Pin to match . . . 80c

3352. Neat Rubber Earrings, dull finished, only 58c
3353. Pin to match $1 09

3354. Very neat Rubber Drops, dull or polished, with 18 kt. rolled gold wires, per pair 50c
3355. Pin to match . . . 50c

3356. Neat style Rubber Earrings, dull or polished, 18 kt. rolled gold wires, per pair 65c

3357. Handsome Rubber Earrings, with 18 kt. rolled gold wires, per pair 59c

3358. Very handsome Bogwood Earrings, dull finished, with 18 kt. rolled gold wires, per pair. . . .35c
3359. Pin to match. . . .30c

3360. Very neat Bogwood Earrings, with 18 kt. rolled gold wires, dull finished only, per pair 35c
3361. Pin to match . . . 51c

3362. Neat Rubber Earrings, dull or polished, per pair, 33c

3363. Neat Rubber Earrings. dull or polished, per pair. 33c

3364. Neat Rubber Earrings. dull or polished, per pair. 31c

3365. Very handsome Rubber Screw Earrings, dull finished only, with sterling silver screws, per pair 33c

3366. Neat Rubber Earrings. dull finished only, with 18 kt. rolled gold wires, per pair 33c

3367. Imitation Ivory Pins, very pretty, entirely new, each $1.39
3368. Same, in Real Ivory $4.79

3669. Very neat Rubber Lace Pin, dull or polished 65c
3370. Earrings to match, per pair 68c

3371. Handsome Rubber Lace Pin. dull or polished 58c
3372. Pin to match 58c

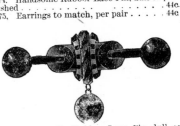

3373. Very neat Rubber Lace Pin, dull or polished 33c

3374. Handsome Rubber Lace Pin, dull or polished 44c
3375. Earrings to match, per pair 44c

3376. Very pretty Rubber Lace Pin, dull or polished 33c

3377. Very neat Rubber Lace Pin, dull or polished 22c

3378. Handsome Rubber Lace Pin, dull or polished 33c

ROLLED GOLD BRACELETS.

3379. Very Handsome Rolled Gold Bracelets, Enameled and Hand Engraved per pair.........................$3 00

3380. Very neat, Hand Engraved and Enameled, per pair. $2 75

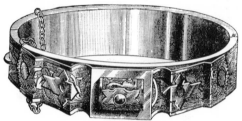

3381. Elegant Rolled Gold Bracelets, Enameled and Hand Engraved, per pair $3 50

3382. Very neat Rolled Gold Bracelets, Enameled and Hand Engraved, per pair.................................$3 75

3383. Very Fashionable Ladies Rolled Gold Bangle bracelet, with fancy cubes, per pair......................$1 39

3384. Very rich Rolled Gold Hinge Bracelets, gold fronts and turquoise setting, per pair...................$2 98

3385. Handsome rolled gold child's bracelets, hand-engraved and enameled, per pair, $1 89

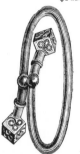

3386. Misse's rolled gold bangle bracelets, with fancy cubes, per pair $1 19

3387. Very neat Misses rolled gold bangle bracelets, knot pattern, inlaid with stone in centre, per pair. $1 89

3388. Handsome rolled gold bracelets, children or ladies sizes, per pair.............59c

3389. Elegant Rolled Gold Bracelets, Hand Engraved and Enameled, per pair................................$3 00

3390. Very Pretty Rolled Gold Bracelets, Enameled and Hand Engraved, per pair...........................$1 50

3391. Very pretty Rolled Gold Bracelets, Enameled and Hand Engraved, per pair..................... ....$5 00

3392. Ladies Rolled Gold Bangle Bracelets, Frosted Knot Pattern, entirely new and stylish, per pair...$2 98

3393. Children's Rolled Gold Hinge Bracelets, Turquoise setting, very handsome pattern, per pair, $2 89

3394. Very neat Rolled Gold Bangle Bracelets, Frosted Balls, inlaid with blue or white stones, per pair...... .... 98c

Genuine Diamond Jewelry, in Solid Gold:

3395. Solid Gold Lace Pin, with one genuine diamond, knot pattern...................$3 49

3400. Solid Gold Lace Pin, with genuine diamond, very handsome, each...........$12 49

3396. Solid Gold Earrings, with genuine diamonds in centre, per pair........$4 98

3397. Very Fine Solid Gold Earrings, with genuine diamonds, per pair............,..$8 69

3398. Very Handsome Solid Gold Lace Pin, with genuine diamond, each...........$8 69

3403. Elegant Solid Gold Lace Pin, with genuine diamond very neat..............$9 49

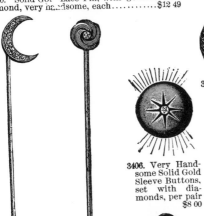

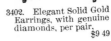

3401. Very Handsome Solid Gold Earrings, with genuine diamonds, per pair, $11 49

3402. Elegant Solid Gold Earrings, with genuine diamonds, per pair, $9 49

3406. Very Handsome Solid Gold Sleeve Buttons, set with diamonds, per pair $8 00

3407. Elegant Solid Gold Sleeve Buttons, set with genuine diamonds, per pair. $11 00

3408. Handsome Solid Gold Sleeve Buttons set with genuine diamonds, per pair.. $9 75

3409. Elegant Solid Gold Sleeve Buttons with genuine diamonds, per pair...... $7 00

3410. Very Handsome Solid Gold Locket, set with genuine diamond.. $19 00

3404. Very Handsome Solid Gold scarf pin, with genuine diamonds, $10 49

3405. Solid Gold Scarf Pin, with one genuine diamond, entirely new, $2 98

3412. Very handsome Solid Gold Collar Button, set with genuine diamond ...$3 50

3413. Neat Solid Gold Collar Button, set with genuine diamond..........$6 00

3411. Elegant Solid Gold Scarf Pin. set with pearls......$6 00

Lace Pins.

SOLID GOLD.

3419. Elegant Solid Gold Lace Pin, handsomely hand-engraved and enameled and set with garnets, each..... ....$4 98

3425. Entirely new hard, enameled and rolled gold Lace Pin, with 3 Brazilian pebbles....$1 49

3426. Polished Rolled Gold Lace Pin, with 1 Brazilian pebble in centre..............$1 69

3420. Elegant Solid Gold Lace Pin, handsomely hand-engraved, and enameled... ....$3 25

3427. Roman Gold Lace Pin, with 2 Brazilian pebbles and 2 garnets.............. ....$1 19

3414. Solid Gold Lace Pin, very handsome and rich, 8 Brazilian pebbles..............$4 50

3421. Very Pretty Solid Gold Lace Pin, handsomely hand-engraved, set with garnets and pearls. $4 50

3428. Roman Gold Lace Pin, with 1 Turquoise garnet and Brazilian pebble..............$1 19

3415. Solid Gold Lace Pin, with Brazilian pebbles........ ....$3 00

3416. Entirely new, solid gold lace-pin, with finely cut Brazilian pebble............:$3 49

3422. Elegant Solid Gold Lace Pin, knife edge, finely cut Brazilian pebble...........$2 89

3429. Rolled Gold Lace Pin, with Brazilian pebble and 4 Turquoises... ....$1 19

3417. Solid Gold Lace Pin, with Brazilian pebbles........ ....$2 98

3423. Solid Gold Lace Pin, Brazilian pebbles..$2 75

3424. Solid Gold Lace Pin, Brazilian pebbles, very neat...................$2 62

3430. Rolled Gold Lace Pin, knot pattern with Brazilian centre.................98c

3418. Solid Gold Lace Pin, knife edge, with 3 finely cut Brazilian pebbles........$2 98

3431.   Solid Gold Lace Pin, Brazilian pebble.....$2 25

3432.   Solid Gold Lace Pin, Brazilian pebble, can also be had set with pearls or garnets..... 1 75

3433.   Entirely new hard enameled and rolled gold lace pin, with three Brazillian pebbles $1 49

3434.   Very neat and unique design rolled gold lace pin, 14 karat gold front.......... .. ..$1 75

3435.   Entirely New Cameo Lace Pin, mounted in rolled gold.........................$1 39

3436.   Polished Rolled Gold Lace Pin, with 1 Brazilian pebble in star............. $1 98

3437.   Elegant Rolled Gold Lace Pin, entirely new, representing a cat holding a Brizilian pebble in her paw, very stylish............$2 98

3438   Elegant Porcelain Lace Pin, hand painted, assorted designs, mounted on 18 karat rolled gold plate....................45c

3439.   Entirely new Cameo Lace Pin, mounted on rolled gold.....$1 39

3440.   Entirely New Hand Painted Porcelain Lace Pin. mounted on rolled gold..............$2 50

3443.   Hard Enameled and Rolled gold Lace Pin, with Brizilian pebble, entirely new.......98c

3444.   Rolled Gold Knot Pattern Lace Pin, inlaid with 1 Turquoise on each end.............69c

3445,   Rolled Gold and Hand Enameled Knife Edge Lace Pin...........................$1 25

3446.   Very Neat Rolled Gold Lace Pin, Turquoise setting...................................79c

3447.   Entirely new Cut Cameo Lace Pin, mounted on rolled gold....... ....$1 98

3448.   Entirely New Rolled Gold Lace Pin, representing a double knot, very stylish $2 98

CUFF PINS.

3455.   Eutruscan Gold Cuff or Bib Pins, each.... ....25c

3456.   Bib Pins, fine rolled gold, black or blue enameled, per pair 25c

3457.   Fine Rolled Gold Cuff Pins, per pair 25c

3458.   Neat Rolled Gold Cuff Pins, per pair. 49c

3441.   Enirely new Roman Gold Knot Lace Pin, very stylish.. $1 39

CUFF PINS.

3442.   Entirely New Enameled Butterfly pattern lace pin. $3 50

3449.   Solid Goid Cuff Pins, per pair $2 50

3450.   Solid Sold Cuff Pins, per pair $3 00

3451.   Unique Rolled Gold Cuff Pins, per pair....................49c

3452.   Fine Rolled Gold, black or blue enameled, per pair....... .75c

3453.   Fine Rolled Gold Cuff Pin, per pair....................59c

3454.   Fine Rolled Gold with "Baby Mine," "Darling" or "Pet," black or blue enameled, per pair 7

EARRINGS.

3459. Elegant solid gold Earrings, with Brazilian pebbles, per pair.. $2 75

3460. Very rich solid gold Drops, with Brazillian pebbles, per pair........ $2 75

3461. Entirely new solid gold Earings with finely cut Brazlian pebbles in centre, per pair........ .....$2 49

3462. Handsome solid gold Earrings, with Brazilian pebbles, per pair.... .$2 75

3463. Neat solid gold Drops, with Brazilian pebbles, $2 50

3464. Solid gold Drops, Brazilian pebbles, per pair... ....$2 00

3465. Solid gold Earrings, with Brazilian pebbles, per pair, $1 75

3466. Very pretty Earrings, solid gold wires, with Brazilian pebbles, per pair.. ....$1 75

3467. Solid gold Earrings, with Brazilian pebbles, per pair............ $1 25

3468. Very handsome rolled gold Earrings· with Brazilian pebbles· per pair... ...... .39c

3469. Solid gold Earrings, very neat, with Brazilian pebbles, per pair... ....$1 25

3470. Handsome solid gold Screw Earrings, with Braziiian pebbles,per pair, $2 25

3471. Solid gold Earrings, with Brazilian pebbles, per pair.... ....$1 25

3472. Solid gold Screw Earrings, with Brazilian pebbles, per pair. $2 25

3473. Very neat solid gold Screw Earrings, with Brazilian pebbles... $2 25

3474. Solid gold Screw Earrings, with Brazilian pebbles,per pr.$1 75

3475. Solid gold Screw Earrings, pearl settings, per pair...$1 50

3476. Solid gold Screw Earrings, Brazilian pebbles, per pair.... ....$1 50

3477. Solid gold Earrings, pearl settings, per pair, $1 39

3478. Solid gold Earrings, pearl settings· per pair.... .. $1 25

3479. Etruscan gold Earrings, gold fronts and wires, very neat and stylish, per pair...... $1 49

3480. Etruscan gold Earrings, gold fronts and wires, per pair....... $1 49

3481 Fine rolled gold Drops, gold fronts and wires, per pair......$1 49

3482. Fine rolled gold Drops, with gold wires, per pair 69c
3482a. Same, solid gold, per pair.$1 59

3483. Very neat rolled gold Ball Earrings, per pair... ....$1 00

484. Neat rolled gold drops with Brazilian pebbles, per pair..25c

3485. Very neat rolled gold drops with solid gold wires, per pair, 93c

3486. Unique rolled gold Drops, per pair.....50c

3487. Fine rolled gold Drops, per pair.....45c

3488. Fine rolled gold Ball Earrings, per pair.... .49c

3489. Handsome rolled gold Screw Earrings Brazilian pebble, per pair..........39c

THIMBLES.

EYEGLASSES, ETC.

3490. Solid gold Thimbles, plain, any size....$2 89

3491. Silver Thimbles, warranted coin silver, all sizes............19c

3492. Silver Thimble warranted sterling silver, handsomely hand engraved. all sizes............49c

3493. Solid Gold Thimbles handsomely hand engraved.$3 98

3499. Frameless Eyeglasses, nickel plated mounting, patent nose spring, to suit all sights, 49, 59 and 69c

3500. Gold Frame Eyeglasses, $3.00, 4 00. 5 00 and 7 00

3501. Spectacles in, gold and silver, $3 00. 4 00, 5 00 and 7 00

3502. Automatic Eyeglass Holders, works same as shade roller, can be adjusted to any length........19c

3494. Silver plated, each............2c
3495. Steel, each..3c
3496. German silver.
3497. Rubber.....8c
3498. Celluloid all colors 3c

Rings and Bangles.

No. 1. $6.49

No. 2. $5.49

No. 3. $5.75

No. 4. $6.00

No. 5. $5.50

No. 6. $5.50

No. 7. $5.00

No. 8. $5.00

No. 9. $5.00

No. 10. $4.75

No. 11. $4.50

No. 12. $4.50

No. 13. $5.62

No. 14. $4.00

No. 15. $4.00

No. 16. $4.00

No. 17. $3.50

No. 18. $3.00

No. 19. $3.00

No. 20. $2.50

No. 21. $2.50

No. 22. $1, 2 and 3.00

No. 23. $1, $2, $3

No. 24. $2.25

No. 25. $2.25

No. 26. $2.00

No. 27. $1.25

No. 28. 75c

No. 29. $1.19

No 30. $2.50

No. 31. $6.50

No. 32. $2.29

No. 33. $1.50

No. 34. $1.19

No. 35. 98c

No. 36. $3.75.

RINGS AND BANGLES.

3503. No. 1. Solid Gold Ring, set with real cameo $6.49
3504. No. 2. Solid Gold Ring. set with onyx and pearls $5.49
3505. No. 3. Solid Gold Ring, set with real cameo $5.75
3506. No. 4. Solid Gold Ring, set with garnet and pearls $6.00
3507. No. 5. Solid Gold Ring, set with onyx, 4 diamond chips in centre and 3 pearls top and bottom $5.50
3508. No. 6. Solid Gold Ring. set with a Parisian diamond $5.50
3509. No. 7. Solid Gold Ring, set with emeralds and pearls $5.00
3510. No. 8. Solid Gold Ring, set with 2 diamond chips $5.00
11. No. 9. Solid Gold Ring, set with garnet 35and pearls $5.00
12. No. 10. Solid Gold Ring, set with real 35cameo $4.75
13 No. 11. Solid Gold Ring, set with garnet 35and pearls $4.50

3514. No. 12. Solid Gold Ring, set with cameo and pearls $4.50
3515. No. 13. Solid Gold band ring, elaborately engraved with pendant, star and crescent, set with genuine diamond chips $5.62
3516. No. 14. Solid Gold Ring, set with real cameo $4.00
3517. No. 15. Solid Gold Ring, set with onyx, $4.00
3518. No. 16. Solid Gold Ring, set with emeralds and pearls $4.00
3519. No 17. Solid Gold Ring, set with real onyx $3.50
3520. No. 18. Solid Gold Ring, set with real cameo $3.00
3521. No. 19. Solid Gold Ring, set with real amethyst $3.00
3522. No. 20. Solid Gold Ring, set with real cameo $2.50
3523. No. 21. Solid Gold set with garnet . $2.50
3524. No. 22. Gold filled band wedding rings . . . . $1.00, 2.00 and 3.00
3525. No. 23. Gold filled wedding rings . . . . $1.00, 2.00 and 3.00
3526. No. 24. Engraved gold filled wedding rings, 18kt. $2.25
3527. No. 25. Solid Gold real cameo ring . $2.25

3528. No. 26. Solid Gold onyx ring $2.00
3529. No. 27. Child's Solid Gold Ring . . $1.25
3530. No. 28. Solid Gold Baby Ring, word "Baby" or "Darling" engraved thereon . . 75c
3531. No. 29. Solid Gold Bangle Ring . . . $1.19
3532. No. 30. Solid Gold Band Ring, handsomely engraved $2.50

3532. No. 31. Black Onyx Glove Ring, set flush stone inlaid gold, and set with three diamond chips, handsomely hand engraved band, any initial or emblem $6.50
3533. No. 32. Misses' Solid Gold Ring, Turquoise horseshoe and pearl centre $2.29
3534. No. 33. Genuine Stone Cameo, set with band shank, neatly engraved for misses or boys $1.50
3535. No. 34. Child's Ring Solid Gold . . $1.19
3536. No. 35. Child's Ring, Solid Gold, real cameo 98c
3537. No. 36. Solid Gold, real Cameo . . . $3 75

BANGLES.

3538. Handsomely Engraved Bangles, Solid Gold, various designs . . . . 18, 25 and 33c

3549. Lady's Plain Nickle Watch, stem-winder and setter, excellent time-keeper, warranted $3 89
3550. Nickel Chatelaine and watch, stem-winder and setter, handsomely engraved, excellent time-keeper $6 39
3551. Lady's Silver Chatelaine Watch, half open face, engraved back, silver cap, stem-winder and setter, warranted, $10 00

3552. Gentleman's Nickel Open Face Watch, stem-winder, good movement, warranted.............. $3 89
3553. Same, in boys' sizes, with white or black dial, warranted............ $3 75
3554. Men's Solid Silver Hunting Case Watches, engine turned case and cylinder movement, key-winder........ $6 98
3555. Solid Silver Hunting Case, Elgin or Waltham movement, stem-winder and setter, engine turned case, warranted good time-keeper........ $9 98

3545. Solid Gold Hunting Case Watch, Waltham movement, handsomely engraved case, stem winder and setter, warranted good time-keeper $35 00
3546. Gentleman's Solid Gold Hunting Case Watch, stem winder and setter, Elgin movement, plain or engraved cases, warranted good time-keeper; a bargain.......... .... $23 98

3547. Lady's Solid Gold Watch, engraved case and gold movement, warranted................... $12 75
3548. Lady's Gold Hunter, stem-winding and setting watch, with anchor-movement..... .... $21 00

Other styles and makes constantly on hand—prices on application.

LOCKETS AND BANGLES.
Solid 14 karat Gold, handsomely hand engraved.

3556. $2 49. 3557. $3 49. 3558. $4 49. 3559. $4 39. 3560. $5 49. 3561. $4 98.

3562. $4 49. 3563. 3564. 3565. 3566. 3567. 3568. 3569.

Bangle Charms, assorted designs, 25c.

SEA BEAN AND ALLIGATOR TEETH JEWELRY.

  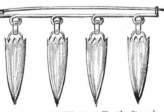

3570. Rolled Gold Sea Bean and Shell Bangle Lace Pin, entirely new, per pair.........69c

3572. Rolled Gold Alligator Teeth Bangle Lace Pin, very stylish......... ....63c

3571. Rolled Gold Bracelet, with assorted shell sea bean bangles, entirely new and very fashionable, per pair.... .... 69c

3573. Sea Bean Ear Drops, rolled gold wires to match pin and bracelets, per pair.......... .... 59c

3574. Alligator Tooth Scarf Pin, solid gold, very neat, $1 39

3575. Rolled Gold Alligator Teeth Earrings, to match pin, very stylish, per pair 50c

CHAINS.

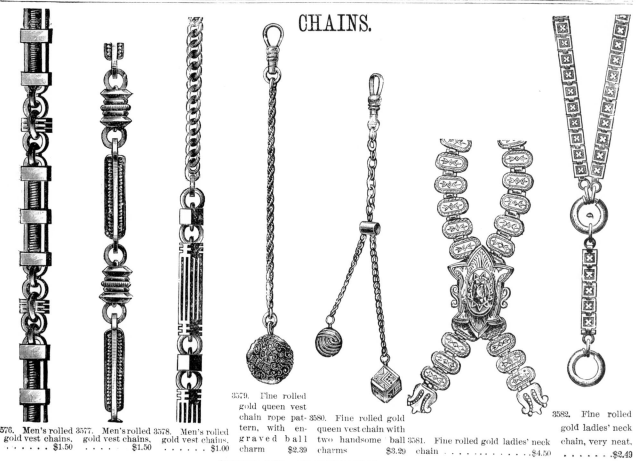

3579. Fine rolled gold queen vest chain rope pattern, with engraved ball charm $2.39

3580. Fine rolled gold queen vest chain with two handsome ball charms $3.29

3581. Fine rolled gold ladies' neck chain $4.50

3582. Fine rolled gold ladies' neck chain, very neat, $2.49

3576. Men's rolled gold vest chains, $1.50

3577. Men's rolled gold vest chains, $1.50

3578. Men's rolled gold vest chains, $1.00

COLLAR BUTTONS.

3583   3584   3585   3586   3587   3588   3589   3590   3591

3583. Rolled Gold   5c
3584. Ladies' Rolled Gold Collar Buttons. solid gold tops each   21c
3585. Solid Gold   59c
3586. Separable Collar Buttons, fine gold front, chased and engraved   50c

3587. Same   45c
3588. Separate Collar Buttons, with solid gold top,   45c
3589. Ladies' Solid Sterling Silver Collar Buttons, with Brazilian pebbles, large, medium or small sizes, each   10c

3590. Ladies' Solid Gold Collar Buttons, Brazilian pebbles, each $1.50
3591. Ladies' or Men's Roman Gold Collar Buttons, genuine diamonds, star setting $3.50, 5.00 7.50 and 10.00

SCARF PINS.

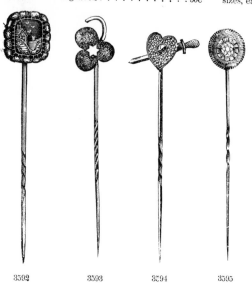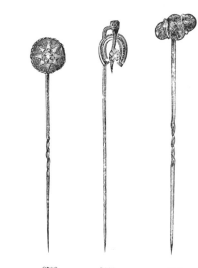

3592   3593   3594   3595   3596   3597   3598   3599   3600   3601

3592. Gold front sterling silver centre   75c
3593. Roman Gold   49c
3594. Rolled Gold, with solid gold trimmings. set with garnet   59c

3595. Rolled Gold, Brazilian pebble   69c
3596.   "   "   "   "   49c
3597. Solid   "   "   " $1.69
3598.   "   "   "   "   98c

3599. Solid Gold, Brazilian pebble   98c
3600.   "   "   "   "   98c
3601. Roman Gold Scarf Pin, very neat   49c

3602. Rolled Gold Hammered link sleeve buttons, per pair. 98c

3603. Separable link buttons, plain gold and stone setting. and fine gold plate, per pair 97c

3604. Patent separable sleeve buttons, rolled gold, plain with onyx, blood-stone, sardonyx and pearl, per pair................75c
3605. Same with any initials. $1 00

3606. Rolled gold link buttons, per pair.........75c

3607. Rolled plate sleeve buttons, patent lever backs. assorted stone, per pair...........25c

3608. Solid gold sleeve buttons assorted designs. $7 50

3609. Rolled gold patent lever initial sleeve buttons, horse shoe patterns, per pair.............89c

3610. Rolled gold patent lever sleeve buttons in onyx, goldstone blood-stone and agate, per pair.....69c

3611. Rolled gold patent lever buttons in onyx-blood'stone gold stone and agate, per pair......79c

3612. One piece, solid white pearl, with rolled plate, patent lever back 8 kt rolled gold, initial, per pair...........89c

3613. Rolled gold hand cut intaglio sleeve buttons, patent lever back per pair.....$1 19

3614. Ladies rolled gold sleeve buttons, horseshoe pattern, per pair, 25c

3615. Very neat rolled gold sleeve buttons, hand engraved, per pair. 25c

3616. Rolled gold hand cut initial sleeve buttons, patent lever back per pair......69c

3617. Solid gold sleeve buttons, very handsomely hand engraved, per pair.....$4 75

3618. Rolled gold patent lever, sleeve buttons, triangular shape, with onyx, gold-stone, agate, or bloodstone, per pair..........88c

SHIRT STUDS.

3619. Solid Gold Shirt Studs, with Briliant Pebbles......75c and $1 00
3620. Brazilian Pebble Studs, plated. each....................39c
3621. Solid Gold Shirt Studs, genuine diamonds..$10 00, 15 00 and 25 00
3622. Rolled gold Spiral Studs, per set.......................50c
3623. Black Onyx. for mourning. in matt or bright finish, per set..50c
3624. White Pearl, best quality, per set.......................50c
3625. White Linen Stone, for evening dress, set of 3............50c

EMBLEMS. Solid Gold.

3 2 i. Engraved Masonic pin, 79c

3627. Enameled Odd Fellows Pin......$1 39

3628. Enameled Knights' Pythias pin. ...$2 00

3629. Odd Fellows pin, $1 29

A Complete line of badges constantly on hand.

STYLOGRAPHIC AND GOLD PENS, PENCILS AND CHARMS.

3630. Plated Lantern Magic Pencil Charm.............. ......$1 67

3631. Gents' Plated Magic Pencil $1 13

3632. Plated Charm Magic Pencil, Snake....$1 50

3633. Celluliod Mercantile Screw Pencil....................45c

3634. Ladies Plated Magic Pencil Charm.... ....$1 35

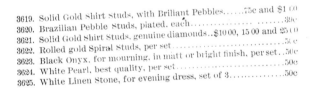

3635. 4 Gold Pens in Plated Pencil Holder........$2 35

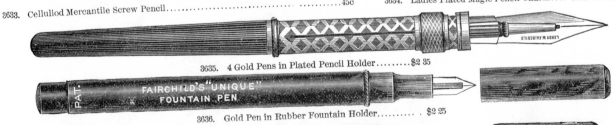

3636. Gold Pen in Rubber Fountain Holder.......... $2 25

3637. The Cross Stylographic Pen, plain............$1 49

3638. 2 Gold Pens, Plated Desk Holder $1 19

3644. 18 kt. rolled plate hard enameled Lace Pin, set with 1 Brazillian pebble in centre, very neat...............39c

3650. Very neat hard enameled rolled gold Earrings, pansy shape with pearl in centre, per pair...........39c

3651. Entirely new rolled gold Earrings, hard enameled, with Brazillian pebbles, per pair...............39c

3656. Very neat 18 kt rolled plate Lace Pin, set with pearls.................. ....39c

3645. 18 kt. rolled plate pansy Lace Pin, set with real porcelain pansy, very stylish....................39c

3652. Rolled Gold Bracelets, handsomely hand engraved, never sold less than $1 00 per pair 25c

3657. Entirely new 18 kt rolled plate Lace Pin, set with 3 pebbles or pearls...............39c

3646. 18 kt rolled rolled plate hard enameled Lace Pin, 1 Brazillian pebble.... ....39c

3658. Very pretty oxydized Mikado Pin, 45c

3647. Very neat Rolled Plate Bracelets, per pair..... ... 25c

3659. Very neat Rolled Plate Bracelet, per pair....25c

3648. Pretty style Rolled Plate Bracelets, per pair..... ...25c

3660. Beaded Bracelets, good gold plate, per pair 35c

3653   3654

3653. Ladies' Watch Chain, with charm, (smelling bottle) very neat, oxydized silver or gilt......................59c

3654. Entirely new, Ladies' Vest Chain, with charm, Mikado pattern, (smelling bottle,) oxydized silver or gilt.......85c

3649. Entirely new oxydized Mikado Pin.............35c

3655. 18 kt rolled plate Lace Pin, cat tail design, entirely new.... ....39c

3661. Very rich oxydized Medallion Pin 35c

OPERA GLASSES. The Celebrated "Lemaire" Make.

3662. Ivory two sizes, $5.00 and 7.50.

3663. White Pearl, two sizes, $7.50 and 8.50.

3664. Leather covered, two sizes. $2.50 and 3.50.

3665. Mother of Pearl, two sizes, $7.50 and 8 50

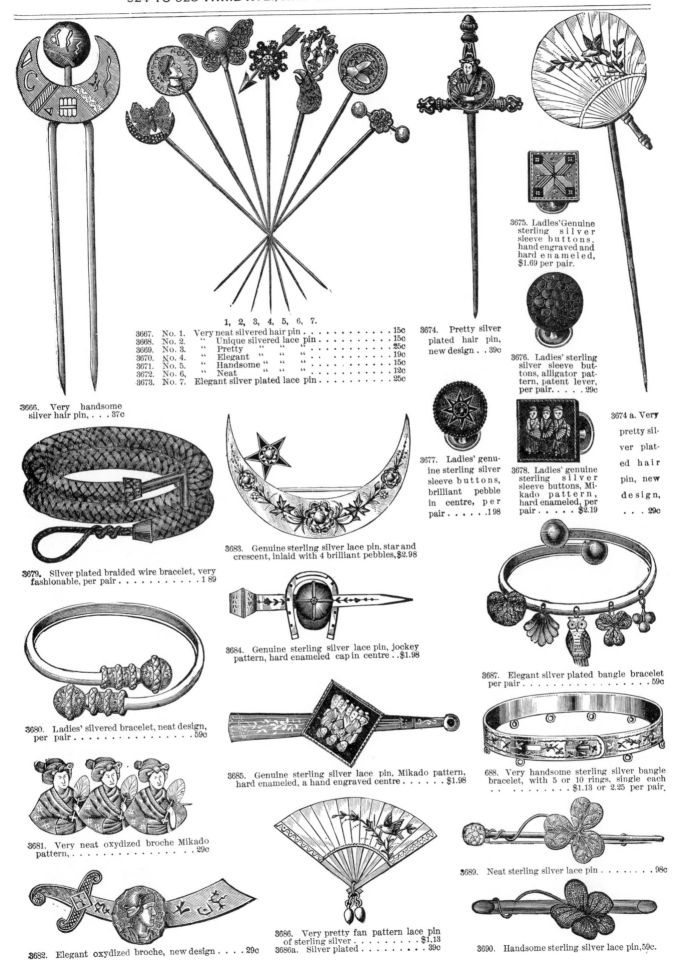

1, 2, 3, 4, 5, 6, 7.

3667. No. 1. Very neat silvered hair pin 15c
3668. No. 2.   "   Unique silvered lace pin 15c
3669. No. 3.   "   Pretty   "   "   " 25c
3670. No. 4.   "   Elegant   "   "   " 19c
3671. No. 5.   "   Handsome   "   "   " 15c
3672. No. 6.   "   Neat   "   "   " 12c
3673. No. 7. Elegant silver plated lace pin 25c

3666. Very handsome silver hair pin, . . . 37c

3679. Silver plated braided wire bracelet, very fashionable, per pair 1 89

3680. Ladies' silvered bracelet, neat design, per pair 59c

3681. Very neat oxydized broche Mikado pattern, ... 29c

3682. Elegant oxydized broche, new design 29c

3683. Genuine sterling silver lace pin, star and crescent, inlaid with 4 brilliant pebbles, $2.98

3684. Genuine sterling silver lace pin, jockey pattern, hard enameled cap in centre . . $1.98

3685. Genuine sterling silver lace pin, Mikado pattern, hard enameled, a hand engraved centre $1.98

3686. Very pretty fan pattern lace pin of sterling silver $1,13
3686a. Silver plated 39c

3674. Pretty silver plated hair pin, new design . . 39c

3675. Ladies' Genuine sterling silver sleeve buttons, hand engraved and hard enameled, $1.69 per pair.

3676. Ladies' sterling silver sleeve buttons, alligator pattern, patent lever, per pair 29c

3677. Ladies' genuine sterling silver sleeve buttons, brilliant pebble in centre, per pair 1 98

3678. Ladies' genuine sterling silver sleeve buttons, Mikado pattern, hard enameled, per pair $2.19

3674 a. Very pretty silver plated hair pin, new design, . . . 29c

3687. Elegant silver plated bangle bracelet per pair 59c

688. Very handsome sterling silver bangle bracelet, with 5 or 10 rings, single each . . . . $1.13 or 2.25 per pair.

3689. Neat sterling silver lace pin 98c

3690. Handsome sterling silver lace pin, 59c.

Metal Clasps.

Clasps represented below are made of the best quality hard metal, handsomely engraved and rich in appearance, entirely new and very fashionable this season; can be had in oxydized or bronze.

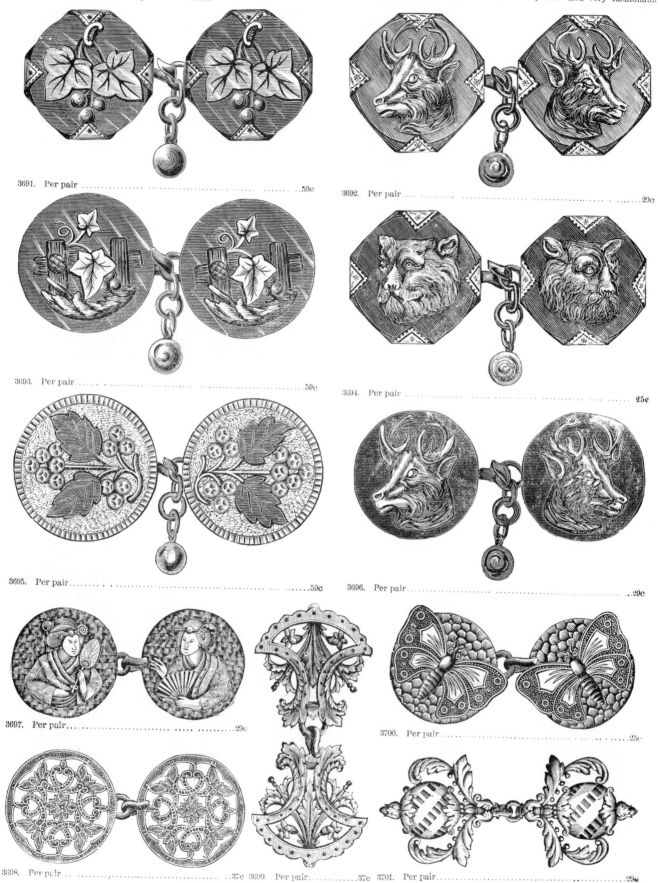

3691. Per pair 59c

3692. Per pair 29c

3693. Per pair 59c

3694. Per pair .... 25¢

3695. Per pair 59c

3696. Per pair 29c

3697. Per pair 29c

3700. Per pair 25c

3698. Per pair .... 37c 3699. Per pair .... 37c 3701. Per pair 29c

3702. Ladies' Silver Plated Collarette, new design $1 13

3703. Genuine sterling silver collar button with Brazilian pebble, hand engraved, 69c

3703a. Ladies oxydized broche 25c

3704. Very neat silver plated drops, per pair . .63c

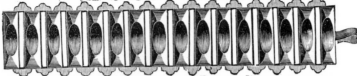

705. Ladies sleeve plated collarette $1 87

3706. Sterling silver ball drops with wires or screws, per pair . . 15c

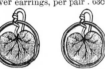

3707. Elegant sterling silver earrings, per pair . 63c

3708. Ladies silver plated collarette $2 25

3709. Very neat sterling silver earrings, per pair, 69c

3710. Very neat sterling silver earrings, per pair. .50c

MOURNING JEWELERY, ENTIRELY NEW DESIGNS.

3711. Ladies patent oxydized sleeve buttons 25c

3713. Ladies oxydized sleeve buttons patent lever par pair.. . . .29c

3714. Onyx lace pin with 4 rolled gold bands, and cut onyx drops $1 69
3715. Drops to match, per pair 98c

3716. Onyx lace pin trimmed with rolled gold bands, leaf inlaid with pearl $1 59
3317. Earings to match, per pair $1 39

3721. Dull finished screw earrings, plated wires, per pair 39c

3722. Onyx screw knobs finely cut per pair . . .39c

3729. Dull finish onyx bead pin, with gold rings 97c

3730. Cut onyx bead pin, with gold plate rings between each bead 69c

3718. Black onyx pin. 25c

3723. Onyx earings with one pearl in centre and rolled gold branch, per pair $1 39

3724. Finely cut onyx earrings, trimmed with 1 rolled gold band per pair. . 98c

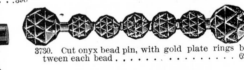

3731. Onyx and rolled gold lace pin, inlaid with pearls, finely cut bead bangles . $1 98
3732. Earrings to match . . . .$1 69.

3719. Polished onyx faceted solid bead bracelet finely cut with rolled gold rings between each bead, per pair $1 39

3725. Dull finish earings, per pair. .75c

3726. Cut onyx earings, gold wires, bright finish, per pair 69c

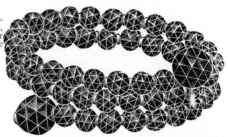

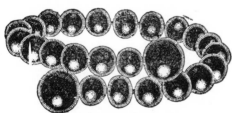

3720. Onyx dull finished bead bracelets, per pair . . 59c

3727. Cut onyx earings gold wires. per pair $1 19

3728. Dull finished earings, pair . 75c

3733. Polished onyx faceted solid bead bracelet, finely cut with rolled gold ring between each bead, per pair $1 98

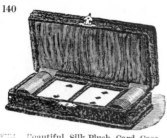

3735. Hand embroidered Silk Plush Cushion and Bottles, all colors, $5 50

Beautiful Silk Plush Card Case, satin lined, containing 2 decks of superior glazed cards and 70 bone chips, $2 50

3736. Handsome Silk Plush Manicure Case, containing 3 pieces bone trimmings and one curved scissors, satin lined $1 49

3738. Combination Plush Toilet and Nail Set, slanting desk shape, size, 11x13, containing large celluloid mirror, brush, comb, nail and tooth brushes, salve box, nail polisher, nail cleaner, nail scissors and manicure brush $11 25

3739. Very handsome Silk Plush Shaving Case, containing mug, razor, comb, scissors, lather and hair brush and swinging beveled mirror, $8 00

3740. Combination Silk Plush Work, Glove, Handkerchief and Odor Case, with following trimmings, viz.; bone glove stretcher, 2 bottles and six work fittings $4 50

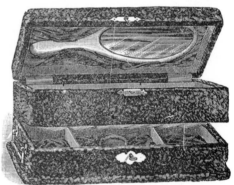

3741. Very handsome Silk Plush Work Box, containing 7 pieces, satin lined $3 00

3743. Handsome Silk Plush Toilet Case, containing zylonite fittings $6 80

3742. Handsome Silk Plush Collar and Cuff Box, satin lined $2 50

3744. Silk Plush Handkerchief Box satin lined, beveled mirror top, $1 89

3745. Silk Plush Odor Case, with extension handle, containing 2 bottles and beveled plate mirror, satin lined $1 87

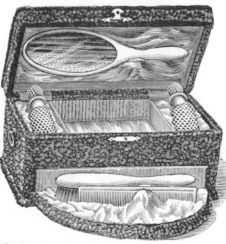

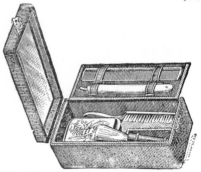

3746. Elegant Silk Plush Jewel Case, satin lined, small size, $2 00; medium size, $2 50; large size, $3 00.

3747. Very handsome Combination Silk Plush Dressing and Odor Case and Handkerchief Box; revolving bottom fitted with zylonite comb, brush, mirror and two odor bottles, satin lined $7 25

3748. Very handsome Gentleman's Dressing Case, imitation leather, complete . . . . $2 7?

3749. Gentleman's Alligator Dressing case, complete....................$5 39

3750. Elegant Silk Plush Frame, with French beveled glass 8x8, 2-inch frame, $1 20; same, 3-inch, frame. $1 50; 10x10 2½-inch, $1 81; same, with 3½-inch frame, $2 15; same,12x12,3½-inch frame $2 81; 14x14, 4-inch frame,.........$3 50

3751. Hand Mirrors, French plate, each............63c

Frames can be had in cardinal, navy blue, old gold and peacock blue.

3752. Whisk Broom Holder of Silk Plush, with brass handle broom, $1 25

3753. Very handsome Silk Plush, Frame, outside size 11x9, imperial oval opening....................................81c

3754. Elegant Silk Plush Frame, Parchment shape, nickle ring, outside size, 9½x6, price............83c

SPECIAL.

3755. Antique Brass Frames, Imperial size..........19c

3756. Elegant Silk Plush Frame, representing a pair of door curtains over an imperial or arch opening outside, size 9x7 price 69c

3757. Very Elegant Silk Plush Frame, combination of cardinal and bronze plush, gilt trimmings, nickle ring and oval opening, outside size, 9x7, price................53c

3758. Very Elegant Silk Plush Frame, square opening trimmed with raised bronze satin and plush, outside size, 9x7, price $1 13

3759. Very Elegant Satin Frame Grecian pattern raised effect, nickel and gilt ring, imperial and oval openings, outside size, 9x7, price............... ...65c

3760. Very elegant Silk Plush frame nickel trimmings, and ring outside, size, 8½x6½, price...... 49c

3761. Fine Silk Plush Album, padded, nickel corners and extension clasps, beveled inside, size 9x10½ inches, price............................$3 89

3762. Very fine Silk Plush Album, padded, fine gilt ornamental shield, round corners, beveled inside, extension clasp $3 75

3763. Fine Silk Plush Album, padded, with handsome silk ornaments, round corners, beveled inside and extension clasp, price..........$3 59

3764. Fine Silk Plush Album, padded, nickel shield on side, round corners, imitation beveled inside, size 9x10½ inches, price... ..$3 25

3767. Fancy Paper Box, containing 24 sheets of paper and envelopes 8c
Postage, 7c.

We will send this Catalogue, free of charge, to any one applying for it by letter or postal card.

3765. Leatherette Cabinet, satin lined, containing 2½ quires of fine white or tinted paper, 1 quire of cards and envelopes to match . . 69c

3766. Plain Glazed Box, containing 24 gilt edge corresponding cards, white or tinted, and envelopes to match . . 15c

3768. Silk Plush Cabinet, satin lined, containing 2½ quires of fine white or tinted paper, 1 quire of cards and envelopes to match $1.49

3769. Thermometer and Storm Glass. 49c
3769a. Thermometers, each. 10, 15, 25, 50, 75c

3770. Olive Wood-Inkstand, pen, pencil and eraser, $1.25

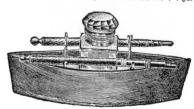

3771 Boat-shape Olive Wood Inkstand, with pen and pencil 85c

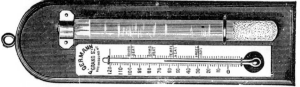

3772. Plain Glazed Box, containing 24 corresponding cards with black border for mourning, and envelopes to match 19c
3773. Same, with 24 sheets of paper and envelopes to match . . . 29c

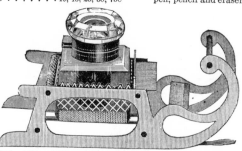

3774. Gilt and Silver Inkstand, 3 inches high and 6 inches wide $1.25

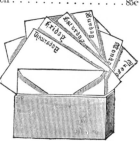

3775. Leather covered Pocket or Traveling Inkstand 17c

3776. Plain Glazed Box, containing 24 corresponding cards, with days of the week on one corner and envelopes to match, white only 25c
3777. Same, with black border for mourning 49c

INKSTANDS.

3778. Olive wood, bronze and bronze, imported and domestic inkstands, in all the novelties, from. . . . . .50c to $5.00 each
3779. " Good Luck" Revolving Inkstands, ebony and gold finish, 4 in. high, 4 in. wide. . . . 39c
3780. Fancy Bronze Inkstand and Rack, one cut glass bottle, ebony and gold finish, 4 in. high, 4½ in. wide. 59c
3781. Fancy Bronze Inkstand, brass finish, new design, with one cut glass bottle, demon shape, 4 in. high, 3 in. wide $1.19
3782. Bronze Inkstand and Rack, French bronze finish, one cut glass bottle representing barrel with lock, entirely new design, 4 in. high, 3 in. wide 35c
3783. Fancy Bronze Inkstand, japan and gilt finish, two glass bottles, 5 in. high, 3 in. wide, 75c

NOTE PAPER IN BOXES

3793a. Plain Glazed Box, containing 24 sheets of initial paper, white or tinted, and envelopes to match any initial 29c
3794. Same, without initial 25c
3795. Plain Tinted Box, containing 24 sheets of paper, with steel engravings on one corner, 4 designs in box, and envelopes to match . . . 22c
3796. Same, plain 16c
3797. Fancy Paper Boxes, for children, containing 24 sheets of paper, fancy designs on one corner and envelopes to match 19c
3798. Same filled with plain paper 10c

Paper By the Quire or Ream.

3799. Crown Irish Linen, white, per quire . 12½c
3780. Envelopes to match, per package of 25, 12½c
3781. Mourning Paper, with narrow, medium or wide borders, per quire 17½c
3782. Envelopes to match, per package of 25. 17½c
3783. Tinted Paper, 24 different colors, per quire 8c
3784. Envelopes to match, per package of 25 8c

No. 3787.
3787. Drinking Glass and leather case 97c

No. 3784.
3784. Brass Calendar, marking days, date and months, works on rollers, can be used for yrs. 59c
3785. Same in olive wood 69c
3786. Same in ivory. $1.19

3825. White Paper Quality, Quality X, per quire, 3c; per ream 50c
3826. Quality XX, per quire, 5c; per ream . 75c
3827. Quality XXX, per quire, 6c; per ream. $1.00
3828. Quality XXXX, per quire, 8c; per ream, 1.25
3829. Envelopes to match, package of 25,
3829a.   Quality X, XX, XXX, XXXX
                      5c,   7c,   8c,   10c
Per box of 250 . . 40c, 50c,   65c,   80c
3830. Foolscap, per quire. 15c
3831. Legal Cap 15c
3832. Letter Paper 15c
3833. Any of the above, per ream $2.50

DIARIES' ETC., FOR 1886.

3815. All sizes,
     9, 15, 18. 20, 29, 31, 33, 39, 45, 59, 75c, $1.00
3816. Memorandum Books, in Russia covers,
     12, 15, 18, 25, 29, 32, 35c to $1.49
3817. Gents' Memoranda, Russia leather, kid lining, money, card and ticket compartments, and a paper memorandum book, in different sizes $1.25, 1.50, 1.75, 2 00, 2.25, 2.50
3818. Gentlemen's Diaries, with bill pockets, card and stamp compartments, and rubber strap $1.50, 1.75. 2.00, 2.50
3819. Leather, gilt edge, with rubber band across the end $1.00

BIRTHDAY CARDS.

3777a. Mounted on handsome satin cards and fringed . . . . 49, 69 and 89c

ENGRAVING FOR BALLS, WEDDINGS, PARTIES, VISITING CARDS, ETC.

3788. Plate and 50 cards, engraved, any name or design 89c
3789. Same, with address $1.00
3790. Monograms, any design . . . . $1.00 to 1.50
3791. Stamping on paper and envelopes, per quire 15c
3792. Same, envelopes per pack 15c
3793. Cards printed from your own plate, per hundred 50c
Printing neatly done in all its branches. Estimates furnished on application.

WRITING DESKS.

3820. Black Walnut, velvet lined, 12 inches long, 75c; 14 inches $1.00
3821. Maple or Rosewood, velvet lined, 12 inch, $1.50; 14 inch $2.00
3822. Alligator Leather, satin lined, padded square top, 8x10¼, $3.75; 8¾x11¾ . . . $4.25
3823. Silk Plush, 8x10¼, $4.75; Same, padded, 8¾x11¼ $5.50

INDELIBLE MARKING INK.

3824. Payson's Indelible Ink, for marking clothing, etc. 21c

STENCIL PLATES.

3825a. Any name put up in a neat box, with brush and ink for marking clothing and linen. Instruction in box 25c

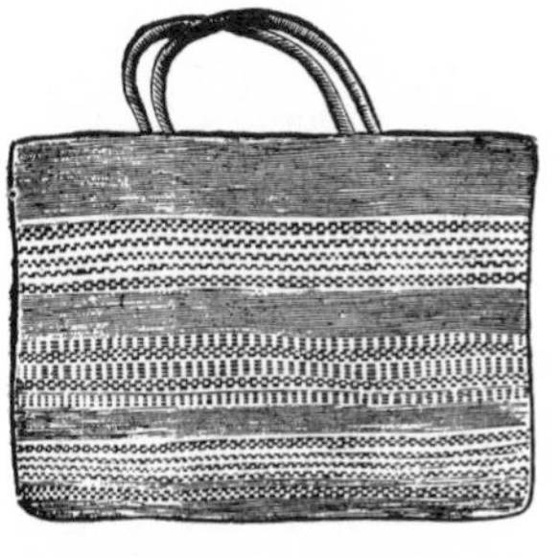

3821. Hemp, quality B, with rope handles, 12 inches wide, 12c; 14 inches wide..14c
3821a. Quality A, 14 inches wide, 15c; 16 inches wide..........................17c

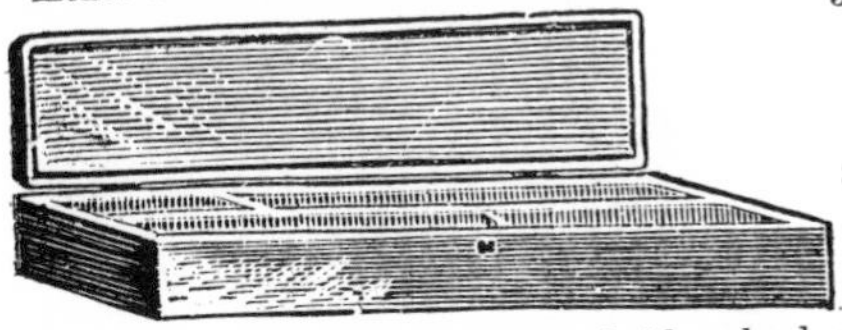

3822. Maple Pencil Box, with pen, holder, lead and slate pencils, chalk, ruler, eraser and sponge..................................15c

MISCELLANEOUS.

3823. Double Silicate Book Slates, each, 5, 10 and 15c; same, with cloth covers, 12, 17, 21 and 33c
3824. Eagle Lead Pencils, inserted rubber tip, as good as any pencil made for ordinary use, per doz..........12c
3825 Eagle Lead Pencils, black, per dozen, 25, 40, and 50c
3826. Faber's black, per dozen.... .25, 40 and 50c
3827. Automatic, each..........................15, 18c
3828. Pen-holders, each...............2, 3, 5, 10c
3829. Gillott's Steel Pens, per dozen..8, 9, 10, 12c
3830. Spencerian, per dozen.......................10c
3831. Esterbrook's, per dozen.........8, 9, 10, 12c
3832. Slate Pencils, German, sharpened, 5½ in., per box of 100..............................15c
3833. Soapstone, sharpened, 6 in., box of 100.23c
3834. Erasers, each.................1, 3, 5, 10, 15c
3835. Writing Books...............2, 5, 10, 12, 15c
3836. Slate Sponges, each, 1c; per dozen......10c
3837. Rulers, 12-inch, each............1, 5, 10, 15c
3838. Nickel Pencil Sharpeners......................9c
3839. Tin Lunch Boxes...............................10c
3840. Pen Wipers, each.......................5, 10, 15c
3841. Blotters, per dozen............................5c
3842. Paper Knives, each.......................25, 50c
3843. Drawing Instruments, per set,39,69,87,$1 19
3844. Book Clamps, each............................15c
3845. Book Straps...........................5, 10, 15c
3846. Spencerian Copy Books, each...............11c
3847. Copy Book Covers, each........................3c
3848. Blank Books, each.....................3, 5, 10c
3849. Memorandum Books..................5, 10, 15c
3850. Paper Pads, 100 sheets ruled and plain, all sizes, each, from.......................3 to 15c
3851. Thaddeus Davids Co.s' Black Ink, per bottle.......................................3 and 6c
3852. Carter's black, per bottle........................6c
3853. Mucilage, per bottle.............................5c

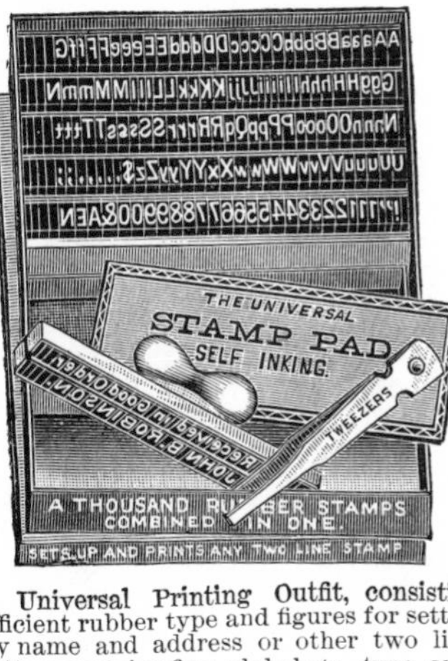

3854. Universal Printing Outfit, consisting of sufficient rubber type and figures for setting up any name and address or other two lines of matter; contains five alphabets, type and figures, two line type holder, a self-inking stamp pad, a pair of type tweezers and full directions 95c

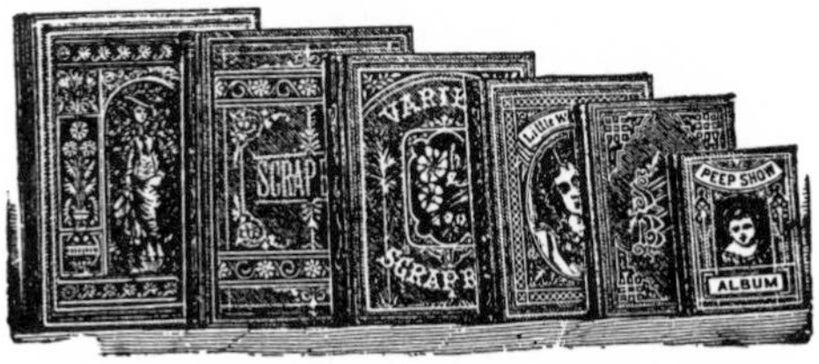

SCRAP BOOKS.

3855. The Plain Series: Imitation cloth, assorted colors, embossed, black, buff paper, size, 8¼x10, 19c. 8¾x11½, 22c; 9½x12, 29c; 10¼x12¾, 35c; 11½x14. 42c; 12½x15..50c
3856. The "Rose" Series: Imitation leather, embossed gold and black, illuminated with beautiful card center, round corners, buff paper inside, 8¾x11½, 75c; 9½x12, 89c; 10¼x12¾, $1 00; 11½x14, $1 15; 12½x15.......$1 35
3857. The "Staple" Series: Imitation Russia back and corners, cloth sides, spring back, lettered "Scrap Book" on side, heavy white paper inside, 8¼x10 $2 00: 8x11, $2 25; 9¼x12, $2 50; 11½x13¼.....................$3 00

SCRAP PICTURES.

3858. All the latest designs in scrap pictures to be had per sheet from..............................3 to 10c

AUTOGRAPH ALBUMS.

3859. Children's Series, imitation cloth, assorted colors, decorated with flowers, etc., 2⅝x4¼, 9c, 3x4½, 11c; 3¼x4¾...16c
3860. The "Season" Series, imitation leather, embossed in gold, elegantly illuminated with flowers, panels, etc., nickle edges and cream tinted paper, containing exquisite illustrations after Giacomelli, 3x4½, 42c; 3⅜x5⅜, 69c; 3⅞x6¼, 83c; 4¼x7, $1 10; 5x7¾, $1 33; 7x 8½...$2 00
3861. The Nouveaute" Series, entirely new, leatherette alligator, plush back, word "Album" inlaid in plush, stamped gilt, heavily padded, gold edges and cream tinted paper, 3⅞x6¼, $1 25; 4¼x7, $1 50; 5x7¾, $1 92; 7x8½...$2 50

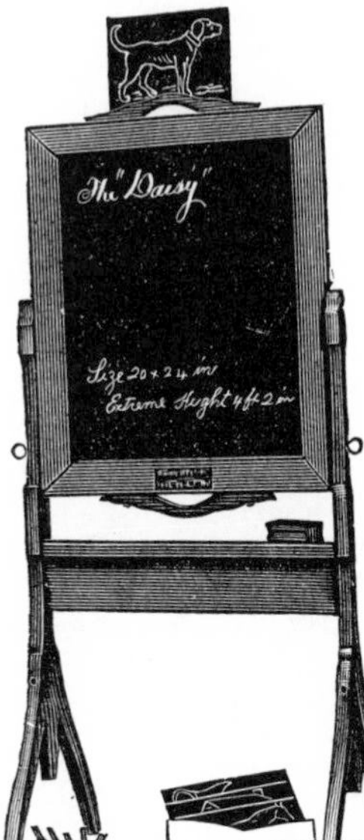

3862. The "Daisy" Revolving Blackboard and Easel combined, with set of drawing cards, rubber and crayons; size, 20x24 inches, extreme height, 4 feet 2 inches......................$2 60

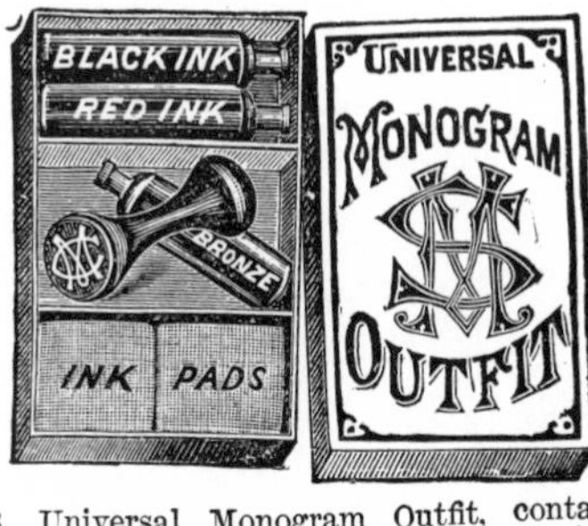

3863. Universal Monogram Outfit, containing one rubber monogram stamp, one bottle indelible ink, one bottle bright red ink, one ink distributer, one bottle bronze, ink pads, directions for use, etc.; cut represents ¼ size......35c

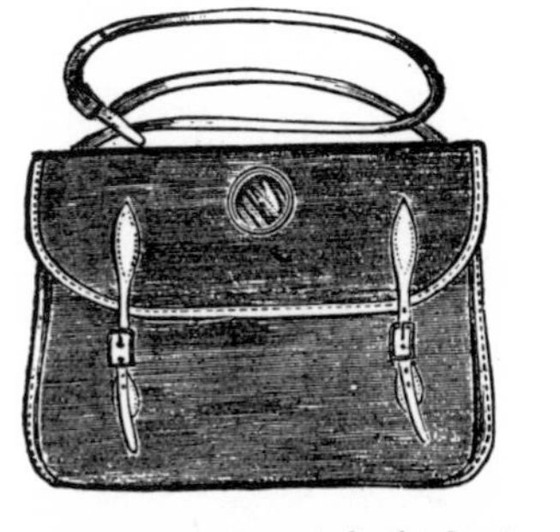

3864. Rubber cloth, or imitation leather, strong lined inside, with straps to buckle as illustrated, and strap to go around shoulder, or handles, 17 inches wide 49, 65c
3865. Same, leather.........97c and $1 59
3866. Same, duck...........50c and $1 00

SHAWL & TRUNK STRAPS.

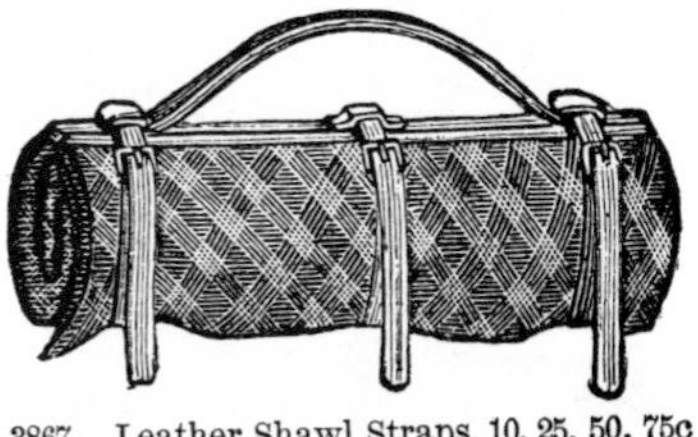

3867. Leather Shawl Straps, 10, 25, 50, 75c
3868. Patent Shawl Strap, with roller and handles.........................25, 50c, $1 00
3869. Trunk Straps, 8 to 9 feet long, 1 inch wide......................59, 69 and 89c

SCHOOL SUPPLIES' ETC.

In these necessities we have every article for School use. Below we give a short list of such as we have on hand. For School Books refer to Book Department.

3870. Writing Sets (entirely new); Box shape of a closed parasol, with silk tassel, containing pen, holder, ruler and pencil.................15c
3871. Paper box, containing olive wood penholder with pen; knife eraser, olive wood handle, and olive lead pencil with nickel tip and eraser...10c
3872. Wood-frame hinged box, with ruler, lead pencil, knife eraser, olive wood handle, and olive wood pen-holder.......................15c
3873. Ebony-wood box, nickel trimmings, two rulers, lead pencil with nickel protector and rubber, and knife eraser; pen-holder with olive wood handles and pen.........................29c
3874. School Knives, wood handles, one blade, 5c
3875. White bone handle, two blades, 10c; pearl handle...21c

SLATES.

3876. Noiseless Slate, bound with cloth, very strong and durable, 5x7, each, 9c; per dozen, 90c. 6x9, each, 12c; per dozen, $1 30. 8x12, each, 15c; per dozen.......................................$1 70
3877. School Slates, best quality, 5x7 in., each, 3c; per dozen, 30c; 6½x10, each, 5c; per dozen, 50c; 8x12, each, 6c; per dozen.....................60c

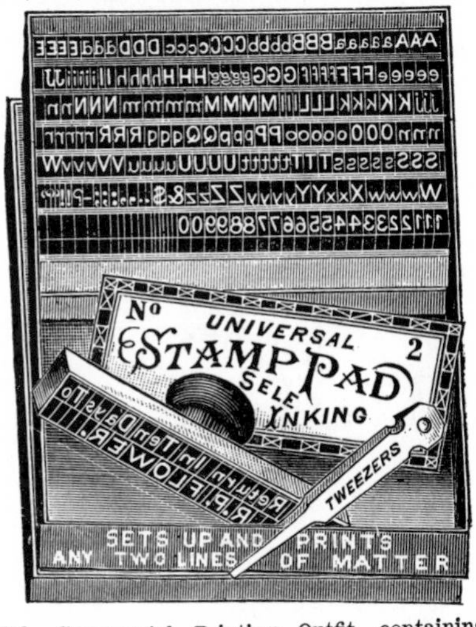

3878. Commercial Printing Outfit, containing 200 rubber letters (8 alphabets and figures), one three line holder, self-inking stamp pad and a pair of type tweezers, sets up three lines..$1 35

MUSIC CASES.

3879. Imitation Cloth, bands of pansies, roses, etc 39c
3880. Morocco Cloth, lettered "Music" 49c
3881. American Russia Leather, lettered "Music" 75c
3882. Japanese Leather Hinge Box, nickel catch, 75c
3883. Silk Plush, satin lined $2 69

STERESCOPES.

3884. Without shaft, screw handle and slide, 25, 50 and 75c; on stand . . . . . 50c, $1 00 and 1 50
3885. Views of kinds, 3c each; per dozen. . . . 33c

SAALFIELD MUSIC ALBUMS.

A book nicely bound with paper covers, containing all the latest airs in vocal and instrumental music:

3886. Small, 124 pages 25c
3887. Large, 248 pages 39c
3888. Same, handsomely bound with cloth covers, large size 89c

MUSIC WRAPPERS.

ENGLISH STYLE, ENTIRELY NEW.

3889. Japanese leather $1 79
3890. American Russia leather. $2 00
3891. Alligator. 2 49
3892. Plush, satin lined 2 89
3893. Plush, satin lined, word "Music" in hammered silver letters 3 75
3894. Leather 1 00
3895. Antique leather, fern pattern. 1 50

SPRING BACK MUSIC FOLIOS.

3896. Morocco, cloth back, paper sides. 69c
3897. Leather back, cloth sides full gilt. . . . $1 19
3898. Japanese leather band and corners. cloth sides, stamped on side "Music" in black and gilt $1 49
3899. Imitation Alligator, back and corners, cloth sides, embossed word "Music" on side in nickel $2 50
3900. Half Plush, with elegant full size chromo lithograph on one side $3 75
3901. Silk Plush, assorted colors, with monogram "Music" in nickel round corners, very fine $5 50

GAMES.

3902. Game of Peerless 20c
3903. " " Pictorial Dominoes 15c
3904. " " Logomachy 42c
3905. " " Animals and Birds 10c
3906. " " Shakespear's Characters and Quotations 35c
3907. Game of House that Jack built 20c
3908. " " Merry Goose 35c
3909. " " Chinese Puzzle 35c
3910. " " Word Making and Taking . . 25c
3911. " " Old Maid . . .10, 18, 21 and 23c
3912. " " Words and Sentences. . . . 17c
3913. " " Lotto . . . . . 25, 50 and 67c
3914. " " Dominoes 49, 69, 79, 88c and $2 00
3915. " " Chess Men, wood, per set, 50, 69 and 73c
3916. Game of Chess Men, bone, per set. 1 00, 1 50 and $2 00
3917. Game of American Jack Straws, No. 2 25c
3918. " " Little Red Riding Hood 20c
3919. " " Where's Johnny. 20c
3920. " " Checker Boards 24, 41, 49, 54 and 61c

PLAYING CARDS.

3921. Good bristle board, full deck 7c
3922. Double edges, enameled, heavy card, full deck with Joker 25c
3923. Fine satin finish, round corners, full deck with Joker 39c
3924. Extra fine double heads, pearl enamel finish, full deck with Joker 49c

FIREARMS.

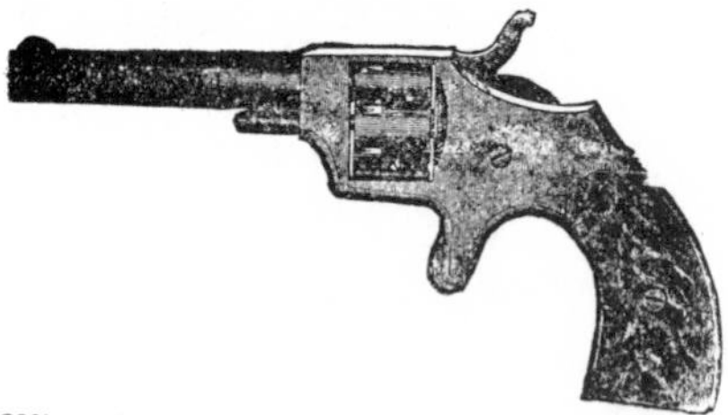

3925. Blue Jacket No. 1, 22 cal., 6 shot, wood handles 75c
3926. Ivory Handle $1 49
3927. Pearl Handle $2 50
3928. The Continental, Hard Pan or Defender, 32 cal., short cyl., plain, nickel plated, wood stock, (Padlock) $1 40
3929. Rubber $1 75
3930. Bulls-eye, Robin Hood, Defender or sterl- 32 cal., long cyl., fluted, nickel, wood stock, (Parcel) $1 54
3931. Sterling or Defender No. 1, 22 cal., long fluted, wood, (Package) $1 07
3932. Rubber (Paint) $1 20
3933. Octagon wood (Packet) $1 25
3934. Octagon rubber (Pain) $1 40
3935. Sterling Defender or Dash, 32 calibre, 5-shot, round fluted, rubber stock (Path) . . $1 75
3936. The celebrated Smith & Wesson's Revolvers. The new No. 32 double action, 9-shot, central fire, with automatic cartridge ejector; weight, 12½ oz., 32-100 calibre, 3 and 3½ inch barrel, blue or nickel plated, rubber stock $12 50
3937. Ivory stock, extra $2 00
3938. Pearl stock, extra 3 00
3939. Engraved, extra . . . . $1 50 to 5 00
3940. Gold plated trimmings, extra $1 50
3941. Cartridges, per hundred 1 10

Other revolvers including all makes, such as Harrington & Richardson's Texas Bull Dogs or Western Stars, the American Bull Dogs, Colts' and Smith & Wesson's at regular prices. A full line of firearms, sporting goods and ammunition constantly on hand. Prices on application.

THE GEM OIL STOVE.

This Stove has become renowned for its excellence. It has so been improved that the tank, by a slight turn, can be separated from the top, leaving the inside exposed, so it can be easily cleaned and repaired.

3942. No. 1. Single Stove, with one 4-inch burner and wick $1 09
3943. No. 2. Single Stove, with two 3-inch burners and wicks $1 39
3944. No. 3. Single Stove, with three 4-inch burners and wicks $2 50
3945. No. 4. Double Stove, with four 3-inch burners and wicks $2 29
3946. No. 5. Double Stove, with four 4-inch burners and wicks $3 75

Also, a complete line of other popular Stoves. Description and prices furnished on application.

All our goods are marked at the lowest prices, which do not include postage. No goods sent by mail, except sufficient money accompanies the order, for postage; otherwise we will reduce orders, and take out part of goods to the amount of postage required.

Whenever you send us money with an order for goods, and fail to hear from us within ten days after sending the order, please inform us of the fact by letter or postal card, as lost money can be more readily traced when looked after at once. Customers in California or on the Pacific Coast should write within fifteen days after sending.

SKATES.

In ordering skates, please mention size of shoes they are intended for.

Inches, compared with sizes of shoes, by numbers.

Skates, inches	7,	7½,	8,	8½,	9,
Nos. Shoes,	9½,	11,	12½,	1,	2½
Skates, inches,	9½,	10,	10½,	11,	11½
Nos. Shoes,	4,	5½,	7½.	9,	10½

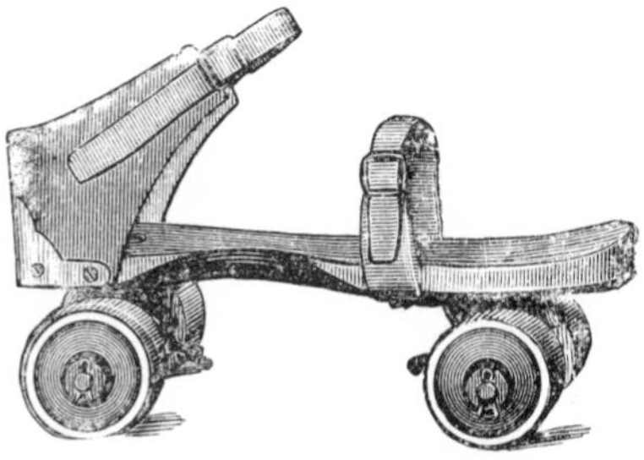

3947. New patent Rink Skate, sizes 7½ to 11½; polished beech wood, oak-tanned black grain leather trimmings, patent buckles, nickel-plated heel band, malleable iron frame, japanned steel axles, box-wood rolls, per pair $2 49

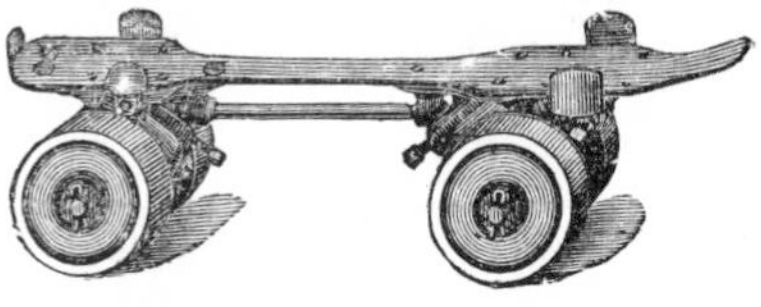

3948. Double Clamp Roller Skates, sizes 8 to 11½ inches; these skates have steel foot plates, blued or nickel plated, and highly polished clamp, operated by a right and left screw for holding both the toe and the heel of the shoe, malleable iron trucks, steel axles, rubber springs, with adjustable screw for loose or tight tension, Turkish box-wood wheels, nickled foot plate, per pair $5 98
3949. Blued foot plate, per pair $4 98
3950. Sidewalk Roller Skates, for boys and girls, sizes 7 to 11 inches, polished beechwood, trimmed with black leather nickel plated heel band, patent buckles, steel frames and axles, hardwood wheels, each 59c
3951. Same, better quality, made like rink skates, each 89c

DOLLS!

A Full Line of

DOLLS

OF ALL KINDS.

From 5 Cents to 12 Dollars.

PRICES ON APPLICATION.

For particulars, refer to previous catalogue.

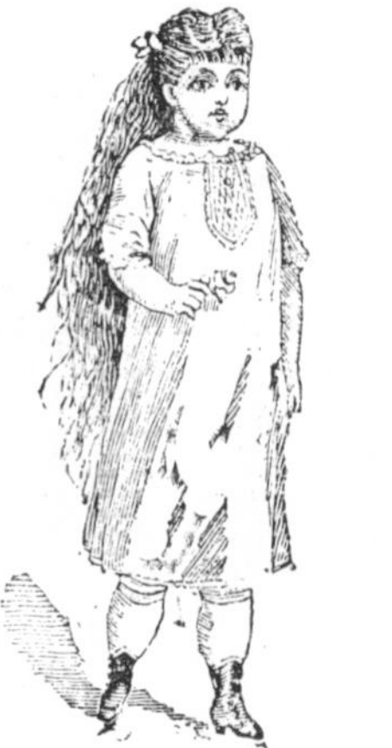

TOYS!

A complete Line of

TOYS

OF EVERY DESCRIPTION.

PRICES ON APPLICATION.

Refer to previous catalogue.

Our next number of this Price List will be issued early in the Fall; we will send a copy free of charge to any one applying for it by postal card or letter.

In this Price List we do not give illustrations and prices for Winter goods, but we have always on hand a large assortment suitable for cold climates; and we will cheerfully furnish prices of such articles on application.

Book Department.

We will obtain any book not in our catalogue on receipt of price and publisher's name, at less than the regular price. Books for Children and school books far below publishers' prices. Want of space prevents us from describing our entire stock, we therefore describe the most popular works.

STANDARD WORKS.

WORTHINGTON'S PUBLICATIONS.

These books are well bound, large type and nicely illustrated.

3854.	Washington Irving, 6 vols	$4 98
3855.	George Eliot, 8 vols	4 39
3856.	Dickens', 15 vols (reduced)	6 98
3857.	Thackeray 11 vols (reduced)	6 98
3858.	Scott's Waverly Novels, 12 vols	7 49
3859.	Bulwer, 13 vols	9 67
3860.	Plutarch, 3 vols	2 69
3861.	Lamb's Essays, 3 vols	2 59
3862.	Smile's Self Help, 4 vols	2 69
3863.	Chamber's Encyclopædia, 10 vols	10 98

ROUTLEDGE'S PUBLICATIONS.

3864.	Shakespeare, 13 vols	$4 39
3865.	Shakespeare, Knight's Edition 3 vols	4 98
3866.	Spectator, 3 vols	2 49
3867.	Disraeli's, 6 vols	5 69
3868.	Beaconsfield, 12 vols	8 89
3869.	Ruskin, 12 vols	8 98
3871.	Macaulay's Essays, 3 vols	1 69

HURST'S PUBLICATIONS.

ARLINGTON EDITION STANDARD CLASSICS.

3872. 12 mo., cloth gilt. Per vol, 39c.

Andersen's Fairy Tales,	Corinne,
Grimm's Fairy Tales,	Creasey's Battles,
Bonaparte Family,	Dante,
Buffon's Natural History,	David Copperfield,
Burns,	Famous Boys,
Byron,	Famous Men,
Life of Calhoun,	Favorite Poems,
Life of Fremont,	History of France,
Hypatia,	Poe,
Jane Eyre,	Pope,
John Halifax,	Romolo,
London by Day & Night,	Schiller,
Nicholas Nickelby,	Scott,
Moore's Poems,	Shakespeare,
Paris with Pen & Pencil,	Tennyson,
Pickwick Papers,	Uarda.

HURST' POPULAR CLASSICS.

3873. 18 mo., gilt cloth. Per vol, 28c.

Arabian Nights,	
Burns,	
Byron,	
Children of the Abbey,	
Corinne,	
Creasey's Battles,	
Dante,	
Don Quixote,	
Favorite Poems,	
Goethe,	
Gulliver's Travels,	
Heine,	
Jane Eyre,	
John Halifax,	
Tom Brown,	
Uarda,	Virgil,
Tennyson,	Romolo,
Pope,	Scott,
Poe,	Schiller.

PORTER & COATES' PUBLICATIONS.

3874. Alta Edition, 12 mo., cloth gilt, nicely illustrated, 39c per vol.

Robinson Crusoe,	Arabian Nights,
Swiss Family Robinson,	American Family Robinson,
Scottish Chiefs,	son.
Thaddeus of Warsaw,	Children of the Abbey,
Vicar of Wakefield,	Don Quixote,
Gascoyne,	Freaks on the Fells,
Shifting Winds,	Floating Lights,
Bear Hunters,	Gorilla Hunters,
Kangaroo Hunters,	Adventures in Canada,
Life of Napoleon,	Life of Washington,
Paul and Virginia,	Pilgrim's Progress,
Child's History of England,	Æsop's Fables,
land,	Baron Munchausen,
Last Days of Pompeii,	Ivanhoe,
Guy Mannering,	Waverly,
Tom Brown,	Dog Crusoe,
Wild Man of the West,	French Fairy Tales,
Standard Fairy Tales,	Stories from History,
Pique,	Orange Blossoms,
Cook's Voyages,	Complete Letter Writer.

3875. Standard Works at 69c.

Kenilworth,	Pirate,
Lady Jane Grey,	Grimm's Fairy Tales,
Andersen's Fairy Tales,	Lady of the Lake,
	Travels in Africa.

NOVELS.

HOUGHTON & MIFFLIN'S CLOTH PUBLICATIONS.

3881.	The Gates Ajar	$1 23
3882.	Beyond the Gates	1 23
3883.	Zooroaster, by Crawford	0 94
3884.	In War Time	0 77
3885.	A Captive of Love	1 08
3886.	At Love's Extremes	1 08
3887.	Aulnay Tower, by Howard	1 08
3888.	Countess of Albany	0 60

APPLETON'S PUBLICATIONS.

3889.	Glenaveril, by author of Lucile	$1 08
3890.	How to be Happy, Though Married	1 08
3891.	Mulhbach's Works	0 95
3892.	The New King Arthur	1 08
3893.	As is was Written	0 79
3894.	Infelice	1 19
3895.	St. Elmo	1 10
3896.	Bessie's Fortune, by Holmes	0 86
3897.	A Mortal Antipathy, by Holmes,	1 14
3898.	The Lady with the Rubies	1 13
3899.	The Dynamite	0 79
3900.	The Scarlet Letter	0 98
3901.	An Original Belle, by Roe	0 85
3902.	Othmar, by Ouida	0 89

RED LINE EDITION OF THE POETS

HURST'S PUBLICATIONS.

3903. Each vol. is beautifully printed on toned paper, with a scarlet border round each edge, and is illustrated with several engravings. They are bound in cloth gilt edges $0 59

3904.	Half Russia	0 75
3905.	Alligator	1 19

Arnold,	
Browning,	
Burns,	
Byron,	
Campbell,	
Chaucer,	
Cook,	
Coleridge,	
Cowper,	
Dante,	
Dryden,	
Eliot,	
Favorite,	
Goethe,	
Goldsmith,	
Heine,	
Hemans,	
Hood,	
Hugo,	Poets of America,
Illiad,	Proctor,
Ingelow,	Shakespeare,
Keats,	Shelley,
Kingsley,	Schiller,
Lalla Rookh,	Scott,
Lucile,	Swinburne,
Meredith,	Tasso,
Milton,	Tennyson,
Moore,	Thompson,
Odssey,	Willis,
Petrarch,	Wordsworth,
Poe,	Religious Poems.

HOUGHTON & MIFFLIN'S PUBLICATIONS.

Longfellow, Whittier, Bryant, Lowell, Bret Harte, Poems.

3906.	Diamond Edition	$0 60
3907.	Household Edition	1 49
3908.	Fireside Encyclopædia	3 85
3909.	Alice Carey Poems	1 49
3910.	Wm. Cullen Bryant's selection of poetry and song	$3 69
3911.	Poems, bound in calf	3 79
3912.	Poems, bound in cloth and gilt, large type, illustrated	$2 49

MISCELLANEOUS.

3913.	Mark Twain's Works	$1 89
3914.	Marion Harland's Cook Book	1 25
3915.	American Popular Dictionary	0 39

DICK & FITZGERALD'S PUBLICATIONS.

3916.	Dream Book	12, 28, 39c each
3917.	Fortune Telling Book	28, 39c
3918.	Dick's Quadrille Call Book	56c
3919.	Frost Dialogues	23 and 39c
3920.	How to amuse an Evening Party	39c
3921.	Recitation Book	7, 21, 39c

BOOKS FOR BOYS.

3922.	Sailor Boys' Series, 3 vols	$3 00
3923.	Oliver Optic's Works	94c each
3924.	Boys' Book of Games	59c "

BOOKS FOR GIRLS.

3925.	Holmes Works	89c
3926.	Alcott Works	99c
3927.	Elsie Book	69c
3928.	Mildred	69c
3929.	Dr. Gilbert's Daughter	94c
3930.	A Little Country Girl	89c
3931.	Lulu's Library	89c

Also a complete line of Books for Girls, Boys and Children, at less than publishers' prices.

INDEX.

(Continued on page 146.)

INDEX.

(Continued from page 145.)

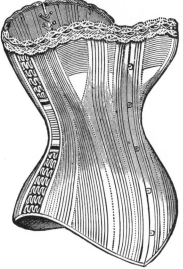

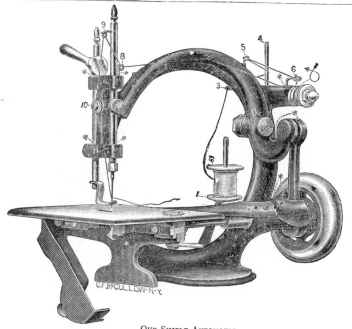

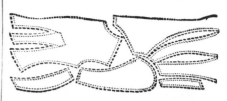
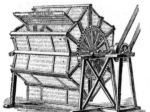

Boulevard Velveteen.

Black and Colored.

Rivals Silk Velvets in Lustre and Finish at One-third the Cost.

For Dresses, Suits, Trimmings and Millinery Purposes,
HAS NO EQUAL.

From the Lowest to the Finest qualities are made in all shades to match all fabrics. ORDER NONE OTHER.

Ship Brand and Velous de Genoa Silk Velvets.

DRESS SHIELDS.

LADIES

Should be very particular in the selection of their Dress Shields, so that they have those which really shield the dress from discoloration under the arms, thereby having the full benefit of the dress as long as they wish to use it. There are numerous styles in the market, but the only one which can be relied on, and which we GUARANTEE or REFUND THE MONEY, are those—

BEARING THIS      TRADEMARK

THE NAME   WITH

KLEINERT "   IN THE CENTRE,

And all these we cheerfully recommend.

To the Ladies!

We beg to draw your attention to our importation of

SILK WARP HENRIETTAS.

We have examined all other makes and find that ours are Superior in

MAKE, QUALITY, FINISH AND DURABILITY,
TO ANY IN THE MARKET,

We Guarantee them in Every Particular. A regular list of prices can be found on page 94. We quote here a few special prices,

36 inch,	formerly	$1.25,	now	$1.00.	
40 inch,	"	1.75,	"	1.25.	
40 inch,	"	1.90,	"	1.40.	
40 inch,	"	2.00,	"	1.50.	

BLOOMINGDALE BROS.

THE PIVOT CORSET.

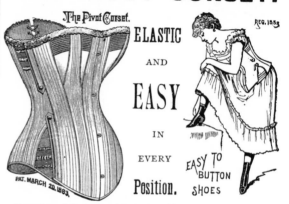

ELASTIC AND EASY IN EVERY Position.

EASY TO BUTTON SHOES

Expands and Contracts with the breathing, and yields to any position of the wearer.

The best fitting Corset in the market.   ONLY $1. TRY IT.

For explanation and cuts of
MADAM FOY CORSET AND
C. N. C. NURSING CORSET.
See page 34, Cuts Nos. 37, and 40.

FAY, HARMON & CHADWICK, Manufacturers,
New Haven, Conn.

WE RECOMMEND

BEST SIX CORD, for HAND AND MACHINE USE.

Bloomingdale Brothers.

——— USE ———

PRIDE OF THE KITCHEN
SOAP.

For Scouring Tin and Woodenware.   For Sale by
BLOOMINGDALE BROS.

THE MADONNA
EMBROIDERY COTTON.

Superior needle work can only be produced with the right kind of Embroidery Cotton. An improperly twisted Cotton, however excellent its other qualities may be, renders the best work indifferent, washes thick and lumpy, contracts and wears out the material.

The MADONNA EMBROIDERY COTTON is recognized as the best by the trade, by art embroiderers, and by competitors who try to introduce their makes by imitating it or referring to it. It combines with the greatest perfection in quality, and the largest variety of *fast colors*, a reasonable price. *Use no other.*

MADONNA
CROCHET COTTON.

In White and Colors. Best article for the Crochet Lace Work.

MADONNA
MENDING COTTON.

In White and Colors, for every day, and art mending and darning.

UTOPIA LINEN
Embroidery Thread.

In 40 beautiful FAST Colors. A new Embraidery Material, particularly to be recommended for linen and wash goods. Cotton and silk hose, but the colors of this thread improve, by washing,

*** Inquire of dealers, specially for the above materials

JAMES L. SHARP,

MANUFACTURER OF

GAS AND OIL
STOVES,

10 MURRAY STREET, NEW YORK.

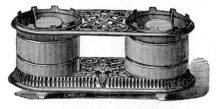

The above goods are for sale by
BLOOMINGDALE BROS.

H. B. MERRILL'S
BALANCED CHRONOMETER AND REGULATOR VALVES.

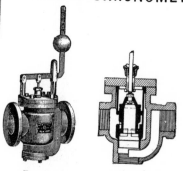

FIG. 1—Represents the Balanced Chronometer Valve

FIG 2—A sectional view of the same. The black portion represents the composition metal. which is proving by each additional year's use, its great superiority over iron valves or seats of any form or degree of hardness, as they have *never been known to steam cut or corrode.*

The valve seats. which are four in number, are all in one casting. which fits the iron body at the ends *only*, thus providing perfectly for free expansion and contraction,

The construction of the valve is such, as will be seen by Fig. 2, that the steam pressure is equal on all sides, making it a perfectly balanced valve, and relieving it from any extra friction. These valves are used for a great variety of purposes, where a simple, durable, and easy working valve is required, as in steam, water and gas pressure regulators, as float valves for large locomotive or other tanks, on water pumps, hydraulic elevators, etc., etc.

FIG. 1.   FIG. 2.

The following are a few of the prominent buildings in this city in which they are used :

The New Cotton Exchange,
The Standard Oil Company's new building.
The Mortimer Building,
Knickerbocker Apt. House, 5th Av. and 28th St.

Madison Avenue Apt. House, Mad. Av. and 30th St.
W. & J Sloane's Carpet Warehouse.
Astor Building, Broadway.
Navarro Apt, Houses, etc., etc.

ALSO DEALER IN

Worthington
STEAM PUMPS.

H. B. MERRILL,

86 Liberty St., N. Y.

N. B. The above valves and pump are to be used in our building now in course of erection cor. 3d Av. and 59th Street.

BLOOMINGDALE BROS.

LADIES!

LADIES, we would like to call your attention to OUR NEW

TISSUE PAPER FLOWER

OUTFIT. This Outfit has been specially put up by us with the view of making it the most COMPLETE and CHEAPEST ONE OF THE KIND EVER OFFERED. It contains a choice lot assorted colors of imported Tissue paper, Wire, Rubber Stems, Leaves, Culots, Sprays, Flower Centres, a large assortment of Stamped Flowers, etc. *ALL THE MATERIALS ARE WARRANTED TO BE OF THE BEST QUALITY.*

A new feature of our outfit is an ILLUSTRATED BOOK of Directions for Making Flowers, etc. *The Directions are so plain and explicit that any person, old or young, can make flowers.* We have two outfits—No. 1, 50c. No. 2, \$1; Postage Free, Agents Wanted.

JEROME NOVELTY CO., 150 Nassau St., N. Y.

The Finest in the World for producing a Brilliant and Lasting Polish without Scratching.   Send for Sample.

BORSUM BROS., 91 Cliff St., New York.

M. HEMINWAY & SONS,

SPOOL SILK,

BUTTON-HOLE TWIST,
EMBROIDERY SILK,
PURE DYE KNITTING SILK

AND

JAPAN ETCHING SILK,

ARE KEPT BY

All Leading Dry and Fancy Goods Houses, and we
Recommend them as Superior to all other Makes.

Bloomingdale Brothers.

M. Heminway & SONS' 48-page book on ART EMBROIDERY, profusely
illustrated, and explaining all the latest stitches, sent on receipt of five 2-cent
stamps.

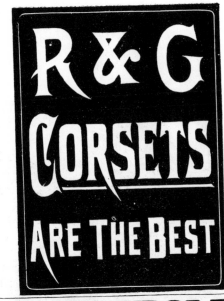

GLYCEROLE !

FOR OILING AND DRESSING

LADIES' AND CHILDRENS'

SHOES.

FAR SUPERIOR TO SHOE
DRESSINGS.

The only OIL PREPARATION and LEATHER PRESERVATIVE in
Existence. Do not ruin your shoes with Shoe Dressing; you can avoid it by using

GLYCEROLE !

25c per Bottle. For Sale in all First Class Shoe Stores.

GAS STOVES,

FOR COOKING AND HEATING.

On Exhibition and for Sale at the Office of the

CONSOLIDATED GAS COMPANY,

METROPOLITAN BRANCH,

BROADWAY, and 46th STREET.

INSTRUCT SHIPPERS TO FORWARD GOODS BY

UNITED STATES EXPRESS COMPANY.

From NEW YORK CITY,

To Secure Quickest Time! Lowest Rates! Safe Transportation!
THROUGH CARS! THROUGH TRUNKS FOR PAPER PARCELS!

ORDERS FOR GOODS.—Orders for goods, to be returned by United States Express, will be carried and delivered FREE OF CHARGE. Goods promptly forwarded as soon as received.

PARCEL RATES.

Table of **Lowest** and **Highest Rates,** from **New York City** to all offices of the **United States Express Co., Pacific Express Co., Northern Pacific Express Co., Wells, Fargo & Co.'s** Express and **Denver & Rio Grande R. R. Express Co.,** reached by railroad lines in the following States:

	1 lb. or less.	Over 1 to 2 lbs.	Over 2 to 3 lbs.	Over 3 to 4 lbs.	Over 4 to 5 lbs.	Over 5 to 7 lbs.
NEW JERSEY	25 cts.	25 cts.	25 cts.	25 cts.	25 cts.	25 cts.
NEW YORK	25 "	25 "	25 "	25 "	25 "	25 "
PENNSYLVANIA	25 "	25 to 30 "	25 " 35 "	25 to 40 "	25 to 45 "	25 to 50 "
OHIO	25 "	25 " 30 "	25 " 35 "	25 " 40 "	25 " 50 "	25 " 55 "
INDIANA	25 "	30 "	35 " 40 "	35 " 50 "	40 " 55 "	45 " 60 "
ILLINOIS	25 "	30 "	35 " 45 "	40 " 60 "	50 " 70 "	55 " 80 "
MICHIGAN	25 "	30 "	40 " 45 "	45 " 60 "	50 " 70 "	55 " 80 "
WISCONSIN	25 "	30 "	35 " 45 "	40 " 55 "	50 " 65 "	55 " 75 "
IOWA	25 "	30 "	40 " 45 "	50 " 60 "	55 " 70 "	60 " 95 "
MINNESOTA, KANSAS & NEBRASKA	25 "	30 "	45 "	55 " 60 "	65 " 70 "	75 " 95 "
INDIAN TERRITORY	25 "	30 "	45 "	60 "	70 " 75 "	80 " $1.00
MISSOURI	25 "	30 "	45 "	60 "	70 "	80 " 90 cts.
DAKOTA & TEXAS	25 "	30 "	40 to 45 "	50 to 60 "	55 to 70 "	60 " 90 "
MONT., COLORADO, UTAH & N. MEXICO	25 to 35 "	30 to 40 "	45 to 50 "	60 to 65 "	70 " 75 "	90 " $1.00
WYOMING	25 "	30 "	45 "	60 "	75 " 85 "	$1.00 to $1.15
IDAHO	25 to 35 "	30 "	45 "	60 "	75 "	$1.00
WASHINGTON TERRITORY	25 to 35 "	30 to 45 "	45 to 55 "	60 to 75 "	75 to 90 "	1.00 to 1.25
CALIFORNIA AND OREGON	35 " 40 "	40 " 50 "	50 " 60 "	65 " 80 "	85 " $1.00	1.25 " 1.50
ARKANSAS	35 " 40 "	40 " 50 "	50 " 70 "	65 " 95 "	85 " 1.15	1.15 " 1.60
ARIZONA	25 "	30 "	45 "	60 "	70 cts.	80 " 95 cts.
	25 to 40 "	30 to 50 "	45 to 60 "	60 to 80 "	75 to $1.00	$1.00 to $1.50

Advantages of Shipping by United States Express Company.

1. **There is no limitation as to weight of parcels.**
2. **Prepayment of charges is not required.**
3. **Receipts are given and taken for all shipments.**
4. **Deliveries can always be proven.**
5. **The Company is liable for loss and damage according to the conditions of its receipts.**

SEND REMITTANCES BY UNITED STATES EXPRESS ORDER.

CHEAPEST, SAFEST, MOST CONVENIENT.
FOR SALE AT ALL THE COMPANY'S OFFICES.

$5.00 and under... 5 cents.	Over $20.00 to $30.00.12 cents.	
Over 5.00 to $10.00 ... 8 "	" 30.00 to 40.00.15 "	
" 10.00 to 20.00....10 "	" 40.00 to 50.00.20 "	

☞Apply to Agents of the United States Express Company, and other Companies named, for further information.

Principal Office, 82 BROADWAY, New York.

MANHATTAN BOOK AND JOB PRINT, 109 E. 13th St., and 328-330 7th Ave., N. Y.